THE ROMAN HISTORIANS

The Roman Historians provides a clear survey and a critical analysis of five centuries of historical writing in and about ancient Rome. The book examines authors of various historical genres – narrative, biography, and autobiography – and places them within the political and social framework of the late Roman Republic and the Roman Empire. Since Roman historiography is an extension of political conflict and moral discourse, all these writings are examined within the context of Roman public life.

The book begins with Cato and the early Roman annalists, and includes major chapters devoted to Sallust, Livy, Tacitus, and Ammianus Marcellinus. In these chapters Ronald Mellor brings together each historian's political experience with his particular rhetoric and style. Chapters on biography and autobiography treat Suetonius' *Lives of the Caesars* and Julius Caesar's *Commentaries on the Gallic War*. Other chapters examine such issues as censorship, literary style, and the moralism of Roman historical writing.

This book illuminates how and why Roman authors told the stories of their past. All Roman historical writing is highly political and deeply moral, and we see here how the political experience and moral vision of the historian shape the historical narrative and intimately inform the content, the rhetoric, and the literary style of the history.

Ronald Mellor is Professor of History at UCLA. He is the author of *Tacitus* (1993) and *The Historians of Ancient Rome: An Anthology* (1997).

THE ROMAN HISTORIANS

Ronald Mellor

London and New York

First published 1999
by Routledge
11 New Fetter Lane, London EC4P 4EE

Simultaneously published in the USA and Canada
by Routledge
29 West 35th Street, New York, NY 10001

©1999 Ronald Mellor
The right of Ronald Mellor to be identified as the Author of this
Work has been asserted by him in accordance with the
Copyright, Designs and Patents Act 1988

Typeset in Garamond by Routledge
Printed and bound in Great Britain by
Creative Print and Design, Ebbw Vale, Wales

British Library Cataloguing in Publication Data
A catalogue record for this book is available from the British Library

Library of Congress Cataloging in Publication Data
Mellor, Ronald.
The Roman historians / Ronald Mellor.
p. cm.
Includes bibliographical references and index.
ISBN0–415–11773–9 (hb). – ISBN 0–415–11774–7 (pb)
1. Rome—Historiography. 2. Historians—Rome—Biography.
3. Rome—History. I. Title.
DG205.M45 1999
937'.0072022—dc21   98–27442
CIP

ISBN 0–415–11773–9 (hbk)
ISBN 0–415–11774–7 (pbk)

FOR ANNE
TRICESIMO ANNO NOSTRO

CONTENTS

PREFACE

This book is designed as an introduction to the masterpieces of Roman historical and biographical writing. Even after two millennia, these books remain enjoyable and intellectually stimulating, but they were written for a very different audience and the contemporary reader needs to understand their political and literary context. My aim is to provide the necessary setting and entice new readers to these books which have had such a lasting impact on the western tradition. Since this slim volume is necessarily unencumbered by scholarly apparatus, I apologize to those scholars, past and present, whose ideas appear unacknowledged in these pages. I have appended brief suggestions for further reading.

The Roman Historians is intended as a companion to T.J. Luce's *The Greek Historians* (Routledge, 1997) and also owes its birth to a kind invitation from Richard Stoneman of Routledge. I am grateful to UCLA for a sabbatical leave, and to the UCLA Research Council for its continuing support. The book was largely written during a year as a visitor in the School of Historical Studies at the Institute for Advanced Study in Princeton. I am grateful to Professors Glen Bowersock, Christian Habicht, and Patricia Crone for making the Institute a hospitable place to work, and to colleagues in Classics and History at Princeton University for their welcome. Colleagues at those institutions kindly took time from their own work to give me suggestions on this book: Graeme Clarke and Ben Isaac read a draft of the entire manuscript, and Glen Bowersock, Robert Kaster, and Geoffrey Rickman read one or more chapters. They, and especially the anonymous readers, gave me much useful advice; for the errors and idiosyncratic views that remain I am wholly responsible. Translations unattributed to another source are my own.

The manuscript was also read, and vigorously corrected, by my wife, Anne Mellor. As a professor of English, her views on grammar and syntax are invaluable. But her real contribution to this book is in her love and support over the past thirty years. With love and continuing admiration, I dedicate it to her.

Princeton, March 1998

INTRODUCTION

The Romans' devotion to their ancestral and national past pervades their literature and art, their architecture and city planning, their political and legal institutions, their religion and legends, their festivals and funeral celebrations. They were proud of their traditions. What had begun as tribal exploits retold and celebrated around the family hearth was transformed over the centuries into a collective national mystique – to be tended by poets and politicians as assiduously as the Vestal Virgins tended the flame of the civic hearth. It is important to remember that for the Romans the past was a validation of their present greatness: it had to be preserved to give meaning to the present. In the words of the Roman orator and statesman, Marcus Tullius Cicero (106–43 BCE):

> To be ignorant of what has happened before your birth is to remain always a child. For what is the meaning of a man's life unless it is intertwined with that of our ancestors by the memory of history.
>
> (*Orator* 120, tr. Hubbell (Loeb))

To say that the Romans greatly valued their history raises a series of important questions. How much of the raw material of history had been preserved through oral transmission? When did Romans begin to study and write their history? For what reasons did the first historians take up their craft? How do Roman historians differ from their Greek predecessors? How did the early historians use their sources? What sources were available to them, and how reliable were those sources? Where, indeed, can the history of the Roman people be found?

The past – whether real or imagined – survives in a remarkable range of ways. The most important for the Romans would include *myth* (Romulus and Remus suckled by the she-wolf); *legend* (exploits attributed to historical figures, like the Tarquin kings); *language* (which preserves otherwise forgotten data, like the etymology for money, *pecunia* from *pecus*, sheep, showing the important early form of wealth); *buildings and urban plans* (which show Etruscan influence); *objects* (funeral masks and portrait busts); *religion* (exact preservation of words and rituals long after their meaning was forgotten); *lists* (names of magistrates); *oral tradition* (funeral speeches preserved in family memory); *inscriptions* (early treaties); *written poetry*; and, last but not least, *historical writing*. This range is particularly important since the earliest historians in any culture must perforce use a diversity of sources. In the course of this book, we will see most of these sources used by Roman historians.

I have already used the word "history" – a word the Romans borrowed from the Greek *historia* ("investigation") – in two different ways: firstly, the events of the past; secondly, a written text that contains the reconstruction of past events. This point is an old one, which Hegel made almost two centuries ago in his *Philosophy of History*: "The term *history*...comprehends not less what has happened than the narrative of what has happened." Modern scholars know that these meanings are closely intertwined since the events of the past can only survive in a written text and the separation of the events and the text is impossible. Yet we normally accept (or pretend) that a "History of Rome" exists independent of any texts. The study of Roman history is the attempt to recover and understand the substance of that sequence of events.

If we are to study the history of the Roman people, where do we find it? The answer is quite simple. To an overwhelming degree it survives in the historical writings of the Romans themselves: Cicero, Caesar, Sallust, Livy, Tacitus, Suetonius, Ammianus Marcellinus, and the Historia Augusta. In addition, Greek writers who lived under Roman rule also left histories of Rome: Polybius, Dionysius of Halicarnassus, Plutarch, and Dio Cassius. Is this so very surprising? It certainly is by the standards of later history – from the Middle Ages to the very recent past – for which a contemporary scholar seeks eyewitness evidence in archives, memoirs, diaries, letters, and (very recently) tape and film. Every scholar of the Renaissance or Louis XIV or U.S. Grant would regard as primary evidence the private documents written at the time or soon after, and that same scholar would regard public material written long afterwards with some suspicion. For Roman history we are heavily dependent on Greek and Roman writers who lived long after the events, even centuries later. (Cicero's letters might approximate a contemporary archive, but they may have been revised for publication after his death.) The modern scholar may use inscriptions, papyrological texts from Egypt, coins and archaeological remains to learn much about Roman society and culture, as well as to gain insights into their private life. But we remain overwhelmingly dependent on historical reconstructions by a handful of great storytellers, and the study of Roman history must start from the writers who have left us these impressive documents.

"Historiography" is both the writing of history and the study of historical writing – once again the close connection between events and the examination of them. This book will examine the aims and achievements of those Latin historians of ancient Rome. My purpose is not to retell or summarize the historical narrative contained in these writers, but to provide an introduction to the historians and their books and thus to help the reader understand why and how these histories were written. For the Romans, history, biography, and autobiography were quite distinct literary genres written to serve different purposes. Modern readers, however, regard biography and autobiography as alternative forms of historical writing, so I will include them here and try to show how these genres differed in the Roman mind from history proper.

Cicero never wrote history as such, but he wrote thoughtfully about how and why history should be written. He said that history should be both useful and moral: useful in keeping the statesman aware of precedents in law, foreign policy, and military affairs; moral in providing models of conduct from Rome's past to help its leaders act virtuously.

> All literature, all philosophy, all history, abounds with incentives to noble action, incentives which would be buried in black darkness were the light of the written word not flashed upon them. How many pictures of high endeavor the great authors of Greece and Rome have drawn for our use, and bequeathed to us, not only for our contemplation, but for our emulation.
>
> (*Pro Archia* 14, tr. Watts (Loeb))

By linking the present with the past, history would illuminate the contemporary state of society and provide both moral and practical guidance. Thus a Roman was encouraged to imitate the personal and civic virtues of his ancestors at the family hearth, in the Forum, or on the battlefield. This closely intertwined code of public and private conduct was called the *mos maiorum* – "the traditions of our ancestors" – and formed the core of moral and political education at Rome.

History at Rome was written mostly by senators for senators: this explains its narrow focus on political conduct. The Romans use this fact to excuse, somewhat defensively, history's slow development at Rome. Sallust suggests it is because Romans are too busy with the duties of public life:

> But because Athens produced writers of exceptional talent, the exploits of the men of Athens are heralded throughout the world as unsurpassed. Thus the merit of those who did the deeds is rated as high as brilliant minds have been able to exalt the deeds themselves by words of praise. But the Roman people never had that advantage, since their ablest men were always most engaged with affairs; their minds were never employed apart from their bodies; the best citizen preferred action to words.
>
> (*Catilina* 8, 3–5, tr. Rolfe (Loeb))

Cicero also thinks clever Romans are too busy in the law courts, whereas he says neither Herodotus nor Thucydides had to do much public speaking. That suggestion is self-serving, since there is more to public life than the law courts. Most great Greek historians were in fact political exiles (Thucydides, Xenophon, Timaeus, Polybius) and others, like Herodotus, lived far from home. Exile gave them leisure for study, and also made them more cosmopolitan in their attitudes. One result of the obsessively political Roman historical writing was that it was less interesting to the general public (who found diversion in strange customs and appalling portents) than to the political elite. Thus Roman schoolteachers often preferred to find moral exempla for their students in poetry, biographies, or collections of anecdotes. But senatorial historians cared little whether other readers approved of their subject, since their work was an extension of political life and was primarily aimed at those with political power in the Roman state.

If Roman historical writing was political, it was also deeply moral. In this the great Roman historians parted company with their Greek forebears: Herodotus, Thucydides, and Polybius. In other societies, theologians, philosophers, or social theorists may discuss important moral issues that in Rome were the province of historians. For example, the Romans used history to discuss the moral dimension of political questions while the Greeks used philosophy. It is in Sallust, Livy, Tacitus, and Ammianus that we find the most cogent Roman discussions of freedom versus tyranny, the corrupting effect of individual or civic power, and the decline of political and social institutions. Thus the problem of Rome's decline was regarded as a moral question, and historical writing became the conscience of the Roman people. In this book I will examine how these Roman writers were able, through the medium of history, to address the moral and political issues of their time.

A final caveat. I will try to make a sympathetic case for Roman historians for two reasons. I believe we greatly underestimate the difficulties of writing history without libraries, reference works, reliable sources, editorial principles, and even commonly accepted standards for evaluation of earlier material. We need to examine carefully the motives which drove men to take on the immensely difficult and lonely task of writing history. Sallust says that writing history is among the most difficult tasks since the words must equal the deeds themselves, and any criticism is greeted with accusations of malice (*Catilina* 3, 2). Both Livy and Tacitus also complain of the *labor* of writing history, which Tacitus says is "without glory." In addition, modern ideas of historical scholarship have changed dramatically since the academic revolution of the nineteenth century when Herodotus was transformed from the Father of History into the Father of Lies. If we scoff at the Roman historians as a physicist might smile at the poetic science of the Pre-Socratic philosophers, or if we look to the past only for what we still regard as probably "true," we can lose sight of very real human achievements. In a wise address to the American Historical Association, the Association's president Theodore Roosevelt said in 1912:

> The great historian of the future will have easy access to innumerable facts patiently gathered by tens of thousands of investigators, whereas the great historian of the past had very few facts, and often had to gather these himself.
> (*American History Review* 18 (1912–13), 479)

Roosevelt went on to say, citing Thucydides and Gibbon, "When, however, the great historian has spoken, his work will never be undone" (484). Some historians leave masterpieces that may be factually superseded, but can never be replaced. The Roman historians tell us many things about Rome that cannot be swept aside by a modern textbook. In this book, we will investigate why that is so.

1

ORIGINS OF ROMAN HISTORIOGRAPHY

Greek antecedents

While many ancient societies learned writing systems from more advanced neighbors, most worked out their own literary genres in terms of their own intellectual and cultural environment. The Romans adapted their letter forms from the Greek alphabet they received, probably via the Etruscans, from the Greek-speaking cities of southern Italy, but it was centuries before the Romans actually developed a written literature. By 265 BCE, Rome had control of the entire Italian peninsula and its cultural life fell increasingly under the influence of Greeks from southern Italy who came to Rome as tutors, slaves, and prisoners-of-war. Since the Romans had as yet no indigenous literature, they took what they could from the Greeks. The earliest surviving fragments of Latin poetry are from a translation of Homer's *Odyssey* into Latin by Livius Andronicus, a Greek slave captured at Tarentum. In addition to epic, the earliest comic and tragic poetry in Latin were also translations of Greek plays.

Greeks had been writing history for three centuries before the first Roman, Fabius Pictor, turned his hand to historical prose. Homer had long before provided the earliest example of oral poetry which contained praise, or *encomia*, of famous men. In fifth-century Athens Herodotus and Thucydides followed Homer in providing a third-person narrative of great deeds. Their historical masterpieces gave written history some of its notable characteristics. Thus Herodotus wrote his history of the Persian Wars on an epic scale. The early books set forth the geographical and cultural background of the eastern Mediterranean peoples: Persians, Egyptians, Scythians, Lydians, and Ionian Greeks. In the Homeric tradition, he invented speeches for his characters – wholesale fabrications in which he was followed by virtually every subsequent Greek and Roman historian.

Herodotus' goal was to give pleasure to the reader and to recreate the past. But Herodotus also needed to establish the credibility of his story. The poet Homer claimed to be inspired by the Muse, but the historian claimed his authority by his personal observation (autopsy) and by doing research. Hence he dutifully went to Egypt to question local priests on Egyptian culture, but he also embellished his history with imaginative elaborations and thrilling drama. The story of Solon and Croesus bears the hallmark of a Sophoclean tragedy rather than history, but Herodotus knew his audience and their taste. In an age of limited literacy, many more Athenians heard Herodotus' recited performances of his history than could yet read the text. He needed to ensure that his listeners, and his readers as well, be entertained, as they had been by epic poems.

Several decades later Thucydides introduced a more austere way of writing history in his treatment of the Peloponnesian War. He developed a scientific history intended to be useful to statesmen when similar events recur. He regarded the true utility of history to be for the future, when it would be a "possession for all time" for generations to come. He was unconcerned, even scornful, about the entertainment of his reader; he preferred to convey a truthful picture of the war and the motivations of the contending parties. He was without question an "elitist" who addressed his book to future political leaders. Although some see in Herodotus and Thucydides only the stark contrast between historians who seek to entertain by telling stories and those who wish to educate – a contrast said to persist after 2,500 years between purveyors of popular history and academic historians – there is in fact much that they have in common. Both were primarily concerned with contemporary history or the history of the recent past. Most of their sources were oral, since there were few earlier historical writings and no archives available. They truly engaged in an "inquiry," but few of their successors did much of what we would recognize as primary research; they tended to rewrite history that they found in earlier books. Both Herodotus and Thucydides felt free to invent speeches when it seemed appropriate, and both constructed historical scenes to resemble the tragedies then so popular in Athens.

When the Romans turned to Greek models for history, they drew less on Herodotus and Thucydides than on later Greek writers who wrote in the very theatrical world of the Hellenistic city-state. Cicero regarded Herodotus as no more truthful than epic poets like Ennius, and he thought Thucydides deficient as a rhetorical model. Some Hellenistic writers emphasized the dramatic and rhetorical aspects of historical writing that elicited an emotional response from their readers, and that type of historian was pilloried by the Greek satirist Lucian:

> Again, such writers seem unaware that history has aims and rules different from poetry and poems. In the case of the latter, liberty is absolute and there is one law – the will of the poet...So it is a serious flaw not to know how to keep the attributes of history and poetry separate, and to bring poetry's embellishments into history – myth and eulogy and the exaggeration of both: it is as if you were to dress one of our tough, rugged athletes in a purple dress and the rest of the paraphernalia of a pretty whore and paint his face. Heavens, how ridiculous you would make him look, shaming him with all that decoration.
>
> (*How to Write History* 8, tr. Kilburn (Loeb))

The greatest Greek historian of the Hellenistic age, Polybius (202–120 BCE), also harshly criticized the emotional approach to history, and he preferred a more analytical style of history. Since he deeply believed that history is cyclical and thus would "repeat itself," he saw great utility for political leaders to study history carefully. Though Fabius and Cato had already written the earliest Roman histories before Polybius completed his own history of the growth of Roman power, Polybius' historical achievement made him the dominant influence on later Roman historical writers. With Livy and Tacitus, Polybius became one of the three greatest historians of Rome and so, despite his Greek origins and language, he deserves more than cursory mention in this book.[1]

His father was the leading figure in the Achaean League – an alliance of Greek city-states – and young Polybius held military office and also served on embassies. When the Achaean League rose against Roman domination, Polybius was one of 1,000 Achaeans taken to Rome "to stand trial." In fact they were interned as hostages in cities throughout Italy until 152, when the 300 survivors were allowed to return to Greece.

During his years in exile this young Greek transformed himself into a great historian. At a time when the Roman nobles were becoming interested in Greek culture, Polybius' intelligence, education, and political shrewdness brought him into the intellectual circle of Scipio Aemilianus, the adopted grandson of the conqueror of Hannibal. Under Scipio's patronage Polybius was able to travel throughout Italy, as well as gain access to family libraries and state archives in Rome. He abandoned an earlier plan to write a history of the Achaean League, deciding instead to demonstrate to his fellow Greeks how Rome became in little more than a century the greatest power in the Mediterranean world.

Polybius traveled to Spain and Gaul with Scipio, and remained with him and the Roman army throughout the Third Punic War, which ended with the final destruction of Carthage in 146. The historian died about 120 – falling from a horse in his native Greece at the age of eighty-two.

Polybius had a clear idea of his historiographic goals. He wished to write what he called "pragmatic history," which would be, above all, politically useful. In this, his model was Thucydides. A mere factual narrative was not sufficient; the historian must evaluate causes and connections to provide a truly useful explanation of how and why events occurred. Polybius was particularly contemptuous of the Hellenistic attitude toward historical writing as entertainment, and he often attacked by name historians whose books included mythical genealogies, tragic drama, or emotional scenes.

In Polybius' view, the ideal historian should not only search for truth, but he should be exceptionally well prepared for his task. It was Polybius who first argued passionately for the importance of archival research and set out requirements for an historian:

1   political experience to understand the actual practice of politics and to evaluate sources;
2   geographical knowledge, preferably from personal travel;
3   reliance not only on earlier historians, but personal examination of archives, inscriptions, and treaties.

Polybius' initial goal was to write a universal history in Greek of the period from 220 to 168 BCE. Later events caused him to extend the history through the fall of Carthage and Corinth to 144 BCE. Of the entire work of forty books, only the first five are fully preserved, while the others survive in large or small excerpts. The first two books set the background from the outbreak of the First Punic War (264 BCE), and the narrative proper begins in the third book. Since Polybius believed that Rome's strength lay in her institutions, he devoted all of his sixth book to a description and analysis of the Roman constitution and the Roman army. He looked at the Roman constitution through the lens of Aristotle's political theory and found a "mixed constitution" with elements of monarchy, aristocracy, and democracy. He thought its greatest strength was the balance between competing interests. Though Polybius' analysis presents an incomplete picture of Roman political life, it became enormously influential on eighteenth-century thinkers like Montesquieu and Jefferson, and thus formed the basis of the "balance of powers" in the United States constitution.

Polybius was not without bias: his Achaean birth prejudiced him against the Macedonian kings, just as his loyalty to Scipio led him to vilify Scipio's opponents. While his psychological and political analysis never reached the level of Thucydides, it is to Polybius that we owe the creation of history-writing as a professional calling. He set standards for the analysis of sources, for geographical and political knowledge, and for practical experience that few later historians have been able to equal. He had greater influence on Roman historical writing than any other Greek historian.

A final important Greek influence on Roman historical writing was the historian and philosopher, Poseidonius (135–50 BCE). He was educated in Athens by the leading Stoic philosopher, Panaetius, and was in due course himself a teacher of Cicero in Rhodes. Poseidonius saw the Roman Empire as the incarnation of the ideal Stoic world state – the cosmopolis. He had traveled much around the Mediterranean, and his history showed his interest in ethnology, linguistics, and rhetoric. He wished to write a universal history of all peoples, and his important material on the Celts found its way into Caesar's *Gallic War*. Though only fragments of his work survive today, Poseidonius had a substantial philosophical and historical impact on Roman historians.

Despite all these Greek models, the Roman historiographical tradition developed differently. Greek historians demonstrated their competence and credibility by discussing their methods, showing their research, and often engaging in intellectual polemic with other writers. A Roman historian did few of these things; his claim to authority and credibility usually rested on family background, public career, or military achievements. Nevertheless, Roman writers took over such favorite Greek historical *topoi* as the commander's speech on the eve of battle or the siege and capture of a city.

From its very beginnings Roman historical writing was narrower in scope and less tolerant in its attitudes. Roman historians were initially not interested in the history of the whole world nor in the geography and customs of other peoples; instead they focused on the Roman state and the political life of the community. Before the Romans ever wrote history, they read of Greek achievements both in poetry and history and developed a defensive posture toward their accomplished predecessors. Thus Rome's desire to rival the heroic ancestry of the Greeks created a chauvinistic historiography whose ethnocentrism left little sympathy for Rome's opponents. A lack of parochialism allowed Greek historians to exhibit a Homeric sympathy for both sides in a conflict, which can be seen in the accounts of the Persian and Peloponnesian Wars by Herodotus and Thucydides. To the intensely moralizing Romans, the detached and clinical history of Thucydides would most likely seem amoral. The Romans' polemical, partisan, moralizing strain, first used by historians against Rome's enemies, was increasingly deployed against one faction or another in the domestic struggles in Roman political life.

Sources of the Roman past

While the Romans looked to the Greeks as models for the writings of history, important indigenous traditions also shaped the form and subject matter of Roman historiography for centuries. Though no Roman wrote historical prose before the end of the third century BCE, more than five centuries after the founding of the city, the Romans still preserved the real or imagined achievements of their ancestors and there was remarkable agreement on the earliest traditions. To keep the memory of famous forebears before the young, encomia were said to have been pronounced at dinners and wax masks (*imagines*) of ancestors were kept on display in the atrium of an aristocratic Roman home for exhibition at funeral processions. Funeral addresses, which linked the achievements of the recently deceased with the exploits of his ancestors across the centuries, were either kept in family archives or passed orally from generation to generation with embellishments and distortions. However untrustworthy, these encomia are an early expression of the Roman desire to illuminate and guide the present through the past:

> I have often heard that Quintus Maximus, Publius Scipio, and other eminent men of our country, were in the habit of declaring that their hearts were set mightily aflame from the pursuit of virtue whenever they gazed upon the masks of their ancestors. Of course they did not mean to imply that the wax or the effigy had any such power over them, but rather that it is the memory of great deeds that kindles in the breasts of noble men this flame that cannot be

quelled until they by their own prowess have equally the
fame and glory of their forefathers.

(Sallust, *Jugurtha* 4, 5, tr. Rolfe (Loeb))

In the pre-literate culture of the monarchy and early Republic, such
oral traditions could be passed on for centuries.

A number of ancient writers suggest that poems recounting the
heroic exploits of Romulus, Lucretia, and the Horatii were once
sung at banquets:

And would there were still extant those songs, of which
Cato in his *Origines* has recorded, that long before his time
the several guests at banquets used to sing in turn the
praise of famous men.

(Cicero, *Brutus* 75, tr. Hendrickson (Loeb))

Nineteenth-century scholars argued vigorously over the existence of
these songs – which Macaulay "recreated" in his *Lays of Ancient
Rome*. Though the only evidence is this testimony of Cato and later
writers, it is not improbable that such songs were presented at
symposia. In an oral society in which funeral orations might be
preserved for generations, it would be even easier for poetic compositions to be retained in memory.

Other family records were kept in written form. Roman magistrates kept the accounts of their tenure in office, called *commentarii*,
among private documents in their homes, though in some cases
they were also deposited with the priests for incorporation into the
official records. Epitaphs on placards might also be carried beside
the masks at family funerals. These epitaphs, best known from the
group found in the tomb of the Scipios, might contain details of
careers in public life. From the late fourth century, families
preserved particularly famous orations by their ancestors. A. Claudius
Caecus, consul (312 BCE) and dictator, is best known for constructing
the first aqueduct (*Aqua Claudia*) and the first highway to Naples
(*Via Appia*). But he was also known as the first Roman to have a
speech published, and Cicero regarded him as the forerunner of
Cato. The speech must have been preserved for a century or more in
the archives of the proud Claudian family.

Besides these family records, the Romans preserved a variety of
public documents. They had long displayed treaties; thus there is
no reason to doubt Polybius' report that he saw on a bronze tablet a
treaty with Carthage from about 500 BCE. The Twelve Tables were

set up in the Forum in 450 BCE where they remained as "the foun-
tainhead of all public and private law" (Livy 3, 34, 6). Decrees of
the Senate were kept in the public treasury in the temple of Saturn,
and resolutions of the Plebeian Assembly were preserved in the
temple of Ceres. The most important of the early records were the
pontifical tables kept by the *pontifex maximus* (chief priest). This
information was initially written each year in black ink on whitened
notice boards from which they were later erased with a wet sponge.
At the end of the year the records were added to the inscriptions on
the bronze tablets which stood at the Regia in the Forum, probably
called *annales maximi* from the Latin word for year (*annus*) and the
title of the priest. They recorded the consuls, military triumphs,
religious prodigies, and any other important events that required
religious rituals. Cicero describes them:

> For history began as a mere compilation of annals, on
> which account, in order to preserve the general traditions,
> from the earliest period of the City down to the pontificate
> of Publius Mucius, each High Priest used to commit to
> writing all the events of his year of office, and record them
> on a white tablet (*album*), and post up the tablet (*tabula*) at
> his house, that all men might have the liberty to acquaint
> themselves therewith, and to this day those records are
> known as the pontifical annals (*annales maximi*)
>   (*De orat.* 2, 52, tr. Sutton and Rackham (Loeb))

Cato the Elder derided the *annales*:

> It is disagreeable to write what stands on the tablet at the
> house of the Pontifex Maximus – how often grain was
> costly, how often darkness or something else blocked the
> light of the moon or of the sun.
>   (*Origines* Frag. 77; Peter *Historicorum Romanorum Reliquiae*)

Famines and eclipses may have seemed trivial to Cato, but they
required expiation of the gods and so, together with buildings
constructed to fulfill a vow, they were included on the pontifical
annals. Later writers could use the record of eclipses to fix secure
dates, and the consular names alone, if accurate, would be of enormous use in establishing a chronological framework.

A more cogent criticism of the *annales* is one that can be made of
all chronicles: the disconnected entries have no plot, that is, they do

not attempt to establish a causal link between events. Without plot and without causation, there can be no true history. But, on their own terms, from the fourth century onward the annalistic records of magistrates, religious events, and public building seem to have been quite reliable. Though family records were inclined to exaggerate offices held, public scrutiny by competing families seems to have ensured that the names of magistrates recorded in the *annales* were dependable, though other facts may have been manipulated. Despite the fact that the *annales* were not collected until the late second century and perhaps were not published until the first century, they were available to senatorial historians. About 130 BCE the *pontifex maximus* Mucius Scaevola collected and edited 280 years of annals, perhaps supplementing the bare records with additional material from the archives. (There is no evidence that the *annales* were actually published by Scaevola; they were more likely issued publicly in the time of Augustus.) All these annual records decisively shaped the formal structure of Roman historical writing, which tended to follow their year-by-year account. The effect of such a structure continues to appear even in such literary historians as Livy and Tacitus. It has usually been said, not least by Livy (6,1), that the Gallic sack of Rome about 390 BCE destroyed all earlier records. Since at least the Carthaginian treaty and the Twelve Tables survived, scholars are now inclined to believe that other documents may have endured as well. A careful analysis of material preserved in later historians does not show a marked break at 390 BCE, but rather that increasingly reliable information appears gradually in the course of the fourth century. The bronze tablets containing the *annales maximi* were probably finally destroyed in the fire that destroyed the Regia about 36 BCE.

Rome's first historians

As in Greece, the earliest Romans to write about the past were the epic poets, though only fragments of their works survive. Though Gnaeus Naevius (270–201 BCE) was born in Campania in southern Italy, he is identified as a Roman citizen and was the first citizen – as opposed to slaves – to write books in Latin. Heroic legends of Rome's past were transmitted from oral traditions into written epic poems, and the same stories appeared later as prose history and biography. Like the modern films from which many contemporary viewers learn their history, epic poetry was a vibrant and attractive, though usually uncritical, presentation of the past. Naevius' epic poem on the First Punic War, *Bellum Poenicum*, retains certain Homeric elements like gods on the battlefield, despite the fact that Naevius himself had served in the war. A long digression allowed Naevius to include the national myth of Rome's foundation by a Trojan prince, Aeneas, as well as the early history of Carthage. About sixty of 5,000 lines of the poem survive – enough to show that Naevius knew both Homer and Hellenistic poetry. Since he was writing while Hannibal was in Italy during the Second Punic War, Naevius' epic was certainly intended to stir patriotic feelings.

Naevius was better known in his lifetime as a playwright. Though some of his tragedies may be translations or adaptations of Greek plays, he was the first to write original tragedies on Roman themes: a *Romulus*, and a *Clastidium* on the defeat of a Gallic army by Claudius Marcellus in 222 BCE. The play may have been written for Marcellus' funeral games – an example of the use of history for the glorification of a Roman aristocrat. The names of dozens of Naevius' comedies have survived, probably largely adaptations from the Greek. Several of his plays were set in Rome (*fabula togata*), and topical Roman allusions and personal attacks were inserted in many others. Naevius' fierce onslaughts on the aristocratic Caecilii Metelli caused him to spend time in prison, and he died in exile in Africa.

His successor, Quintus Ennius (239–169 BCE), was born at Rudiae in the heel of the Italian boot, where he grew up speaking Greek, Latin, and the south Italic language, Oscan. Though he was brought to Rome by Cato in 204 BCE, he soon moved into the Hellenizing circle of the Scipios which Cato detested. Like Naevius, he was both a tragic and an epic poet. After accompanying his patron Scipio Nobilior to Greece in 189 BCE, Ennius memorialized his victory at Ambracia in a tragedy of the same name. Nobilior rewarded him with Roman citizenship. Another "Roman" tragedy depicted the Rape of the Sabine Women.

Ennius' great epic poem, *Annales*, earned him the title of Father of Latin Literature. The eighteen books brought the history of Rome from Aeneas down to the 170s BCE. Though only some 600 lines now survive, the book was once much studied and imitated by all later Roman poets, especially Virgil. The poem, which took its name from the pontifical annals, focuses on Roman military exploits and uses every opportunity to praise the *virtus* of the ancestors of the aristocrats of Ennius' own time. The celebration of aristocratic ideology has its roots in Hellenistic court poetry, and was precisely the kind of Greek influence that Cato wished to keep away from Rome. Ennius certainly used the recent prose history of Fabius

Pictor, but his other sources are not clear. His emphasis on the national pride and moral power of Rome had a lasting influence on prose historical writing as well as epic poetry. The Romans saw far less difference between history and poetry than is the case in modern times. Augustus was actually praised for his "dedication to history" when he prevented the destruction of Virgil's epic poem, the *Aeneid*. The *Annales* was for generations of Romans the great work of history through which they were uplifted by the heroic achievements of their ancestors.

The first Roman to write history in prose was the senator Q. Fabius Pictor who, late in the third century BCE, wrote an account of Roman history from the beginnings to the Second Punic War. He wrote in Greek, for there was as yet little literary prose in Latin, and Greek was the lingua franca for peoples of the eastern Mediterranean. The Babylonian priest Berossus and the Egyptian priest Manetho both wrote histories of their own people in Greek and, in third-century BCE Egypt, a Jewish scholar named Demetrius wrote a biblical history in Greek. A large team of Jewish scholars in Alexandria also translated the Hebrew Bible into Greek (*Septuagint*). Even some Carthaginian authors wrote in Greek to reach a wider audience. Fabius was himself aware of Greek political life, since he had been sent as a Roman ambassador to Delphi to consult the oracle in the aftermath of their disastrous defeat at Cannae (216 BCE). Thus, in the midst of Rome's life-and-death struggle against Hannibal, who was seeking Greek alliances, Fabius withdrew from public life in order to present the Romans' policy, values, and remarkable resources to the Greek world in the form of a history from Rome's foundation to his own time. His insistent praise of his own ancestors indicates that he was also addressing his book to the Greek-reading Roman elite.

Fabius' task was a formidable and an audacious one: to create the first prose narrative of Roman history when so much existing information was oral. He used what was available: the pontifical *annales*, family records including speeches, earlier Greek historians like Hieronymus of Cardia and Timaeus, and most of all what he had seen and could learn from oral testimony. Fabius must also have drawn on the existing traditions for the foundations of Rome, which seem to have become relatively coherent by his day. Rome had developed a remarkable sense of its past, and the growth of literacy during the third century had not yet obliterated the living, oral tradition. But it is only with written history that true historical self-consciousness can develop. Fabius, who was born about 250 BCE, would have heard from men whose fathers and grandfathers had served in battles from Caudine Forks (321 BCE) through the First Punic War. His personal observations underlay his account of the Second Punic War, and his description of the embassy to Delphi became the source for Livy in Book 22.

Fabius' achievement was remarkable. He created a narrative of Roman history that permanently displaced that of Naevius, while at the same time being taken seriously by Greeks as a "Greek" historian. Fabius' history was very far from the bare *annales* kept by Roman priests; he was the first to bring Hellenistic Greek historical methods into Roman historical writing. While Polybius criticized Fabius' pro-Roman and anti-Hannibal bias, he relied heavily on him for the First and Second Punic Wars. Polybius even assumes the reliability of many speeches found in Fabius. Though few fragments survive, Polybius' use of Fabius allows us to discern the Roman's moralizing anecdotes and nationalistic attitudes: praise for Roman greatness and moral superiority, the wisdom of the Senate, and especially of the Fabian family, with criticism of the stupidity of the popular assembly. In his exaltation of his own family, Fabius was the first to see that the intense competition for glory among the Roman elite could now be transferred to the field of historical writing. Fabius thus introduced prose history to Rome and his moralistic nationalism established its character for centuries to come.

For another generation Roman historians followed Fabius by writing in Greek. We cannot be certain whether this was due to the desire to appeal to a wider readership, the undeveloped state of Latin prose, or cultural pretentiousness. The most prominent of these *annales Graeci* – as they were later called by Cicero – was L. Cincius Alimentus (praetor, 210 BCE), who fought in the Second Punic War and was taken prisoner by Hannibal. His work was praised both by Polybius and by Dionysius of Halicarnassus. The use of Greek soon fell into decline, probably because it no longer served any purpose. In the preface to his history, A. Postumius Albinus (consul, 151 BCE) apologizes for the errors in his Greek, and Cato scathingly asked who had required him to write in Greek. By that time history in Latin was certainly possible; it was being written by Cato himself!

Marcus Porcius Cato (234–149 BCE), later called Cato the Elder, was the first to write history in Latin. Though Cato had been born to a plebeian family in rural Tusculum, he had a brilliant public career after he had served as quaestor under Scipio in Africa in 204; he was consul in 195 and censor in 184. Throughout his public career he had been a renowned orator – Cicero knew 150 of his speeches – so he was well prepared to write in his old age the first important work in Latin prose, *Origines*. He derided Roman annals written in Greek, and defended his literary efforts as a justified use of leisure (*otium* in Latin, as opposed to its opposite, *negotium*: "business") to write Rome's history "in large letters" for his son. The work only survives in fragments quoted by later authors interested in Cato's archaic Latin. *Origines* traced Rome's history in seven books from the beginning down to about 150 BCE, shortly before the historian's death at the age of eighty-five. After the first book on the origins of Rome, Cato devoted two books to the origins of other Italian cities and throughout paid particular attention to the growing unification of Italy.

Cato was remembered for centuries for his scathing criticism of aristocratic families for their personal luxury, political corruption, and servile acceptance of Greek ideas. He fought to keep Greek philosophers from teaching at Rome, and championed the old virtues (*mos maiorum*) of frugality, work, discipline, and piety. He believed in public expenditure and private frugality and boasts in his handbook on agriculture, *De agri cultura*, how little he can spend to feed and clothe a slave and still get him to work effectively. Cato not only rejected the ideology of the Scipios and other great aristocratic families, but he stubbornly avoids mentioning the names of magistrates in his history; he simply refers to "the consul" or "the dictator." He views the Roman people as sovereign, and resents the glory that Fabius, Ennius, and even the *annales maximi* attached to individual Roman families. He sometimes made heroes of ordinary soldiers such as the tribune who fought in a lost cause and saved the Roman army:

> But what a difference it makes where you do the same service! The Laconian Leonidas, who performed a similar exploit at Thermopylae, because of his valor won unexampled glory and gratitude from all Greece, and was honored with memorials of the highest distinction; they showed their appreciation of that deed of his by pictures, statues and honorific inscriptions, in their histories and in other ways; but the tribune who had done the same thing gained small glory for his deeds.
>
> (*Origines* Frag. 83; Peter *Historicorum Romanorum Reliquiae*, tr. Leeman)

There was more than a little posing in Cato's disdain for all things Greek. His famous phrase *rem tene, verba sequentur* ("Grasp the point, the words will follow") was intended to be a rejection of Greek-style rhetoric. When he defined a good orator as simply a "good man skilled in speaking," he again emphasized morality over rhetorical training. He also boasted that he learned Greek so that his son would not learn it from a slave. In fact, he knew Greek quite well and the *Origines* displays many characteristics of Greek historiography, including surprising facts, which he called *admiranda*. For example, his treatment of the geography and customs of Italy relies heavily on the Sicilian Greek historian Timaeus, and Cato relied on other Greek sources for the Carthaginian constitution, including Polybius, with whom he probably discussed history. Cato's disdain for aristocratic self-aggrandizement did not prevent him from including his own speeches in the later books, a practice he took over from the Greek historian Xenophon. But Cato did not only learn from the Greeks; he carefully studied tombstones as well as other inscriptions for his history of Italian cities.

His purpose in writing history was to instruct Rome's future leaders in pragmatic politics, and for that both Cicero and Livy associated him with Thucydides. But Cato also believed the young should learn the moral standards of their ancestors, which needed to be retained to combat the increasing corruption that accompanied Hellenization. The *Origines* was not just didactic history, it was also the beginning of the polemical tradition of factional history at Rome. The last three books dealing with Cato's own times begin the tradition of political autobiography at Rome and set a clear precedent for the partisan nature of later Roman political history. It was also Cato, in describing his political and military career, who first made the historian's own personality the source of authority and credibility, in which he was followed by later Roman writers. He made history an extension of the battles of the Forum in his aggressive attacks on the aristocrats, so that Livy called him "a ferocious attack dog against the nobility."

The Latin annalists

From the century between Cato and Sallust there survive only fragments of the annalistic historians derided both now and in antiquity. With the pontifical annals as their formal model, these historians provided a year-by-year account of major magistrates and important events, but such a structure obviously precluded treatment of long-term political, social, or economic tendencies. They expanded the history by inventing episodes where necessary, but did not raise historical writing much beyond bare chronicle. In the words of Cicero, "they did not embellish their material, but were mere chroniclers" (*De orat.* 2, 54). Cicero meant stylistic embellishment; no one could accuse a writer like Cn. Gellius of being unimaginative, since he wrote fifteen books on Roman history before 389 BCE, though little could have been known of that period.

During the social and political conflicts of the age of the Gracchi, Roman annalists projected the violent confrontations of their day into their histories. Gaius Gracchus himself may have begun this tendency when he wrote a propagandistic biography of his murdered brother Tiberius. L. Calpurnius Piso Frugi (consul, 133 BCE) was an opponent of the Gracchi. His *annales* in seven books reached his own time. While Cicero found his style dry and overly spare, Calpurnius was respected both by Sallust and Livy. Some fragments survive because the second-century CE antiquarian Aulus Gellius found his style charming. A contemporary, C. Fannius (consul, 122 BCE), was the first Latin annalist to represent the pro-Gracchan popular tradition, though he later seems to have become strongly critical of their movement. He was steeped in the Polybian tradition and did try to rise above factional interests to engage the entire Roman people. Sallust strongly praised Fannius for his devotion to truth.

Two slightly younger contemporaries who also diverged politically were able to improve the standards of annalistic history. The plebeian L. Coelius Antipater should perhaps be regarded as the first professional Roman historian, in that he had no public career. He adopted many Greek ideas in his monograph in seven books on the Second Punic War, including an erotic interest in women that owes much to Hellenistic historical writing. He introduced the historical monograph to Rome and was sufficiently skilled in rhetoric to merit praise from Cicero:

> Fannius' contemporary, Antipater, to be sure, blew a somewhat more forceful strain, and showed some power, though of a rough and rustic character, lacking in polish and the skill that comes from training; nevertheless he might have served as a warning to his successors that they should take better pains with their writing.
>
> (*De legibus* 1, 6, tr. Keyes (Loeb))

Though Cicero seems to have been concerned only with Coelius' literary abilities, there are also historical strengths in his work. He placed Hannibal at the center of his narrative, and used sources with an African viewpoint as well as checking documentary sources. He became Livy's chief source for books 21 and 22, including the Spanish campaigns and the disasters at Trasimene and Cannae. The pathos and fantasy in his narrative sometimes approach the sensational, as when he adds a storm to enliven a sea-crossing by the Roman army. But he also shows considerable accuracy in determining Hannibal's route across the Alps and the length of his march. His vigorous style combined with historical accuracy makes Coelius perhaps the best of the annalistic historians.

Sempronius Asellio, who served as military tribune under Scipio Aemilianus in 134 BCE, wrote a history of his own time in fourteen books down to 91 BCE. He was greatly influenced by Polybius, whom he probably knew, and had ambitions to go beyond earlier annalists by explaining as well as narrating:

> But between those who have desired to leave us annals, and those who have tried to write the history of the Roman people, there was this essential difference. The books of annals merely made known what had happened and in what year it had happened, which is like writing a diary which the Greeks call ἐφημερίς. For my part, I realize that it is not enough to make known what has been done, but that one should also show with what purpose and for what reason things were done.
> (Frag. 1, Peter *Historicorum Romanorum Reliquiae*, tr. Leeman)

He wished, like Polybius, that history would be useful to the future in helping the state to prevent harm to itself and, like Cato, he tried to provide examples of virtuous behavior. To do otherwise and to behave like traditional annalists who just listed magistrates and triumphs without explaining the reasons is, for Asellio, "to tell stories to children" (A. Gell. *N.A.* 5, 18, 9). Despite a pose of objectivity, Asellio was hostile to the Gracchi and other popular politicians. It is clear that his historical aspirations took him far beyond the mere recording of facts, but Cicero criticizes Asellio for an inartistic style.

During the political struggles of the first century, the annalists focused their attention on contemporary history, devising fictions to attack or defend the Gracchi, to praise or damn Sulla. Valerius Antias wrote a history in seventy-five books from the origins of Rome to 78 BCE. It is only known from fragments quoted in later writers. He wrote much on the early years; his third book was still concerned with events under the Roman kings. Antias has attracted the most negative attention of all the annalists ever since Livy called him credulous and strongly criticized his lack of accuracy. He had no political experience to help his judgment, and seems to have invented documents recklessly. He most disturbed Livy by exaggerating numbers, usually casualty figures, but he also invented battles, documents, and glorious achievements for his Valerian ancestors. He hated Marius, and therefore exalted his opponent Sulla by calling him a reborn Servius Tullius, after Rome's sixth king.

Another annalist of the Sullan era, Q. Claudius Quadrigarius, wrote twenty-three books on the period from 390 BCE until his own day. His work contained an evident pro-Roman bias and a certain romantic credulity. More of Claudius survives than of any other annalist since his plain, unadorned style greatly appealed to Aulus Gellius two centuries later. There is one passage where we can actually make an exact comparison between Claudius (preserved verbatim in A. Gell. N.A. 9, 13, 6ff. = Frag. 10b, Peter *HRR*) and the transformation of his text by Livy (7, 9, 8). In his preface to this extended quotation of the battle in which Titus Manlius acquired the cognomen of "Torquatus," Gellius gives an ecstatic stylistic appreciation:

> All this Q. Claudius has described in the first books of his Annales with words of the utmost purity and clearness, and with the simple and unaffected charm of the old-time style. When the philosopher Favorinus read this passage from that work, he used to say that his mind was stirred and affected by no less emotion and excitement than if he were himself an eyewitness of their contest.
>
> (*Noctes Atticae* 9, 13, 4–5, tr. Rolfe (Loeb))

The excitement of Favorinus (and Gellius) is difficult to understand when one examines the simple, direct narration of Claudius. In what follows, Claudius is marked in bold italics, with Livy's reworking in ordinary italics:

> ***As soon as silence was secured he called out in a mighty voice that if anyone wished to engage him in single combat, he should come forward.***

Then a Gaul of extraordinary size advanced upon the empty bridge, and making his voice as loud as possible, cried out, "Let him whom Rome now reckons her bravest man come out and fight, that we two may show by the outcome which people is the superior in war."

This no one dared to do, because of his great size and savage aspect. Then the Gaul began to laugh at them and to stick out his tongue.

The young Romans were for a long time silent. Ashamed to decline the challenge, they were loath to volunteer for a service of transcendent peril.

This at once aroused the great indignation of one Titus Manlius, a youth of the highest birth, that such an insult should be offered to his country, and that no one from so great an army should accept the challenge. He, as I say, stepped forth, and would not suffer Roman valor to be shamefully tarnished by a Gaul.

Then T. Manlius, the son of Lucius, who had rescued his father from the persecution of the tribune, left his station and went to the dictator. "Without your orders, General," he said, "I would fain never leave my place to fight, not so I saw that victory was assured; but if you permit me, I would show that beast who dances out so boldly before the standards of the enemy, that I come of the family that hurled the column of Gauls from the Tarpeian Rock." To whom the dictator made answer, "Success attend your valor, Titus Manlius, and your loyalty to father and country! Go, and with Heaven's help make good the unconquerable Roman name."

Armed with a foot-soldier's shield and a Spanish sword, he confronted the Gaul.

The young man's friends then armed him; he assumed the shield of a foot-soldier, and to his side he buckled a Spanish sword, convenient for close fighting. Armed and accoutered, they led him forth to the Gaul, who in his stupid glee – for the ancients have even thought this worth mentioning – thrust out his tongue in derision.

Livy dramatizes the bare story and adds to it the emotions of the principal characters as well as the involvement and motivations of the commander and comrades of Manlius. One amusing difference is Claudius' casual mention of the Gaul sticking out his tongue, while Livy clearly finds it too distasteful for his elevated literary account. First he does not mention it, but then he does so only after having excused himself by attributing it to his source. The Latin of Claudius is far more abrupt and less varied than that of Livy; the former's sentences vary between seven and nineteen words while Livy's range from four to thirty-four. These brief examples demonstrate how the bareness of an annalist could be embellished by a fine writer. It is important to remember that only fifty years lay between these texts.

As for another contemporary of Sulla, Cicero mentions that L. Cornelius Sisenna "easily surpassed all historians up to the present time" (*De leg.* 1, 7). Yet Cicero sees him as still below the level of an ideal Roman historian. Sisenna was personally close to Sulla and served as praetor in 78. At some point he wrote an extended history of the Social War and its aftermath, probably covering the period from 91 to 78 BCE. He was an accomplished rhetorician, who included speeches and dramatic elements like prodigies and dreams. He strove to create a work of literary art and, to some degree, succeeded. Though Sallust criticized Sisenna for being insufficiently critical of Sulla, his own *Histories* took up the historical narrative from 78 BCE where Sisenna ended.

The century of annalistic history in Latin must be judged from fragments, since these works eventually perished after they were superseded by Livy's great history of the entire Republic. The annalists preserved what was still a living tradition of Rome's past but they also expanded the past through invention, borrowings from the Greek, and introduction of later events into the history of early Rome. Family pride and unquestioning chauvinism distorted the material, as did their need to sacrifice all to the annalistic chronological framework. There were different interpretations of what was missing: Asellio believed, with Polybius, that the true historian must ask probing questions while Cicero lamented the absence of true literary art. Thus they set the agenda for Rome's first historians worthy to stand beside the Greek antecedents.

Cicero's view of history

The major intellectual and literary figure of the late Roman Republic, Marcus Tullius Cicero, speculated on the theory of history in his literary and philosophical essays. He distinguished history from poetry by its devotion to truth, yet he believed literary ability to be absolutely essential and had only contempt for the inept products of the annalists.

For who does not know that history's first law is that an author must not dare to tell anything but the truth? And its second that he must make bold to tell the whole truth? That there must be no suggestion of partiality anywhere in his writings? Nor of malice? The groundwork (*fundamenta*) of course is familiar to every one; the superstructure (*aedificatio*) however rests upon the story and the diction.

(*De orat.* 2, 62, tr. Sutton and Rackham (Loeb))

Since the only available literary training was in rhetoric, it followed for Cicero that rhetorical training was fundamental if the historian was to achieve the Ciceronian goal of making his work persuasive and having it affect future political life.

But history — the witness of the age, the light of truth, the life of memory, the mistress of life, the ambassador of the past — whose voice except the orator's can entrust her to immortality?

(*De orat.* 2, 36, tr. Sutton and Rackham (Loeb))

Cicero understood that stylistic adaptation was necessary when the orator turned to history:

History...involves a narrative in an ornate style, with here and there a description of a country or a battle. It has also occasional harangues and speeches of exhortation. But the aim is a smooth flowing style, not the terse and vigorous language of the orator.

(*Orator* 66, tr. Hubbell (Loeb))

Cicero saw the relationship between oratory and history as reciprocal, since the advocate needed historical material in much the same way as he needed a knowledge of law:

He should also be acquainted with the history of the events of past ages, particularly, of course, of our state, but also of imperial nations and famous kings; here our task has been lightened by the labor of our friend Atticus, who has comprised in one book the record of seven hundred years, keeping the chronology definite and omitting no important event.

(*Orator* 120, tr. Hubbell (Loeb))

Here, as so often in his work, we see Cicero differentiate between the pleasurable and the useful. While he deplores the literary barrenness of earlier Roman annalists and calls for a literary form of history that will rival the Greeks, for the practical purposes of the working advocate he seems to find adequate the chronological handbook of his close friend Atticus. That is more likely his discretion, since in his dialogue *On the Laws* he has none other than Atticus address him in the following words:

> There has long been a desire, or rather a demand, that you should write a history. For people think that, if you entered that field, we might rival Greece in this brand of literature also. And to give you my own opinion, it seems to me that you owe this duty not merely to the desires of those who take pleasure in literature, but also to your country, in order that the land which you have saved you may also glorify. For our national literature is deficient in history, as I realized myself and I frequently hear you say.
>
> (*De leg.* 1, 5, tr. Keyes (Loeb))

Cicero's seeming devotion to historical truth in the passage from the *De Oratore* contrasts with his repeated desire to have an historian write a laudatory account of his own consulship and his suppression of the Catilinarian conspiracy. When he sent his preparatory memoir to his teacher Poseidonius, that wily Greek said it was perfect as it stood and needed no further embellishment. Then Cicero sent a letter to his friend Lucceius:

> So I repeat – elaborate my activities even against your better judgment, and in the process disregard the laws of historiography...Please don't suppress that favor if it nudges you strongly in my favor, but simply let your affection for me take a degree of precedence over the truth.
>
> (*Epist. ad fam.* 5, 12, 3, tr. Woodman)

Like other Roman writers, Cicero's concept of truth is somewhat different from our own; he essentially means an absence of favoritism or overt bias. He was a lawyer and, like modern attorneys, sought to construct a plausible narrative based on the facts. The foundation must be true but, in creating the superstructure, the historians, like an orator, must find what is necessary to embellish the case. To Lucceius, Cicero even goes a step further when he urges his friend to show favoritism for the sake of their friendship; he really wants an *encomium* rather than genuine history.

When Cicero calls for the ornamentation of history according to the rules of rhetoric, he does not only mean the language must be more stylistically elaborate. For the skilled orator ornaments his material both in style and in content. The historian, like any other rhetorician, must rely on what was technically called *inventio* to find appropriate material to illustrate the story. He is probably going to read his composition in Roman salons and, like Herodotus, he wishes to keep his audience's interest. Hence he will add storms or pirates to his account of a sea voyage, since they were ever-present dangers on any voyage, and, even if there is no record of them happening, they are plausible, even probable; the embellishment of the material is precisely what an orator would do in court or the forum. It is different from the modern idea of historical truth as an absolute, but it shows us how much ancient historical writing is first and foremost a branch of literature. Before we dismiss the ancient reliance on plausibility, we should recall how often in the modern courtroom the hypothetical (but plausible) narrative is successfully offered to the jury in place of actual argument on the evidence.

Cicero well understood that at Rome history could be a more effective form of moral education than philosophy. The Romans were not by nature a speculative people; they would rather see specific examples of *virtus* than to hear "the good" described in an abstract philosophical dialogue as the ancient Athenians had. Cicero also seems to have preferred a historical monograph, of the sort that Sallust was to write, to the massive survey of Roman history which Livy attempted. In his mind the more focused history would better employ a rhetorical style and would have a greater moral impact.

Although Cicero defined the genre of moral historiography at Rome and was Rome's greatest historical theorist, his political interests and perhaps a fear of making even more enemies kept him from doing for history what he had done for oratory and philosophy: creating a Latin genre based on Greek achievements, but with a uniquely Roman style and form. Indeed, several of his essays are in fact histories of Roman oratory (*Brutus*) or of the Roman constitution (*Republic*), but he never turned to political history. When he had leisure near the end of his life, he preferred to write philosophy.

> This is the only branch of Latin literature which even now
> not only does not match Greece but was left completely

coarse and unfinished by the death of Cicero. He was the
only man who could and should have given history a elegant
voice...I am uncertain whether the fatherland or historical
writing has lost more by his death.

(Cornelius Nepos, Frag. 40, Peter *HRR*)

On the other hand Cicero did leave a remarkable record in his
hundreds of letters to his political allies and friends, but to the
Roman mind those were far from a work of history.

History in the late Republic

Cicero's repeated plea for a Roman historiography that would rival
that of Greece was not in vain. Within a decade of his death in
43 BCE, Sallust had published his monographs and Livy had begun
preparations for his great history of the entire Roman Republic. But
even in Cicero's lifetime there was increasing interest in various
forms of historical writing. As the Republic unraveled, writers
looked to celebrate its glorious past. Caesar's *Commentaries* and
Cornelius Nepos' *Lives of Illustrious Men* will be addressed in the
later chapter on autobiography and biography. Nepos' *Chronicles*
(*Chronica*) in three books was a universal chronology that brought
Roman history into synchronism with events in Greece and the
Near East. (We must recall that Greeks, Romans, Egyptians, Jews,
and other ancient peoples all used different calendars.) Nepos was
himself part of the Ciceronian intellectual circle, since he dedicated
his *Lives* to Atticus and published his (now lost) intellectual correspondence with Cicero. Later Cicero's closest friend, T. Pomponius
Atticus, published a one-volume handbook of all Roman history
down to 49 BCE, called *Liber Annalis*. We should not underestimate
the scholarly importance of such reference books in an age without
libraries, but these compendia as well as Nepos' *Lives* also testify to
the expansion of the general reading audience. In one letter, Cicero
asks Atticus to discover the ten members of an embassy to Greece a
century earlier. Cicero had found two names, and Atticus could add
only one more. Later historians would use such reference works to
build a common framework for their histories.

Though the work of Atticus and Nepos hardly reflected original
historical research, their contemporary M. Terentius Varro (116–27
BCE) was engaged in genuine research into history and many other
subjects. Varro, one of the true polymaths of the ancient world,
wrote over 500 books in his eighty-nine years. Though only his

work on agriculture is fully preserved and his important book on the Latin language has partially survived, the fragments and titles of his other works show an astonishing range of interests: philosophy, law, rhetoric, language, literary criticism, biography, geography, and dozens of books of poetry, drama, and satire. Nowadays Varro is usually identified as an "antiquarian," which in our day carries overtones of dusty irrelevance. In fact, Varro's work in his *Antiquitates* (forty books) more closely resembles the research efforts of a modern cultural historian than do most ancient historical writers. He examined language, literature, customs, and especially religion to show the connections between Rome's present and the past. The erudition of the work astounded contemporaries like Cicero, who thus addresses Varro:

> We were wandering and straying about like visitors in our own city, and your books led us, so to speak, right home and enabled us at last to realize who and where we were. You have revealed the age of our native city, the chronology of its history, the laws of its religion and priesthood, its civil and its military institutions, topography...
>
> (*Acad. post.* 1, 3, 9, tr. Rackham (Loeb))

Yet surviving fragments reveal that Varro's style was dry and rather obscure, and for the Romans, no research achievements were sufficient to outweigh stylistic deficiencies. Cicero may praise his research, but he still called for a Roman to challenge the Greeks in history. Varro was merely a scholar; Cicero awaited a literary artist. Antiquarian research would not be considered true history until the eighteenth century. Varro's vast learning led Caesar to ask him to create a public library. When the library was finally built, Varro was the only living author honored with a bust.

The structure and arguments of some of his *Antiquitates* survive because the early Christian writers, especially St Augustine in his *City of God*, used Varro's treatment of Roman religion as a foil against which to argue. It was particularly his notion that religion is a human creation that led the Church fathers to deride the barrenness of paganism. Varro remained for all antiquity, and even in the Middle Ages, the model of Roman erudition, but his Latin was not sufficiently graceful for the books to be repeatedly recopied as school texts and hence they have been lost.

2

SALLUST

The earliest surviving complete histories from ancient Rome are two monographs written by the retired general C. Sallustius Crispus (86–35 BCE) in the decade following Julius Caesar's death in 44 BCE. These books – *The Conspiracy of Catiline* (*Catilina*) and *The Jugurthine War* (*Jugurtha*) – examine the political, economic, and social changes that racked Rome in the half-century (113–63 BCE) between the collapse of the Gracchan reforms and the rise of Caesar. After being driven from public life, Sallust channeled his disappointment and anger into history to examine the political pathology of the final death throes of the Roman Republic. But it was less his political insight than his literary artistry and fierce moral vision that made him the great Roman historian of decline, and thus left a lasting mark on the way the late Republic was viewed by later readers – from Romans like Tacitus and St Augustine through the centuries to our own day.

Life and works

Sallust was born in the town of Amiternum fifty miles northeast of Rome in 86 BCE. His family was of Sabine origin, but they long held Roman citizenship in that thoroughly Romanized area. Though nothing is known of the historian's boyhood, it is evident from his writings that he received an excellent education in both Latin and Greek language, literature, and rhetoric. He was the first in his family to pursue a political career, which must have required substantial economic resources. Sallust was proud that his advancement rested on his own merits, like that of Marius and Cicero, rather than on family connections. That early struggle for political recognition was doubtless responsible for his contempt for nobles who owed their careers to their heredity rather than their achievements. The historian's view is expressed in words he gives to Marius: "Nobility begins with merit" (*Jugurtha* 85).

Sallust must have migrated to the capital in his late teens to seek a career in politics, and his later success suggests that he pursued it with tenacity and skill. It brought him a turbulent life that was symptomatic of the disorder he described in his picture of political activity in the late Republic. Sallust later claimed that the "weakness of youth" allowed him to become corrupted by politicians, but one might better regard it as the same burning ambition shared by many young Roman aristocrats. At about the age of thirty Sallust was elected *quaestor*, and the first certain date in his political career is 52 BCE when he served as tribune of the plebs. It was a violent year of thuggery and gang warfare, in which the consular candidate Milo was brought to trial for having killed the popular leader Clodius in street fighting. Sallust organized ferocious street demonstrations to exert public pressure on Milo's lawyer, Cicero, which seems to have intimidated that eloquent advocate into giving a substandard performance. (That, at least, was the view of Milo himself.) Though Sallust's actual political alliances at that time are obscure, his enmity toward the followers of Pompey and his loyalty to Caesar's man Clodius make it likely that he had hopes for advancement when Caesar returned from Gaul.

A few years later the censor expelled Sallust from the Senate for unspecified offenses, though some questionable sources attribute it to the sort of lurid personal scandals that were stock invective in Roman politics. In any event, he was saved by civil war and in 49 BCE, after Caesar marched into Italy, Sallust was given the command of a legion in Illyria. This is the first record of any military position. Two years later, as praetor-elect, he was called upon to suppress a military revolt in southern Italy, and barely escaped with his life. Caesar himself had to rescue the situation. Sallust's election to the praetorship returned him to senatorial status, and he accompanied Caesar to north Africa for the successful battle at Utica against Cato and the republican forces. When Caesar established the province of Africa Nova from the former kingdom of Numidia (modern eastern Algeria), he appointed Sallust as its first proconsular governor with three legions under his command. Since the dictator passed over more experienced officials for this important appointment, he presumably either saw in Sallust great administrative skills or chose to reward his unwavering devotion. This was the high point of Sallust's public career – a career that is itself a symptom of the social transformation of the late Republic.

This public career occupied Sallust's energies until the age of forty-one, when it ended in disaster and disgrace. In Africa he had ample opportunity for self-enrichment as he disposed of the royal estates, treasures, palaces, and art collections. In similar circumstances many past Roman governors had provided for their future. But Caesar had recently passed a law on corruption as an indication of his personal strictness and his intention to improve provincial administration. In 45 BCE Sallust returned from Africa to face charges of corruption and extortion. Though such charges were not uncommon, in this case there was probably considerable evidence, since it was widely rumored that Sallust had to bribe Caesar himself to escape from prosecution. More likely, Caesar allowed his old comrade to retire from public life and confiscated a portion of his dubious profits. Despite this episode, Sallust clearly worshipped Caesar and saw in him the only possible salvation for the Republic. After the assassination of Caesar, Sallust retreated to his lavish estate, later called "Gardens of Sallust," on the northern hills of the city near the modern Via Veneto. He was fortunate to survive those years when Octavian and Antony proscribed so many (including Cicero) for political or financial reasons. His famous property was greatly embellished by his adopted son, who never held office but later served as a personal counselor of both Augustus and Tiberius. The estate was later bequeathed to the imperial family and both the emperors Vespasian and Nerva resided there.

In his last decade Sallust turned from politics to history. Despite his earlier misfortunes, he presents historical writing as his own choice and certainly pursued it with vigor and passion. The Roman elite fiercely competed in electoral politics as the only way to achieve the *gloria* that was the ultimate test of a successful career. (Since military commands and provincial governorships were only voted to ex-magistrates, military glory was possible only after earlier political success.) But that was no longer possible for Sallust. Since Romans were scornful of a life of leisure – the *inertia* of old-style aristocrats who preferred hunting and farming to the turbulence of the Forum – Sallust felt the need (as Cicero had done during his exile from politics) to justify his literary pursuits. Cicero's Latin phrase was *otium cum dignitate* – productive leisure. In the prefaces to the two monographs he wrote between 44 and 40 BCE, the novice historian sought to present the writing of history as an extension of public life. There was little point in political or military achievements unless they were recorded for future generations of Romans to use and learn from. History was not disconnected from public life, since the true historian draws on his own political and military experience more than on archives. His first prologue, to *The Conspiracy of Catiline*, is rather defensive in asserting the glory due to an historian:

> It is glorious to serve one's country by deeds; even to serve her by words is a thing not to be despised; one may become famous in peace as well as in war. Not only those who have acted, but those also who have recorded the acts of others oftentimes receive our approbation. And for myself, although I am well aware that by no means equal repute attends the narrator and the doer of deeds, yet I regard the writing of history as one of the most difficult of tasks: first, because the style and diction must be equal to the deeds recorded; and in the second place, because such criticisms as you make of others' shortcomings are thought by most men to be due to malice and envy. Furthermore, when you commemorate the distinguished merit and fame of good men, while every one is quite ready to believe you when you tell of things which he thinks he could easily do himself, everything beyond that he regards as fictitious, if not false.
>
> When I myself was a young man, my inclinations at first led me, like many another, into public life, and there I encountered many obstacles; for instead of modesty, incorruptibility and honesty, shamelessness, bribery and rapacity held sway. And although my soul, a stranger to evil ways, recoiled from such faults, yet amid so many vices my youthful weakness was led astray and held captive by ambition; for while I took no part in the evil practices of the others, yet the desire for preferment made me the victim of the same ill-repute and jealousy as they.
>
> Accordingly, when my mind found peace after many troubles and perils and I had determined that I must pass what was left of my life aloof from public affairs, it was not my intention to waste my precious leisure in indolence and sloth, nor yet by turning to farming or the chase, to lead a life devoted to slavish employments. On the contrary, I resolved to return to a cherished purpose from which ill-starred ambition had diverted me, and write a history of the Roman people, selecting such portions as seemed to me worthy of record; and I was confirmed in this resolution by

the fact that my mind was free from hope, and fear, and partisanship.

(Catilina 3–4, 1–2)[1]

In the preface to *The Jugurthine War* Sallust raises a more assured, even aggressive, voice:

But among these pursuits, in my opinion, magistracies and military commands, in short all public offices, are least desirable in these times, since honor is not bestowed upon merit, while those who have gained it wrongfully are neither safe nor the more honorable because of it. For to rule one's country or subjects by force, although you both have the power to correct abuses, and do correct them, is nevertheless tyrannical; especially since all attempts at change foreshadow bloodshed, exile, and other horrors of war. Moreover, to struggle in vain and after wearisome exertion to gain nothing but hatred, is the height of folly, unless haply one is possessed by a dishonorable and pernicious passion for sacrificing one's personal honor and liberty to the power of a few men.

But among intellectual pursuits, the recording of the events of the past is especially serviceable; but of that it becomes me to say nothing, both because many men have already spoken of its value, and in order that no one may suppose that I am led by vanity to eulogize my own favorite occupation. I suppose, too, that since I have resolved to pass my life aloof from public affairs, some will apply to this arduous and useful employment of mine the name of idleness *(inertia)*, certainly those who regard courting the people and currying favor by banquets as the height of industriousness. But if such men will only bear in mind in what times I was elected to office, what men of merit were unable to attend the same honor and what sort of men have since come into the Senate, they will surely be convinced that it is rather from justifiable motives than from indolence that I have changed my opinion, and that greater profit will accrue to our country from my inactivity *(otium)* than from others' activity.

(Jugurtha 3–4, 1–4)

This image of historical writing as a form of public service had a great effect on Sallust's successors. When he attributes at least part of the renown of classical Athens to its outstanding historians, he appeals to the deep competitive instinct of the Roman elite to give greater value to its historians so that Roman achievements will become better known. There are, however, problems with Sallust's argument, since he suggests that historians merely extol the glories of their leaders. In his own terms, Sallust suggests that the didactic purpose of history is to hold up for display the *virtus* through which the natural gifts of a Roman (*ingenium*) can bring renown (*gloria*) to himself, his family, and the state. Sallust himself certainly does praise Rome's past through the traditional topos of the Golden Age, but his aim is to throw a dark shadow over his contemporaries of the late Republic. His experience with the senatorial nobility in the political maneuvers of the 50s and in the civil war of the 40s led him to a deep bitterness toward the elite. There are few unalloyed heroes in his surviving writings. His prefaces seem to depict history as a eulogy of great achievements, but in fact Sallust's own writings are analytical and deeply critical of the political culture of first-century BCE Rome. What the historian achieved is far more profound and more influential than the program he proposed at the outset of his work.

The Conspiracy of Catiline

For his first attempt at history, Sallust announced his desire to write history selectively and thus avoided writing narrative history in an annalistic framework. He turned rather to a narrowly focused monograph on a dramatic political episode of his youth: the failed *coup d'état* of Lucius Sergius Catiline in 63 BCE. He professed to see in the Catilinarian conspiracy an unprecedented danger for the state. In doing so, he accepted the perhaps overly dramatic account of the consul Cicero who suppressed the insurrection. (Modern historians are more skeptical that the state was in any real danger from such a disorganized cabal.) Cicero had unsuccessfully asked the historian Lucceius to write a sympathetic account of his consulship; Sallust's work is different, and far more ambitious. Not only does his account of the drama make Catiline the protagonist and consign Cicero to a supporting role, but the historian placed the "conspiracy" in the wider context of political and social crisis. Though Sallust often emphasizes his desire to use history to promote virtue, what usually attracts him are stories of personal and political corruption. Thus the dissipation and corruption of the impoverished aristocrat Catiline are matched by the social and political disorder of the times. If Sallust wished to begin his new career preaching high-minded morality, he could not have chosen a better subject.

Catiline, twice a failed candidate for the consulship, organized a revolutionary movement in the countryside. He drew his support from a combination of profligate young nobles and farmers whose lands had been confiscated under Sulla two decades earlier. Sallust sets this movement against a background of the terrible conditions in rural Italy in the post-Sullan era. At the center of the monograph, a digression analyzes corresponding changes in political behavior:

> But the city populace in particular acted with desperation for many reasons. To begin with, all who were especially conspicuous for their shamelessness and impudence, those too who had squandered their patrimony in riotous living, finally all whom disgrace or crime had forced to leave home, had all flowed into Rome as into a cesspool. Many, too, who recalled Sulla's victory, when they saw common soldiers risen to the rank of senator, and others become so rich that they feasted and lived like kings, hoped each for himself for like fruits of victory, if he took the field. Besides this, the young men who had maintained a wretched existence by manual labor in the country, tempted by public and private doles had come to prefer idleness in the city to their hateful toil; these, like all the others, battened on the public ills. Therefore it is not surprising that men who were beggars and without character with illimitable hopes, should respect their country as little as they did themselves. Moreover, those to whom Sulla's victory had meant the proscription of their parents, loss of property, and curtailment of their rights, looked forward in a similar spirit to the issue of a war. Finally, all who belonged to another party than that of the Senate preferred to see the government overthrown rather than be out of power themselves. Such, then, was the evil which after many years had returned upon the state.
>
> (*Catilina* 37, 4–11)

Though Catiline may have received some support from Caesar and other "popular" politicians – those deriving support from the popular assembly as opposed to the Senate – he essentially took his movement outside the political system and was finally prepared to launch a civil war to bring himself to power. Cicero, whose four speeches "Against Catiline" survive, provoked the conspirators into open revolt, where they could be crushed by the army.

After the Ides of March in 44 BCE and the murder of Cicero the next year, all the principals of the Catilinarian era were dead and Sallust was free to use a wealth of source material, including Cicero's speeches and his now lost memoir on his consulship. Sallust mentions having heard Crassus later declare "with his own lips" that Cicero had slandered him, thus adding to the historian's authority. Otherwise Sallust gives no indication of his own observations during the Catilinarian episode, so he may have been on military service outside of Rome. Though Cicero's speeches provide more details on the stages of the revolt and the diplomatic activities, it is only Sallust who reveals the widespread discontent throughout Italy and the crushing burden of debt that inspired some of the revolutionaries. It is here that we learn of promises of debt relief as well as the proscription of the rich. Though he relies primarily on Cicero as a source, he gives far greater prominence to Cato and Caesar as antagonists in the senatorial debate on whether to execute the captured conspirators. The pair of speeches are the climax of the monograph, and that rhetorical structure recalls Thucydides' treatment of the outbreak of the Peloponnesian War. Like Thucydides, Sallust has written the speeches himself. The historian makes the debate into a contest of virtue between Cato and Caesar and gives a remarkably fair-minded account of figures whose supporters venomously vilified each other. It is in fact Cato's ideals that seem most to approach those of Sallust. This is not so surprising as it might seem, since Sallust recognized that Cato despised the *optimates* despite the fact that he later would become their moral leader. The figure of Cicero is allowed to fade quietly into the background. Since Sallust opposed Cicero in politics and, as importantly, in style, he is clearly reluctant to accord him a dominant role.

Though Catiline is introduced as an utterly corrupt reprobate whose guilt is never in question, Sallust occasionally allows a certain nobility to emerge. Catiline's speech before the final battle is so noble that one scholar has denounced it as "fraudulent," and the reader can see that Catiline's death is given a certain specious heroism for dramatic reasons. There are other elements in the book — the chronology and the account of the "first" conspiracy — that modern historians are unwilling to accept. But as an initial effort, Sallust has produced a rhetorically powerful and politically illuminating account of personal and public depravity. It is a successful beginning of his new career.

Perhaps the more immediate political purpose of *The Conspiracy of Catiline* was a plea for common sense, since it was written during the worst of the proscriptions of the Second Triumvirate. The speech of Caesar against the death penalty for the conspirators can be held up to the murderous actions of those calling themselves the heirs of Caesar: Octavian and Marc Antony. Sallust wished to take the debate beyond the personal iniquity of Catiline to examine the weakness in the state that allowed such a rebellion to arise and grow.

The Jugurthine War

Immediately after completion of *The Conspiracy of Catiline*, Sallust turned to another tale of avarice and corruption. In this case he would show the connection between Rome's overseas conquests and the corruption of domestic politics. Between 112 and 105 BCE the Romans fought a frustrating series of wars against the north African prince Jugurtha. Jugurtha was a wily adversary: a master of both desert warfare and the corruption of Roman officials. Thus *The Jugurthine War* enabled Sallust to develop his argument that Rome's decline was due to the venal and bungling aristocracy:

> I propose to write of the war which the people of Rome waged with Jugurtha, king of the Numidians: first, because it was long, sanguinary and of varying fortune; and secondly, because then for the first time resistance was offered to the insolence of the nobles – the beginning of a struggle which threw everything, human and divine, into confusion, and rose to such a pitch of frenzy that civil discord ended in war and the devastation of Italy.
>
> (*Jugurtha* 5, 1–2)

Though some Romans regarded the earlier Gracchan episode as the first serious challenge to "the insolence of the nobles" which presaged future violence between the orders, Sallust preferred to emphasize the aristocratic corruption during the struggle against Jugurtha as the beginning of the revolution of the first century.

Sallust begins with a disquisition on the nature of man and the connection between body and soul. This preface, though highly derivative of Greek authors, is more assured than in his earlier book and is reasonably well integrated with the subsequent historical narrative. For the history proper Sallust used an earlier annalistic history, which he supplemented with material from the autobiographies of Aemilius Scaurus, Rutilius Rufus, and Sulla. It is Sulla's version of the surrender of Jugurtha that Sallust adopts at the end of his book. The treatment of military matters is unbiased, but the work suffers from the author's uncertain grasp of chronology and a typically Roman weakness in geography, though it does successfully evoke African desert warfare. He is more convincing when he writes on the personal corruption of Jugurtha (as he did earlier of Catiline), and on the political corruption that stemmed from the transformation of the Roman state in the post-Gracchan era. What is ostensibly a monograph on a foreign war becomes an analysis of internal factional strife, much as did Thucydides' treatment of the Peloponnesian War. In both Periclean Athens and Republican Rome, the acquisition of an overseas empire had brought the arrogance of conquest and the wealth to transform traditional values. While the Sallustian account may be overly schematic, there is an essential truth in his linking of imperialism with social degeneration.

Sallust's increasing self-confidence and mastery of his craft are clear in his skillful use of dramatic construction and his sharper moral critique of the senatorial class. He attributes Rome's reluctance to fight Jugurtha to the African's successful bribery of senators, and his antipathy to the senatorial class leads him to play down the genuine reasons of cost and military difficulty. The historian admits that the young Jugurtha, who fought at Numantia and was befriended by the Scipio Aemilianus, was seen as "a tough fighter and a wise counselor" who had "a generous nature and a shrewd intellect." It would hardly be surprising if Roman senators who had served with him twenty years earlier were slow to believe the treacheries attributed to him. In addition, some senators might have been reluctant to commit forces to an African war while there was a chance that the Germanic tribe called Cimbri was still threatening Gaul and possibly Italy. Such reasonable objections are ignored; for Sallust, all who opposed a war against Jugurtha had been corrupted. He reinforces this picture when he portrays Jugurtha as shocked on the one occasion that bribery was no longer effective. While he does not castigate the senatorial general Metellus, Sallust does portray the nobles at Rome – especially M. Aemilius Scaurus – as unscrupulous in using civil strife (*factio*) and rhetorical skill to maintain their dominance. Hence he gives pride of place to the anti-aristocratic speeches by Memmius (31) and Marius (63), and to the digression on the factionalism of the post-Gracchan period (42). Sallust does not fully exempt the *plebs* from blame for the internal dissension, and he recognizes that both sides bear some responsibility. The Republic is up for sale, and tribunes are bought through bribery as well as senators. But despite the obvious corruption of some popular leaders, Sallust regards the nobles' arrogance and greed as the fundamental causes of the conflict.

Sallust's desire for the dramatic leads him to exaggerate the speed of Marius' rise to power. Marius had progressed methodically through the established career pattern. When he was elected consul and replaced Metellus as commander of the African troops, it was not merely a personal triumph but the rise of a new political elite. He even devised a completely new way of staffing a professional army, using volunteers rather than relying only on conscripts. Marius becomes an icon rather than an individual. Like Cato before him and Cicero forty years later, Marius was a "new man" (*novus homo*) who reached the highest office despite having no consular ancestors. Sallust says he can display only his weapons and scars, instead of the wax masks of his ancestors. He did not speak Greek, but his military success allowed him first to defeat Jugurtha and later to campaign in the north for five years until he successfully repulsed German invaders. Despite this generally positive portrait, Sallust does not refrain from mentioning Marius' weaknesses. Marius, Sulla, and even Jugurtha receive positive initial introductions, but in each case the historian's expectations are disappointed.

In *The Jugurthine War* Sallust shows a greater literary skill in including, for structural reasons, the set-piece narratives of the battles at Zama and at Thala as well as political and cultural digressions. The African setting allowed the author to embellish his story with foreign landscapes and exotic descriptions for the entertainment of his reader. The historian says that he used Latin translations of Carthaginian books about the original inhabitants of Africa; he also took ethnographic material from Greek sources like Poseidonius. The book is far from a narrow political or military monograph; it gives the impression of being designed as part of a continuous historical record. He uses the African setting to evoke memories of the Carthaginian Wars and the danger Hannibal posed to Rome. Sallust regards the final destruction of Carthage in 146 BCE as the apex of the rise of Rome; thereafter the absence of a serious rival propelled the Roman elite into the arrogance, self-indulgence, and corruption that led to the post-Gracchan civil conflict. In this picture of Roman political history Sallust is genuinely original. Hence this disgraceful, and divisive, African war is contrasted with the more heroic invasions led by Scipio Africanus (202 BCE) and Scipio Aemilianus (148 BCE) when the Roman people were united in support of their armies.

The Histories

In his final years Sallust undertook what he intended to be his greatest literary achievement: an annalistic history beginning from the death of Sulla in 78 BCE where the annalist Sisenna concluded his history. The book, called *The Histories*, only reached 67 BCE and was left unfinished at the author's death. The metrical form of the first words announced the author's ambition to write a large-scale history that would rival epic poetry – the goal of ancient historical writers since Herodotus. The metrical beginning was also used by Livy and Tacitus in their annalistic histories. The aim of *The Histories* was to trace the collapse of the "constitution" that Sulla established to secure senatorial dominance. For this reason the first book seems to have devoted a good deal of attention to Sulla, perhaps to alert the triumvirs to the dangers of a bloody and repressive regime. Once again personal ambition reduced Roman politics to factional strife as men like Pompey and Crassus struggled for preeminence.

The Histories only survives as a series of fragments. Nearly all the 500 fragments are very short passages or phrases incorporated in later Latin authors, but there are a small number of substantial speeches and letters excerpted in antiquity for use in school. The surviving phrases are often one-line epigrams that probably distort the general character of the book. Likewise, the surviving speeches often include extended political analyses and these too may distort the author's focus. As a result, scholars differ on the overall tone of the book, but they agree that it certainly was annalistic in structure with ethnographic and geographical digressions.

Sallust makes no attempt to capture the style of Roman politicians in the speeches contained in *The Histories*, just as he did not imitate Cato or Caesar in *The Conspiracy of Catiline*. The speeches may include ideas, arguments, and even deceptions that were appropriate to the speaker, but the style was the historian's own. While Sallust may have seen a copy of the letter Pompey sent to the Senate in 74 BCE, his concern was likewise not to repeat Pompey's words but to provide a forceful impression of the vanity and ambition of the man. Sallust despised Pompey, whom he always saw as the bloodthirsty gangster in Sulla's employ rather than the later, far more respectable, leader of the senatorial party and defender of the Republic. So he perhaps exaggerated the self-importance, self-pity, and thinly veiled threats of the young *condottiere* in the letter he composed for him:

(1) If it had been against you and my country's gods that I had undertaken all the toils and dangers which have accompanied the many occasions since my early manhood when under my leadership the most dangerous enemies have been routed and your safety secured, you could not, Fathers of the Senate, have taken more severe measures against me in my absence than you are now doing. For, in spite of my youth, having exposed me to a most cruel war, you have as far as you were able destroyed by starvation, the most wretched of all deaths, me and an army which deserves your highest gratitude. (2) Was it with such expectations that the Roman people sent its sons to war? Are these the rewards for wounds, for blood shed so often for our country? Tired of writing letters and sending envoys, I have exhausted all my personal resources and even my future prospects, while in the mean time for a three-year period you have barely given me the means of meeting even one year's expenses. (3) By the immortal gods, do you think I can play the part of a treasury or maintain an army without food and pay?

(4) For my part I admit that I set out for this war with more eagerness than discretion, for, having received from you only a titular command, within forty days I raised and equipped an army and drove an enemy who was already at the very throat of Italy from the Alps into Spain; and through those mountains I opened up a route different from that which Hannibal had taken and more convenient for us. (5) I recovered Gaul, the Pyrenees, Lacetania, and the Indicetes; I withstood the first onslaught of the victorious Sertorius in spite of the rawness of my troops and the enemy's superiority in numbers. I spent the winter in camp surrounded by the most savage of foes, not in the towns nor in boosting my own popularity. (6) Why need I enumerate battles or winter expeditions or the towns we have destroyed or captured? Actions speak louder than words: the taking of the enemy's camp at the Sucro, the battle of the

river Turia, the destruction of the enemy general C. Herennius together with his army and the city of Valentia – all these are sufficiently known to you. In exchange for them, grateful senators, you present me with famine and shortages.

(7) Thus the situation of my army and that of my enemy is the same: for neither is being paid and either, if victorious, can march into Italy. (8) I draw your attention to this state of affairs and ask you to take notice of it and not to force me to solve my difficulties by abandoning the interests of the state for my own. (9) That part of hither Spain which is not in enemy hands has been laid waste, either by us or by Sertorius, to the point of extermination, except for the coast towns, to the stage where it is actually an expense and a burden for us. Last year Gaul provided Metellus' army with pay and provisions; now, because of a failure of the crops, it can hardly support itself. I have exhausted not only my means, but even my credit. (10) You are our last resort; unless you come to our aid my army, against my wish but as I have already warned you, will cross to Italy and bring with it the whole Spanish war.

(*The Histories* 2, 82, tr. P. McGushin)

Likewise the famous letter of the defeated Asian king Mithridates (4, 67) provides a bitter attack on Roman imperialism from the point of view of the conquered, much as the Scottish chief Calgacus is given, in Tacitus' words, an eloquent denunciation of Roman greed and cruelty. Sallust's rhetorical training allowed him to construct appropriate discourses even for those he detested.

Style and method in Sallust

Sallust was quite aware that he had no immediate historical predecessors worthy of emulation. He looked back four centuries to classical Athens and boldly took as his model the greatest of the ancient historians, Thucydides. *The Peloponnesian War* was a contemporary history in which Thucydides critically examined how the Athens of Pericles had degenerated under the twin forces of war and political ambition. Sallust was attracted by both Thucydidean political and psychological themes, which he transferred to the Roman context. This influence, along with Sallust's Latinization of Thucydides' idiosyncratic style, led later Roman writers like Velleius,

Quintilian, and the elder Seneca to suggest that the image of Thucydides was always before him.

Yet Sallust could not approach his master in intellectual profundity, his critical use of sources, or dispassionate analysis of causation. He had no room for the clinical objectivity of Thucydides since the writing of history at Rome demanded a moral and political commitment; Latin historical writing was deeply and unashamedly subjective. Thucydides' discussion of the civil war in Corcyra influences many passages in Sallust, but neither Sallust nor any other ancient historical writer can equal his penetrating examination of political causality. Yet the Roman has a more modern touch in his tracing of political consequences to social and economic causes, though he admittedly only wished to use them for moralistic reasons. Likewise Sallust dismissed the role of chance in history – which had been so important for Polybius – since he saw single acts or individual political figures as driven by greater historical forces. This was a bold innovation in a historical tradition that tended to personalize all events. Some of his arguments permanently transformed the way the Romans saw their own history. For example, for almost five centuries everyone in the Roman world, including St Augustine, accepted Sallust's view that the decline of the Roman Republic was due to the destruction of Carthage.

The other great influence on Sallust was Cato the Elder, whose harsh moral vision and terse, acerbic style were equally appealing to the later historian. Just before Cato's censorship in 195 BCE Rome had triumphed over both Hannibal and King Philip V of Macedon. The state was hardly in danger and there was no political crisis, but Cato saw the conquests as posing a serious moral threat to Rome. He opposed an attempt to repeal restrictions on luxury goods that had been imposed in wartime, and he feared (with good cause) that the Roman aristocrats and especially their wives would begin to emulate the debauched style of life that they saw in Greece and Africa. A century after Cato's death the Roman aristocrats had indeed adopted eastern luxuries, and now Sallust turned Cato's critique to political purpose. The political invective of the day was charged with moral overtones and Sallust's concern was that this decline of *virtus* would destroy the state itself. He would no longer accept the unspoken assumption that Roman aristocrats – called *boni* or "good men" as their Athenian equivalents had been called *aristoi* – were essentially better than anyone else. His hostility to the hereditary aristocracy led Sallust, like Cato, to regard true *virtus* as something a man earned rather than inherited. Sallust, as much as any ancient author, is responsible for our modern conception of the late Republic as having two competing factions. He used the harsh word *factio* to describe a political grouping that Cicero might less offensively call an *amicitia* ("alliance"). Though his schematic analysis often seems to overlook the fact that popular politicians were no more blameless than the aristocrats, Sallust was not an uncritical admirer of the Roman masses and their leadership.

Sallust much preferred the compressed, austere style of Cato to the more elaborate style popularized in his own time by Cicero. Hence Sallust constructed a powerful style of his own inspired by Cato and Thucydides, whom Cicero also disliked. Using the naturally "archaic" prose style of Cato, the historian invented a contrived archaism characterized by imbalance, speed, and mordant epigrams. If his prose seemed to some harsh and obscure, it was because Sallust distrusted and consciously avoided the smooth periods of Cicero. He preferred to avoid stylistic balance to give the impression of abruptness, to make his prose reflect the devious and convoluted political events recounted in his histories. In the second century CE Apuleius contrasted the stylistic *opulentia* of Cicero with the *parsimonia* of Sallust.

Sallust was the first Roman historian we know to characterize great figures through carefully drawn obituaries. His surviving characterizations of men like Jugurtha, Marius, and Catiline may not be subtle but they are certainly forceful. These portraits are often drawn through speeches and letters – not using the precise words of the subject but, like Thucydides, constructing speeches with ideas and arguments appropriate to the specific personality. Sallust also looks back to his fifth-century model in preserving elements of dramatic construction but avoiding many of the tawdry devices adopted by Greek historians in the Hellenistic period: erotic elements, melodramatic bathos, and the use of omens and prophecy. Sallust was less concerned about history as entertainment than as political education.

Sallust does not attempt to reproduce the style of the speakers; rather the historian uses speeches, as Thucydides does, for historical and political analysis. The only voice is Sallust's own, and it is most forceful in his pungent epigrams:

> [Fulvia] danced and sang better than necessary for an honest woman
>
> (*Catilina* 25, 2)

[Catiline] was as envious of others' possessions as he was prodigal with his own; an eloquent speaker, but lacking in wisdom.

(Catilina 5, 4–5)

Verbose rather than eloquent

(Hist. 4, 43)

[Pompey was] noble in countenance, but shameless in character

(Hist. 2, 17)

[Pompey was] moderate in all things except in his thirst for power

(Hist. 2, 18)

Despite the brevity of Sallust's literary career, his talent was recognized even in his lifetime, since he was asked to write a speech for a general's triumph in 38 BCE. If Livy preferred Ciceronian to Sallustian Latin, writers in the later first century CE still regarded Sallust as the great historical master. The poet Martial called him preeminent in Roman history and the great teacher of oratory, Quintilian, called him the "Roman Thucydides." The rhetorician further suggested that, even if Livy was more suitable to be read by boys – presumably for patriotic uplift – Sallust was the greater historian. As a stylistic innovator of genius, he had his greatest impact on Tacitus, who called him the "most distinguished writer of Roman history." In the second century CE, renewed taste for archaic Latin made Sallust popular with writers like Aulus Gellius and Fronto, the tutor of the emperor Marcus Aurelius. Yet Sallust's most lasting influence was not his style but his moral vision of the late Republic. Later writers followed him in seeing in 146 BCE the great turning point in Roman Republican history. As a moralist, he was seen as the most profound critic of foreign extravagance and its corrupting effect on the Roman people. Even St Jerome called him "very reliable" (*certissimus*). Sallust became, with Virgil, Cicero, and Terence, one of the four Latin authors most favored for reading in the schools – paralleling the Greek canonical authors of history (Thucydides), epic (Homer), oratory (Demosthenes), and comedy (Menander). Thus many copies were made for ancient schools and in medieval monasteries, where his monographs were favored reading material. But by the nineteenth century scholars were scornful of his evident bias and partisanship along with his chronological and geographical errors; Sallust was regarded as a political pamphleteer. Perhaps the most important issue for modern readers is that the powerful critique of the moralist is blunted by his sanctimonious tone and by ancient accusations of corruption, which have made him out to be a remarkable hypocrite.

His passionate analysis of the political consequences of the ineffi-ciency of the senatorial government, the venality of its leadership, and its resistance to allowing new men of talent into the system still stands as a useful antidote to Cicero's elegiac lament for the loss of the Republic. Sallust had been a senator as well as a general, and he knew politics from the inside, even if he idealized conditions in Rome before 146 BCE. His motives for writing history have been questioned, but that does not make his history any less revealing as a treatment of the moral decline and political failure of the Roman state. His anti-establishment view, propelled into the Christian tradition by St Augustine, remains central to our understanding of the fall of the Roman Republic. But perhaps the most compelling vindication for his analysis came in the generation after his death, when Augustus, in revitalizing the Roman state, reduced the power of senatorial administrators, checked the corruption of tax collectors, and promoted the entry of Italians into imperial administrative positions.

3

LIVY

In the long line of Roman politician-historians who combined public life with the literary craft of history, there is one startling exception. Not only did Livy (59 BCE–17 CE) never sit in the Senate nor command a Roman army, but there is no evidence that he ever held any public office or even served in the military. But even though he did not have the practical experience that Polybius argued was essential for an historian, Livy has left us perhaps the most important single work in the Roman historical tradition, his *Ab Urbe Condita* (*"From the Founding of the City"*). Though only a quarter of his enormous history of Rome from its origins to his own day survives, the extant books still constitute the largest single Latin work to have survived from pagan antiquity. And, more than any other author, Livy has shaped the image, for ancients and moderns alike, of the tough, self-reliant Roman of the Republic.

The historian was born in the northeast Italian city of Padua. Though Romans snobbishly considered the province of Cisalpine Gaul to be an intellectual and cultural backwater, our own perspective is more favorable. Though it was only incorporated into Italy (and hence given universal Roman citizenship) by Julius Caesar in 49 BCE, the municipal elite were already highly Romanized. The area produced the poets Catullus and Virgil, as well as Livy, and Padua was perhaps the wealthiest city in Italy outside the capital itself. The city was proud of its ancient origins, and was not yet subject to the luxury and corruption that infected Rome. Its citizens nurtured traditional Roman values and, like much of the municipal elite, greatly preferred the political order, moral rectitude, and piety of the past to the corruption, demagoguery, rapid change, and civil war of the first century BCE. Thus Livy's history might be seen as representing the moderately conservative political views and moral standards of the non-political classes of Italy. This is precisely the group to which Augustus would appeal to rebuild the state in the aftermath of the civil wars.

We know little of Livy's life – much less than of Cato, Sallust, Tacitus, or Ammianus. There are two reasons: Livy did not have a public career to be recorded by other writers, nor did he tell us much about himself. Autobiographical details usually only appear in history where the writer treats the events of his own time, when he might include personal anecdotes. But the last 150 years of Livy's history are lost. No other writings of his survive, so scholars have been forced to make deductions from Livy's text and to pry a few details from other ancient authors. The historian was educated, and educated well, in Padua. In another era such a promising young man would have completed advanced studies with a professor of rhetoric at Rome and embarked on an intellectual pilgrimage to Greece. But civil wars convulsed the Roman world from 49 to 30 BCE and Livy had to make do with the teachers and books available in Padua. It would be interesting to know how he avoided military service, but there is no evidence to enlighten us. In any event, even before he moved to Rome Livy was well enough trained in history, oratory, and philosophy to publish some historical and philosophical essays and embark on his grand project of writing seven centuries of Roman history.

Motivated by patriotism, Livy seems to have begun writing his history before he came to Rome at the end of the civil war. He was present at Augustus' triumph of 29 BCE and published his first book not long after. In his Preface Livy sets out a plan that only decades of unremitting hard work and the good fortune of a long life allowed him to complete. Though his initial idea may have been to conclude his history in 120 books with the death of Cicero in 43 BCE, his intellectual restlessness and energy led him to extend the work to 9 BCE. The final product was 142 books – almost 8,000 modern pages – of which 35 books survive. Livy was nearly coeval with the emperor Augustus (63 BCE–14 CE). At his death in 17 CE in his seventy-sixth year, the historian, like the politician, could look back with satisfaction over a task completed.

Ancient sources provide a few biographical nuggets: that Livy's public readings were sparsely attended; that he was personally rather prudish; that his two sons also pursued literary careers and that his daughter married a mediocre rhetorician; that he returned to Padua to retire and to die. But these details pale in importance beside Livy's massive achievement. He was the first Roman to take on history as a full-time task and to become what we would call a professional historian. He wrote history from books, and he was not ashamed to do so. While his work lacks some of the political acumen of a senator or the military awareness of a general, it gains much from the immense scope that only a full-time historian could bring to it. That scope allowed Livy to link the present with the remote past in ways that no historian in the Greek and Roman tradition had yet been able to do.

> Moreover, my subject involves infinite labor, seeing that it must be traced back above seven hundred years, and that proceeding from slender beginnings it has so increased as now to be burdened by its own magnitude; and at the same time I doubt not that to most readers the earliest origins and the period immediately succeeding them will give little pleasure, for they will be in haste to reach these modern times, in which the might of a people which has long been very powerful is working its own undoing. I myself, on the contrary, shall seek in this an additional reward for my toil, that I may avert my gaze from the troubles which our age has been witnessing for so many years, so long at least as I am absorbed in the recollection of the brave days of old, free from every care which, even if it could not divert the historian's mind from the truth, might nevertheless cause it anxiety.
>
> (Preface, 4–5)[1]

Livy's early philosophical writings are lost, but they probably reflected the neo-Stoicism prevalent in Rome at the time. This Roman form of Stoicism placed its emphasis on ethics rather than on the fatalism of classical Stoicism, though both are present. Since nearly all Roman historical writing contains Stoic phraseology in its criticism of greed, lust, and ambition, it is difficult to tell when Livy is expressly alluding to Stoic ideas and when he is merely using the conventional language of moralization.

Nevertheless, Livy's Stoicism does appear in his allusion to the civil wars of his youth. In contrast to the triumphant chauvinism of the early books of his history, the preface shows that his account of the last decades of the Republic is likely to have been more pessimistic. The loss of the final ninety-seven books of *Ab Urbe Condita* not only deprives us of a continuous account of the last century and a half of the Roman Republic, but it leaves us with a deceptive image of Livy as a genial raconteur who mixes his stirring praise of individual heroism and his accounts of great Roman victories with curious legends and peculiar old wives' tales from the remote past. We must never forget that the accident of preservation has forever distorted our view of this remarkable writer, and our generalizations based on his books must be speculative.

About the time of Livy's birth, Cicero was urging Roman writers to match Greek achievement in writing history as, in his mind, he had equaled or surpassed Demosthenes and other Greek orators. It was a daunting task, and Cicero had some contradictory ideas about how such Roman historiography should be written. Cicero hoped above all for a Roman Herodotus: a wonderful storyteller who was also a fine stylist. But in addition to an elegant style, Cicero wished for accuracy and attention to the ethical function of history – he called history the *magister vitae* ("guide to life"). During the previous three centuries Greek historians used exaggerated rhetorical strategies and sensational episodes to divert and amuse the reader. Some historians included tragic elements in their histories to arouse the emotions of their readers. (Even Herodotus and Thucydides structured their histories like dramas, but the historians of the Hellenistic era included scenes of overt pathos, such as women and children lamenting as they are led into slavery.) The purpose of historical writing had moved from utility to entertainment. These were the traditions that Cicero hoped Roman writers would challenge and surpass.

Though Livy returned to the annalistic form of his history – that is, the year-by-year structure even dividing military campaigns if necessary – he pursued the Ciceronian goal of rhetorical history. As Cicero demanded, Livy avoids the fabulous – save in the first book where there were few other sources – and also emphasizes his moral purpose while he continues to entertain his readers. Cicero's contemporaries who wrote history – Caesar, Sallust, and Asinius Pollio – were political men whose writings were primarily concerned with their political message. It was only the politically detached Livy who could indeed bring Cicero's prescriptions for Roman historiography into reality:

> There is this exceptionally beneficial and fruitful advantage
> to be derived from the study of the past, that you see, set in
> the clear light of historical truth, examples of every
> possible type. From these you may select for yourself and
> your country what to imitate, and also what, as being
> mischievous in its inception and disastrous in its issues,

you are to avoid. Unless, however, I am misled by affection for my undertaking, there has never existed any commonwealth greater in power, with a purer morality, or more fertile in good examples; or any state in which avarice and luxury have been so late in making their inroads, or poverty and frugality so highly and continuously honored, showing so clearly that the less wealth men possessed the less they coveted.

(Preface, 10–11)

Ab Urbe Condita (From the Founding of the City)

When Livy arrived in Rome at the age of thirty, he had already done much general reading for his projected history of the Romans from the arrival in Italy of Aeneas and the Trojans to his own lifetime. Some scholars have suggested that his original plan was more modest but, spurred by the positive reception of his first book, he added a new preface that set forth a grander conception. This seems unlikely, since the desire to apply the lessons of the past to the present pervades his work from the beginning. Nevertheless, he could not have had any idea how much work lay before him. His preface to Book 1 conventionally promises that he will work "to the best of my ability," but by the beginning of Book 31 he realizes the true immensity of the task. The book would consume his entire life, and would only be completed if he were fortunate enough to live to an exceptionally advanced age:

> Whether the task I have undertaken of writing a complete history of the Roman people from the very commencement of its existence will reward me for the labor spent on it, I neither know for certain, nor if I did know would I venture to say…However this may be, it will still be a great satisfaction to me to have taken my part, too, in investing, to the utmost of my abilities, the annals of the foremost nation in the world with a deeper interest.
>
> (Preface, 1–3)

I, too, feel as much relief in having reached the end of the Punic War as if I had taken a personal part in its toils and dangers. It ill befits one who has had the courage to promise a complete history of Rome to find the separate sections of such an extensive work fatiguing. But when I consider that the sixty-three years from the beginning of the First Punic War to the end of the Second take up as many books as the four hundred and eighty-seven years from the foundation of the City to the consulship of Appius Claudius under whom the First Punic War commenced, I see that I am like people who are tempted by the shallow water along the beach to wade out to sea; the further I progress, the greater the depth, as though it were a bottomless sea, into which I am carried. I imagined that as I completed one part after another the task before me would diminish; as it is, it almost becomes greater.

(31, 1, 1–5)

Though only 35 books of Livy survive, brief ancient summaries called *Periochae* exist for all but two of the 142 books. These summaries vary in length from a few lines to a page, and the author(s) seem to have based them on an abridged version of Livy rather than the full text. Ancient writers described Livy's history as organized in pentads and decades, and this structure had a great effect on his interpretative framework. Nevertheless, the *Periochae* show that he did not invariably force his material into such a rigid framework. The surviving books of Livy can be summarized as follows:

Book 1 (753–509 BCE) The self-contained first book actually begins with the arrival of the Trojans in Italy four centuries before the founding of the city by Romulus. It includes the regal period, tracing the reigns of seven kings to the expulsion of Tarquin the Proud in 509.

Books 2–5 (509–390 BCE) Book 2 begins with a second brief preface: "The new liberty enjoyed by the Roman people, their achievements in peace and war, annual magistracies, and laws superior in authority to men will henceforth be my theme. This liberty was the more grateful as the last king had been so great a tyrant." The pentad contains the Romans' early struggles against their neighbors with the sagas of Horatius at the bridge, Coriolanus, and Cincinnatus. After the establishment of the Twelve Tables and the rape of Verginia, the pentad ends with the destruction of Veii and the Gallic sack of Rome in 390.

Books 6–10 (389–292 BCE) The second pentad is primarily concerned with Rome's victories over the Etruscan, Latin and Samnite peoples of central and southern Italy. These books also include the early struggles between the patricians and plebeians which led to the first plebeian consuls in 367. One thread concerns the Manlius family: the execution of Marcus (6), the heroism of Titus in freeing his father from the tribune's persecution and defeat of a Gaul in single combat (7), and Titus' own cruelty for executing his son for disobedience (8).

Books 11–20 (290 and 220 BCE) These books are lost. They contained Rome's victories over the Greek cities in southern Italy, King Pyrrhus, and Carthage in the First Punic War.

Books 21–25 (218–212 BCE) An account of the Second Punic War beginning with the conflict over Saguntum and Hannibal's invasion of Italy. The pentad includes disastrous Roman defeats at Trebia, Lake Trasimene, and Cannae while the Roman commanders in Spain, the Scipio brothers, fell in battle. Marcellus is successful in Sicily.

Books 26–30 (211–201 BCE) The tide turns when the twenty–four year-old Publius Scipio is sent to Spain and begins a series of successful battles. Conclusion of a peace treaty with Philip V of Macedon. Scipio invades Africa and Hannibal is recalled from Italy to confront him. After his victory at Zama in 202, the triumphant Scipio is called "Africanus."

Books 31–35 (201–192 BCE) This pentad traces the Second Macedonian War, in which Flamininus defeats King Philip. The Greek cities are given their freedom by the Senate. In 195 the luxury laws were repealed despite the opposition of the censor Cato. Scipio and Hannibal meet at the court of King Antiochus of Syria.

Books 36–40 (191–179 BCE) Antiochus invades Greece and is defeated first at Thermopylae and later at Apamea in Asia Minor by Lucius Scipio. Roman victories over the Galatians in Asia and the Aetolians. Scandalous behavior is attributed to Asian luxury brought back to Rome. Deadly rivalry between the sons of Philip; the pentad ends with the death of Philip.

Books 41–45 (178–167 BCE) Triumph of Gracchus in Spain. Complaints about King Perseus of Macedon lead to the Third Macedonian War. Increasing cruelty and arrogance of Roman commanders. Defeat of Perseus and triumph of Aemilius Paullus.

Books 46–142 (167–9 BCE)   These are lost. It is clear from the summaries that Livy often abandoned the framework of pentads and decades in favor of a more flexible organization to better incorporate his material.

This summary outline shows that the early books of Livy, which contain many of his famous episodes, are a mere tip of the iceberg of his immense narrative. While the first book covers 240 years and Books 2–5 another 120 years, in the second century BCE Livy's books contained on average two years, and by the first century most years require an entire book. The expansion was obviously due to greatly increased source material, but Livy knew well (as Cato had) that Roman readers were also more interested in the history of the recent past: "I have little doubt, too, that for the majority of my readers the earliest times and those immediately succeeding, will possess little attraction; they will hurry on to these modern days..."(Preface). Though the first five books may have been largely written before the battle of Actium in 31 BCE, a few references to Augustus were added later. The first pentad was published no later than 25 BCE and the second by 20 BCE. Livy's initial ending point was probably the death of Cicero in 43 BCE, which concludes Book 120. He kept working as long as he could and brought his story down to the death of Drusus in 9 BCE – still a hopeful time of high imperial ambitions, before the deaths of Gaius and Lucius drove Augustus to adopt Tiberius. Though Livy wrote twenty-two books (Books 121–142) on the triumph and reign of Augustus, he withheld publication of these books until the emperor's death in 14 CE.

Such a summary inevitably emphasizes the major military events, not least because the surviving books focus on the Hannibalic and eastern wars in which Livy returns to traditional war history in a Thucydidean vein. But we cannot ignore Livy's rich tapestry of social, constitutional and religious history through which threads the historian ties together his enormous work. An obvious one is his report of census figures of Roman citizens. Through the third century the number of citizens climbs from about 270,000 to over 380,000 at the outbreak of the First Punic War in 264. It then declines during the war to 240,000 and returns to 270,000 just before the Second Punic War in 218. Near the low point of the Hannibalic War the citizen census was only 137,000 and did not again reach 300,000 until two generations later in 167. This invaluable information demonstrates the human consequences of Rome's incessant wars.

Likewise Livy details many constitutional changes, from the first plebeian praetor in 337 to two praetors (242), four praetors (228), and six praetors (198), demonstrating the growing need for administrators in the provinces. Other narrative threads include the expansion of colonies in northern Italy, the construction of highways, the corruption of officials, and recurring appearances of great families. One of Livy's favorite themes concerns the religious history of Rome. He often includes prodigies and sacrilege, as when the flame of Vesta is allowed to go out, as well as the introduction of new religions from Juno of nearby Veii and Diana of the Latin city of Aricia to the transfer of the Great Mother Cybele from Asia and the Bacchanalia scandal. The range of Livy's interest is much wider than that of the senatorial writers Sallust and Tacitus, who are more focused on political history.

Livy's Preface

The Preface displays a combination of self-confidence and diffidence. It is only in the prefaces – there are brief prefaces to Books 2, 6, 21, and 31 – that Livy uses first-person verbs, but he also expresses concern over the value of his project. He must certainly have been aware that, in writing as a scholar from the provinces rather than as a statesman, he was in danger of having his work dismissed out of hand. Hence the first book was published separately – a "prose epic" of Rome's legendary past where political expertise and military experience would be of little importance. Once that book received a favorable reception, whether in recitations or through written copies, Livy would have aroused sufficient interest and perhaps the necessary patronage for his project.

Livy knew that his practical compatriots wished for a history that would be useful, and it could only be useful if it were a clear monument to be read by all. Then the *exempla* he provides could be applied by his readers to present circumstances. Hence his Preface invites the personal engagement of every reader: "from these you may choose for yourself and for your own state what to imitate." He relates it to the present by explicit parallels of personalities (Tarquin and Catiline) or situations. The central theme of Livy's history is the creation of the Roman character, and he tended to see both Romans and other peoples in stereotypic terms. Both environmental and historical conditions were important in shaping the virtues that made the Roman people great, yet unlike a modern historian Livy would only rarely describe institutions, cults, or antiquarian structures in an analytical excursus. He describes those conditions indirectly through his narratives.

> The subjects to which I would ask each of my readers to devote his earnest attention are these – the life and morals of the community; the men and the qualities by which, through domestic policy and foreign war, dominion was won and extended. Then as the standard of morality gradually lowers, let him follow the decay of the national character, observing how at first it slowly sinks, then slips downward more and more rapidly, and finally begins to plunge into headlong ruin, until he reaches these days, in which we can bear neither our diseases nor their remedies.
>
> (Preface, 9)

It is immediately clear to the reader that Livy sees the *res Romanae* in moral terms. At times he may exaggerate virtue or vice – the pride of Tarquin or the rashness of Flaminius before his defeat at Trasimene – to emphasize the moral dimension of his narrative. To remember the past is not merely a pleasure; it also embodies the duty of *pietas* toward earlier generations of Romans. Livy's book is the collection and shaping of that collective memory of the Roman people to show the erosion of its moral character – its collective *virtus*. The past was not a lost utopia; there were tyrants like Tarquin and monsters like Appius Claudius. But even Rome's historical villains contributed to the shaping of the national character: before he was destroyed for his cruel mistreatment of Verginia, Appius Claudius helped construct Rome's earliest legal system. The noble actions of the ancestors not only provided models for behavior, but allowed Livy to demonstrate the decline of the Roman people. He prefers not to make explicit appeals to antique virtue in his own voice, so he puts them into speeches or weaves them into the descriptions of such characters as the elder Cato.

While Livy repeatedly advocates *pietas* toward the gods, these are far from the anthropomorphic gods of epic poetry. Livy was deeply influenced by Stoicism and, like many other Roman intellectuals, skeptical about the old gods who might intervene directly in the affairs of men. But he was not among those who regarded the ritual elements of Roman religion as detached from morality and ethics. He believed in the social value of religion, and that the neglect of traditional ritual often led to moral decline. Hence the consul Flaminius' neglect of the auspices and refusal to go to the temple of

Jupiter (21, 63) is made to seem responsible for his defeat at Lake Trasimene. Polybius' use of *Tyche* as a capricious force was too fickle for Livy's Stoicism, so his use of *Fortuna* is much closer to the traditional Roman concept of destiny (*fatum*).

Though Livy saw the past in terms of his own age, he was fully aware that religious attitudes had changed. While he accepted the traditional equation that piety resulted in divine favor which brought military success, his use of such ideas was far more sophisticated. His own concerns were primarily ethical and his Stoicism made him as uncomfortable with Roman savagery as it did with Scipio's mystical approach to religion. Nevertheless, his history faithfully recorded prodigies and sacrifices since he knew that for centuries the Roman people had believed implicitly in their effectiveness:

> The traditions of what happened prior to the foundation of the City or whilst it was being built, are more fitted to adorn the creations of the poet than the authentic records of the historian, and I have no intention of establishing either their truth or their falsehood. This much license is conceded to the ancients, that by intermingling human actions with divine they may confer a more august dignity on the origins of states. Now, if any nation ought to be allowed to claim a sacred origin and point back to a divine paternity that nation is Rome. For such is her renown in war that when she chooses to represent Mars as her own and her founder's father, the nations of the world accept the statement with the same equanimity with which they accept her dominion. But whatever opinions may be formed or criticisms passed upon these and similar traditions, I regard them as of small importance.
>
> (Preface, 6–8)

For Livy the Romans themselves made their own destiny, and if their history in his own century was one of decline, they could only blame themselves.

Livy's literary art

The modern reader must never lose sight of the prodigious size of Livy's undertaking, since that bulk had an effect on every aspect of its literary style and historical content. It is difficult even to grasp conceptually such an enormous book, which originally contained about two million words – between twenty-five and thirty modern volumes. The poet Martial claimed his library was not large enough to hold all those papyrus rolls. In the composition of a work of such scope, stretching over almost a half-century, there will be historical errors and stylistic infelicities. The ancients themselves did not expect perfection in such immense works; as Livy's contemporary, the poet Horace wrote: "Even great Homer nods." Modern critics sometimes seem to regard Livy's prose as a carefully crafted essay in which minor stylistic lapses show he was bored or historical errors show his lack of judgment. It is important to retain a perspective on his achievement. Even the surviving books, though all written within a fifteen-year period, show significant differences in their composition; the entire work must have displayed even more dramatic changes during its forty years of composition.

Cicero stressed the importance of the architecture (*aedificatio*) of a work of history. The ancients believed that memory was architectural, and architecture was used in the schools of rhetoric as a mnemonic aid. Livy also used this metaphor in his work, both in its overall organization and in his stress on monuments to call to mind famous deeds. Aside from the annalistic framework with its alternation of domestic and foreign events, the reader needs guideposts to find his way through Livy. The recent work of T.J. Luce has especially illuminated the architectural structure of Livy's history. Luce emphasized its division into pentads and showed that the prefaces mark important transitions. Livy used two principal methods to give coherence to his narrative. One is to link a section, usually a book, together with a continuing thematic thread. His preface to Book 2 announces the theme of *libertas*, while Book 5 is focused on *pietas*. In later books, where Rome's conquests and savage treatment of subject peoples have a negative impact on the Republic, Livy probably used themes like *luxuria* and *ferocia*.

A larger narrative strategy lies in architectonic patterns within or between books. Book 5 falls into two contrasting halves: the arrogance of Rome in the sack of the city of Veii, and Rome's own capture by invading Gauls. Other structures may stretch over several books or even over an entire decade. Books 21–30 treat the Hannibalic War from the Carthaginian's invasion of Italy until his eventual defeat. The first pentad is generally disastrous for the Romans while the second sees them recoup their fortunes. The mid-point comes in Book 26, with the lowest ebb of Roman fortunes: Hannibal's march on Rome. The city withstood his siege and Roman military successes followed. The ten books form a coherent unity.

Livy also uses the many detailed notices in his sources – foundations of colonies, triumphs of generals, deaths of priests – to set off his narrative or to provide contrast to another episode. He did not necessarily have a particular interest in such material, but he found a use for it in the architecture of his history. Some larger patterns – like foundation, rise, decline, and refoundation – occur several times in the history as a shaping device. Hence through the pages and volumes of the history the reader sees the gradual accretion of the institutions and characteristics that came to define the Roman state and the Roman people.

The Romans considered history to be a branch of rhetoric, since oratory and history were virtually the only forms of literary prose written in Latin during the Republic. Livy would certainly have agreed that literary history demands rhetorical polish. While there is no evidence that he ever delivered orations in public, he became a masterful writer of speeches for his characters, placing them at strategic points in his narrative. Whether written in direct or indirect discourse, the speeches were an important means of delineating character and injecting the historian's opinions into the narrative. Like other ancient historians, Livy rewrote speeches in his own style even if they had been preserved in family records or published like Cato's, or, more often, created appropriate speeches where none survived. More than other historians, Livy was also skillful at composing brief, but lively, speeches to add vigor and color to his narrative. Both Quintilian and Suetonius praised Livy's speeches and they were later published separately for study in schools.

Another rhetorical element that flourished among the Hellenistic historians was the use of dramatic devices. Livy was a master of drama, both in individual scenes and in larger dramatic constructions. We have already seen, in the single combat between Manlius Torquatus and the Gaul (pp. 22–3), how he can elaborate and dramatize an episode which was only a brief anecdote in his source. Livy also foreshadows a future event by dropping a hint of what is to come. For example, Scipio is briefly mentioned in Book 21, at the very beginning of the Hannibalic War; his name remains mutely present during the Carthaginian triumphs, until he destroys their army in Book 30. In Livy's treatment of the sack of Alba Longa by the Roman king Tullus Hostilius, he adds to the tragedy by describing the scene as though one could hear the shouting of the Roman troops and the weeping of the Alban women. It is a deeply anachronistic scene, probably based in part on the poet Ennius' account. Livy describes Alba as a large city at a time when it could have been little more than a primitive village, but the scene captures the reality of the terror of the refugees, which is more important than the size of the walls. In this and other accounts of sieges and sacks, Livy arouses through pathos the fear and pity that Aristotle saw as the essence of tragedy.

In an historical work as enormous as Livy's, it is no surprise that many of the battle scenes become stereotyped. Since the sources were often sketchy and Livy had no military experience, the battles greatly resemble each other. Though the civic assemblies or military gatherings also have similarities, Livy's psychological insight into group behavior makes such encounters dramatically powerful. He also introduces dramatic meetings between individuals, such as that between Scipio and Hannibal on the battlefield before the battle of Zama (30, 30). Though that meeting is fictitious, it encapsulates the confrontation better than any description of battle tactics. Characterizations of less important characters, especially in the early books, often take on stock elements; one doubts whether *all* virtuous women in early Rome were equally beautiful. Where Livy did not have reliable information and his narrative required a description, he often resorted to stereotypes. After Book 21 characterization improves and major figures like Hannibal are often treated with subtlety and insight. Livy becomes more skillful at conveying the thoughts and feelings of the participants. As in drama, characterization is accomplished indirectly, usually through speeches and the reactions of other characters. Livy often uses an obituary as an opportunity for an extended characterization of a major figure. His tribute to Cicero, which is in the lost books but is preserved by the elder Seneca, is sincere and moving. It also demonstrates that Livy was far from uncritical in his admiration for his stylistic model; he includes two very sharp jabs at Cicero's obvious self-pity and at his potential for ruthlessness. Yet he concludes with a powerfully touching tribute.

"He lived sixty-three years, so that even if he had not died by violence his death cannot seem untimely. The rich products of his genius were amply rewarded; he enjoyed long years of prosperity: but his long career of good fortune was interrupted from time to time by serious disasters – exile, the ruin of the party he championed, the sad and untimely death of his daughter. Of all these disasters he bore as became a man none but his own death. A true judgment might have found this less undeserved in that he suffered at the hands of his enemy no more cruel fate than he would himself have inflicted if he had been equally fortunate. Yet if one weighs his virtues with his faults he deserves a place in history as a truly great man, and another Cicero would be required to praise him adequately." With that impartial judgment with which he weighs all men of genius, Titus Livius has rendered the amplest tribute to Cicero.

(Seneca Rhetor, *Suas.* 6, 22, tr. Edward)

Livy rejected the bare prose of the annalists and the abrasive style of Sallust for something more befitting his ambition to produce a literary and polished history of the Roman People. He admired neither the politics nor the style of Sallust, since for a Roman the two were inherently linked. Like Sallust, he chose a style appropriate for his view of the world. As might be expected of an admirer of Cicero, Livy wrote clear Latin in easily flowing periodic sentences. This was especially true in the speeches. He also learned much from the prose of Julius Caesar, but he recognized that Caesar's clarity was achieved at the cost of variety. Livy preferred to produce variety through a wider range of grammatical constructions in his periodic sentences. Though Book 1 was somewhat archaic in diction, perhaps as a result of using Ennius as a source, Livy's prose soon became what we regard as conventionally classical. The great teacher of rhetoric Quintilian referred to Livy's *lactea ubertas* ("milky richness" 10, 1, 32), and describes his style as *dulcis et candidus et fusus* ("sweet and open and flowing" 10, 1, 73) in which *omnia leniter fluunt* ("all flows smoothly" 9, 14, 18). When the historian Asinius Pollio, who had been Marc Antony's brutal governor in Padua, scornfully dismissed Livy's *Patavinitas* ("Paduan provinciality"), he may have been referring to his dignified style or to his provincial moral rectitude. For Pollio, both would go together.

Like any skilled rhetorician, Livy would vary both his diction and syntax to what was appropriate in a given situation. He was indeed even experimental in syntax and contributed to the continued vitality of Latin in the post-Ciceronian age. Livy would sometimes resort to a more emotive vocabulary with the richness and color of poetic language and poetic figures of speech, with the result that he has been called a "prose poet." Perhaps more surprisingly, he sometimes uses a Sallustian imbalance for added effect. It is true that many passages of Livy read as though he has merely taken a source and recast it in elegant periodic Latin. That is understandable; his task was enormous. But the many passages that show careful craftsmanship, use of deliberate variation, and poetic diction demonstrate the genuine literary ability of the historian.

Livy's historical method

The great Greek historians relied heavily on visits to the sites of battlefields to see the geography with their own eyes ("autopsy"), and where possible they personally spoke to participants in the events. But after Herodotus and Thucydides, historians tended to rely primarily on the narratives of their predecessors. Even Polybius, who certainly consulted archives and even inscriptions, relied on earlier narratives in Greek and in Latin. We cannot know with any certainty how Livy would have prepared himself for the history of his own time, but we know he was acutely aware of the lack of any contemporary evidence for his first five books:

> The history of the Romans from the foundation of the City to its capture, first under kings, then under consuls, dictators, decemvirs, and consular tribunes, the record of foreign wars and domestic dissensions, has been set forth in the five preceding books. The subject matter is enveloped in obscurity; partly from its great antiquity, like remote objects which are hardly discernible through the vastness of the distance; partly owing to the fact that written records, which form the only trustworthy memorials of events, were in those times few and scanty, and even what did exist in the pontifical commentaries and public and private archives nearly all perished in the conflagration of the City. Starting from the second beginnings of the City, which, like a plant cut down to its roots, sprang up in greater beauty and fruitfulness, the details of its history both civil and military will now be exhibited in their proper order, with greater clearness and certainty.
>
> (6, 1)

Livy was not indifferent to good sources for the early history of Rome; there were simply none available. He read all six annalist versions of the early period, as well as poetic treatments, myths, and legends. He also took account of the family traditions that continued to circulate orally in the city. He is fully aware that those annalistic accounts could not derive from any secure sources, since nearly all primary documents were destroyed in the Gallic sack of

390 BCE. How and why did he provide a "fictitious" reconstruction of Books 1–5?

Livy believed it was his duty to present the best possible account of the entire history of Rome to understand how the unique character of the Roman people developed. Since much was "known" or thought to be known through received legends, he was determined to do as best he could. Possible analogies might be found in the history of some European colonies. Until a generation ago, the history of North America usually began with Columbus and that of Australia with Botany Bay. Then American historians like Gary Nash and Australian historians like Manning Clark used archaeology and anthropology to begin their surveys thousands of years earlier with the sketchy "history" of indigenous peoples. It was in no way comparable in detail to the history after colonization, but such inclusive history recognized the existence of pre-European populations and thus took a first step toward assessing their importance.

For the earliest period Livy used the principle of verisimilitude – what is believable; in fact he used the phrase explicitly more than a dozen times:

> At this point a tale is introduced to the effect that whilst the king of the Veientines was offering sacrifice, the soothsayer announced that victory would be granted to him who had cut out the sacrificial parts of the victim. His words were heard by the soldiers in the mine, they burst through, seized the parts and carried them to the Dictator. But in questions of such remote antiquity I should count it sufficient if what bears the stamp of probability be taken as true. Statements like this, which are more fitted to adorn a stage which delights in the marvelous than to inspire belief, it is not worth while either to affirm or deny.
>
> (5, 21)

By modern standards Livy's practice may not seem to be very satisfactory, but we must recall that he believed it was his duty to pass on tradition and thus keep it alive. Even poetic fables had symbolic value for him. In addition, ancient writers believed the cyclical patterns inherent in history made the study of the past useful for behavior in the future. If history was indeed cyclical, Livy could also reconstruct the remote past by examining later patterns and projecting them backwards in time. Scholars have criticized Livy for "doubling" descriptions of battles and attributing constitutional innovations to distantly separated members of the same family. An alternative view might be that this is an original form of historical reconstruction relying upon the cyclic philosophy of history. It is important to recall that no other ancient historian even attempted a history of the remote past on anything like this scale.

What were Livy's sources and how did he use them? For nearly a century scholars regarded this as the most important issue in the study of Livy. These scholars, who practiced what is called *Quellenforschung* ("source examination"), regarded Livy as heavily dependent on a single source for each portion of his narrative. He closely followed that source and turned it into elegant Latin prose. Some scholars even suggested that Livy did not read ahead, but consulted his sources only as he was actually writing. During the last two decades most scholars have become more sympathetic to Livy's plight. He did not regard it as his primary duty to consult documents, and in any case systematic consultation was impossible. Any existing state archives were chaotic, and most important documents were still held (if at all) by the descendants of the magistrates. As a non-senator, Livy could not have had easy access to family archives until he became well established. He did a great deal of preparatory work to plan the structure of his pentads and decades, and to determine which sources to rely upon most heavily. No one could possibly have created such a history by, as it were, wandering through the sources, papyrus roll by papyrus roll, and rewriting them.

The early books were obviously the most difficult, since ancient writers did not have the critical tools to deal with the history of the remote past. It was only in the early nineteenth century that scholars like Niebuhr developed the analytic tactic of breaking down sources and reconstructing them to yield a more reliable narrative. Livy was reduced to choosing among several competing early versions. Yet, unlike many of his predecessors, he did not embellish the legends with additional fictions. His treatment of the monarchy is only one quarter as long as that of his contemporary Dionysius of Halicarnassus, since he tries to tone down the more obvious fantasies. He explicitly warns of his skepticism and, unlike Dionysius who argues the date of the foundation of Rome, Livy merely accepts the consensus, since he knows certainty is impossible. Yet he could not omit a popular legend like the birth of Romulus and Remus merely because he disbelieved it. The story of the twin sons of Mars was indigenous to Latin sources, and over the centuries such myths helped to shape the Roman self-image. The emphasis on Romulus as a self-sufficient hero of rustic origins, rather than stressing his divine heredity, seems to be Livy's own contribution. Since comparisons of the founder Romulus and the re-founder Augustus were current in Livy's own day, his treatment of Rome's first king was shaped in response to contemporary ideological questions.

Livy was no antiquarian interested in peculiar ancient institutions for their own sake, nor did he make much use of antiquarian writers of his own day like Varro. He does try to link legends to surviving monuments to provide visible evidence. But he knows that the mere existence of a monument or an inscription proves little, since inscriptions can be faked and the meaning of monuments is interpreted in the light of oral tradition:

> I believe that the true history has been falsified by funeral orations and lying inscriptions on the family busts, since each family appropriates to itself an imaginary record of noble deeds and official distinctions. It is at all events owing to this cause that so much confusion has been introduced into the records of private careers and public events. There is no writer of those times now extant who was contemporary with the events he relates and whose authority, therefore, can be depended upon.
>
> (8, 40, 4–5)

In Book 1 Livy traces the origin of the Lacus Curtius in the Forum to a Sabine, Mettius Curtius, whose horse became stuck in the swamp during a battle. Then, in Book 7, the historian gives another story in which the Roman Marcus Curtius sacrificed himself to appease divine anger. Only then does Livy indicate that he prefers the second version. His report of both stories is not sloppiness, but a simple awareness that, while certainty is impossible, transmission of Rome's legendary heritage is an important part of his task.

When Livy moves beyond 390 BCE at the beginning of Book 6, he acknowledges that some writings survived. These were, however, merely priestly records of triumphs, calamities, and the names of magistrates. It seems likely that the lists of consuls, censors, dictators, and triumphators were reliable for the fourth century. Otherwise there is no sudden change in the quality of Livy's source material until Book 10 (290s BCE) when a wider range of material becomes more reliable. For both the fourth and third centuries, Livy still relies on Greek authors or the Roman annalists, whom he claims to have read in their totality. In the early parts of his history,

Livy structures his material year by year in an annalistic form, but with increasing amounts of source material he eventually becomes far more flexible and relied on thematic threads rather than strict chronology as his organizing principle. The constitutional and religious material grows as Livy's sources improve, and he is able to differentiate more frequently between sources and even to argue in favor of a particular version. A good example is the scandal surrounding the ex-consul Lucius Flamininus in 186 BCE, which Valerius Antias blames on his love for a courtesan, Placentia, for the cruelty which had him expelled from the Senate. Livy tartly comments that the annalist, "as if he had never read the speech of Cato," ignored the surviving contemporary speech in which the censor attributed Lucius' behavior to his passion for a degenerate Carthaginian boy, Philippus (39, 42–3). Livy did on occasion consult primary documents, and he knew their value.

After his wide general reading in the history and poetry of the past, there seem to have been three stages to Livy's composition. First he read the principal sources for a large period of history – in the case of the First and Second Punic Wars, fifteen books (16–30). He then evaluated sources, blocked out the structure, and determined what themes could be threaded through the narrative. The next step was to read carefully the principal sources for a shorter segment – perhaps a war, or a book, or later a single consular year. Here he would choose his principal source on the basis of reputation, verisimilitude, and fullness of detail. The third phase was to break down the material into small blocks – from a few lines to a few pages – and turn them into his own prose, occasionally including divergent versions. He worked quickly, taking more time only over the writing of speeches, so it is hardly a surprise that there are factual errors or stylistically bland passages.

To a modern reader, Livy's best source for the Hannibalic War (Books 20–30) and Rome's conquest in the East (31–45) was Polybius. Livy soon recognized this, and after Book 24 Polybius becomes not only his principal source but the inspiration for his vision of Rome's climb to world power. Polybius is the only earlier historian whom Livy actually praises, and not once but twice. Most commonly Livy abridges Polybius to give the story a more rapid narrative flow. We can reasonably imagine him writing with a scroll of Polybius open beside him. On occasion, Livy follows the Polybian account almost word by word, especially where technical or military details are involved. In other cases, Livy recasts the material to add dramatic or rhetorical flavor to the narrative. Yet despite his respect for Polybius there are occasions when he re-orders the Polybian narrative or inserts chauvinistic material from the Roman annalists. Livy recognizes Polybius as his most reliable source on the East, but for his purpose more material had to be found and added. Hence his account of the Hannibalic War is more extensive than Polybius' or any earlier version. Livy could be skeptical of a dubious source, but he sometimes forsook skepticism in his quest for material that would illuminate the historical transformation of the Roman people.

It is for his use of sources that Livy has been most often, and most justly, criticized. He fell under the patriotic spell of Fabius Pictor and he did not work hard enough to root out falsifications by annalistic historians. Though Livy is distrustful of numbers given by the annalists he still includes them when no better material was available. For example, in one discussion of the size of Hannibal's army, he includes three figures for infantry, ranging from 100,000 to 20,000. He does not report, however, that the smallest number was given by Polybius, who said that he had seen it on an inscription set up by Hannibal himself.

> The authorities are hopelessly at variance as to the number of the troops with which Hannibal entered Italy. The highest estimate assigns him 100,000 infantry and 20,000 cavalry; the lowest puts his strength at 20,000 infantry and 6,000 cavalry.
>
> (Livy 21, 38, 2)

> [Hannibal] had with him the remains of his African army – 12,000 infantry – and his Spanish army (8,000), and, in addition, not more than six thousand cavalry, as he himself makes clear on the column set up at Cape Lacinium which has an inscription of the numbers.
>
> (Polybius 3, 56, 4)

There are times when Livy confuses topographical information; it is still impossible to trace Hannibal's path through the Alps on the basis of his account. It must be said, however, that had Livy pursued strict historiographical methods, he would never have finished his book. Even today, with the most advanced scholarly techniques, we are not certain of the history of early Rome or archaic Greece.

Perhaps the most noticeable structural elements in Livy's history are the links between past and present. These thematic patterns show how the Romans kept alive and used their past history. Thus the Rape of the Sabine Women tells much about the Roman conception of marriage: how marriage, like other forms of alliance, is fundamentally an expression of political, social, and economic relations among men. The stories of the early kings provide a framework to illustrate how men without hereditary rights – what Romans in the late Republic called "new men," like Marius and Cicero – were able to achieve high office and legitimacy. Livy understood that traditional legends were a distillation of ancient debates and thus had enduring importance for how the Roman people came to be who they were.

The surviving books of Livy show Rome's development from a village on the Palatine to mistress of the Mediterranean world. Yet we have seen from the Preface that the history also intended to show how Rome had declined. Less than a generation earlier Sallust had argued that Rome owed its decline to the destruction of Carthage in 146 BCE. Without the fear of a foreign enemy to focus them on the good of the state, he believed the Romans allowed self-indulgence, corruption, and personal ambition to lead the state into decline. While Sallust's analysis is explicit, Livy's interpretation of Rome's decline must be teased from his narrative. There he attributes the decline after 200 BCE to the foreign influence that corrupted Rome with eastern luxury and a loss of discipline: eastern religious rites like the Bacchanalia enticed the Romans into sexual license, and greed impelled Roman generals and magistrates to treat allies and conquered subjects with unprecedented brutality.

> For it was through the army serving in Asia that the beginnings of foreign luxury were introduced into the City. These men brought into Rome for the first time, bronze couches, costly coverlets, tapestry, and other fabrics, and – what was at that time considered gorgeous furniture – pedestal tables and silver salvers. Banquets were made more attractive by the presence of girls who played on the harp and sang and danced, and by other forms of amusement, and the banquets themselves began to be prepared with greater care and expense. The cook whom the ancients regarded and treated as the lowest menial was rising in value, and what had been a servile office came to be looked upon as a fine art. Still what met the eye in those days was hardly the germ of the luxury that was coming.
>
> (39, 6, 7–9)

A good example of moral decline is the death of Hannibal almost twenty years after Zama. The old general had fled in exile to the court of King Prusias in Asia, and with the arrival of the Roman emissary Flamininus, he prepared to take poison:

> "Let us," he said, "relieve the Romans from the anxiety they have so long experienced, since they think it tries their patience too much to wait for an old man's death. The victory which Flamininus will win over a defenseless fugitive will be neither great nor memorable; this day will show how vastly the morale of the Roman People has changed. Their fathers warned Pyrrhus, when he had an army in Italy, to beware of poison, and now they have sent a man of consular rank to persuade Prusias to murder his guest."
>
> (39, 51, 9–11)

A century earlier the Senate had rebuffed as disgraceful and cowardly a traitor's offer to poison their still potent adversary Pyrrhus. Livy saw in the treatment of Hannibal and other examples of Roman cruelty and arrogance a clear indication of how the old Roman character had been changed by their conquests. Could such a decline be reversed? Livy would seem to believe so, since the Romans themselves, not the gods nor fate nor some foreign power, were responsible for their moral decline. It was only they, under strong moral leadership, who could bring about a rebirth.

Livy and Augustus

The emperor Augustus is closely connected with the great writers of his time: Horace and Propertius dedicated their lyrics to him; he personally countermanded Virgil's dying request that the manuscript of the *Aeneid* be burned; and, for reasons still debated, he exiled Ovid to finish his life on the remote shores of the Black Sea. What of Livy – the greatest Augustan writer of prose, whose surviving books were written in the first fifteen years of Augustus' reign and who eventually became a welcome guest in the imperial palace and encouraged Augustus' step-grandson, the future emperor Claudius, to pursue his interest in writing history? He must surely have approved of the new regime that had revitalized Rome after a generation of civil war. Or did he?

Livy would certainly seem to be an "Augustan author," since the great patriotic themes are present in his work: regeneration and rebirth, *pietas*, clemency, the traditions of the ancestors, the value of peace and, on the other hand, moral decay, the greed of the rich, and the pain of civil strife. And yet Livy's Preface, written soon after Augustus' victory at Actium, strikes a pessimistic note: "a downward plunge has brought us to the present time, when we can endure neither our vices nor their cure." The "cure" for Rome's vices could be taken to be the rule of Augustus. We should remember that no one knew what would follow Actium: the bloody ruthlessness of Sulla and the young Octavian or the general clemency of Julius Caesar. The Preface contains no fawning dedication or allusion to the emperor, and the first mention of him early in Book 1 is rather restrained: "the gods allowed our age to witness the closing of the temple of Janus after the battle of Actium when Caesar Augustus restored peace on land and sea" (1, 19, 3). The other surviving mentions of Augustus are factual and respectful, but without flattery.

This is enough to show that Livy was not, and did not want to be considered, a court historian. There is no ancient evidence of who brought him into court circles, of any connection to Maecenas, or any specific financial rewards for him. This suggests a remarkable independence. Yet historian and emperor, who lived as contemporaries for more than seven decades, were indeed friends for forty years. It is only a few years after their deaths that Tacitus has the historian Cremutius Cordus, arguing for literary freedom, say that Livy "praised Pompey to such heights that Augustus called him a 'Pompeian,' but this did not detract from their friendship" (Tacitus, *Annales* 4, 34).

Yet Livy, with the conservative Italian values of Horace and Virgil, deeply believed in much of the "Augustan program" on his own account. Since Augustus shaped the ideology of his regime to appeal to an Italian elite damaged by civil war, it is hardly surprising that his views coincided with those of Livy, who had been hostile to Marc Antony. His sympathy with Cicero's ideas of *concordia* and even his respect for Brutus and Cassius posed little threat to Augustus after Actium; by that time Augustus was emphasizing the conservative elements in his program. Though Livy was not politically engaged, he was ideologically so close to the Augustan program that it is possible that the court adopted Livian ideas. Livy's early books, probably conceived and largely written before Actium, perhaps affected the emperor's religious program of rebuilding temples and reviving abandoned rituals. His idea of

Camillus as a second founder (*conditor alter*) of Rome may be connected to Augustus as re-founder of the state. Scholars disagree, however, on whether Livy's history was used in the sculptural and ideological program of the Forum of Augustus with its statues of great Romans (*conditores*). If so, he might have disapproved since in his mind there was only one hero, the Roman People themselves.

Strong but humane leadership was obviously needed, and Livy at one time thought that Augustus might provide it. Here the bourgeois Paduan reveals his yearning for peace and concord instead of civil war. Yet, as the years of Augustus' domination turned into decades, Livy may have become disappointed in the concentration of power into dynastic government. We know he did not publish his final twenty-two books on the Augustan era until after the emperor's death. The reason for this was more likely *pietas* than fear, since Livy's treatment of Augustus was hardly used by later historians. His treatment must have been rather gentle, since his successors preferred authors who wrote more frankly after the emperor's death. While Livy honorably refused to become a court historian, he perhaps did not have the political acumen and sharp wit necessary to write a truly probing history of those complex times. Without his final books, there is no way to be certain.

Livy as historian

Livy's book was far too long for most ancient readers. It was soon summarized and then the summaries shortened again. Though his original text survived until the sixth century, it was more commonly read in abridgments. It was also excerpted in handbooks; later critics were respectful but they preferred the briefer books of Sallust. Hence Livy was not much read in the Middle Ages, and few manuscript copies were made. The humanist Petrarch found texts of thirty books and was the first scholar since antiquity to unite the surviving sections. It was perhaps Boccaccio who translated Books 21–40 into Italian in the fourteenth century. By the fifteenth century Livy had become a stylistic and political model for Renaissance Italy. Humanist scholars ransacked monastery libraries on a treasure hunt for additional books of Livy. Perhaps the first modern work of political theory is Machiavelli's *Discourses on the First Ten Books of Livy* (1531), which uses Livy as a point of departure for political analysis.

From the Renaissance to our own time, Livy has almost always been read as an historical source rather than as an historian. He tells us the legends of Romulus and Remus, the dramatic tales of the Rape of Lucretia and the brothers Horatii, the accomplishments of the brilliant Hannibal and the righteous Cato. His stories were dramatized by Shakespeare, Racine and Corneille; they were used in operas from Francesco Cavalli's *Scipio Africano* (1665) to Benjamin Britten's *The Rape of Lucretia* (1946); and paintings of Livian scenes range from numerous sensual Renaissance depictions of the Rape of the Sabine women to Jacques-Louis David's earnestly revolutionary *Oath of the Horatii*. Livy would have been delighted to learn that his tales have shaped the European image of Republican Rome for 2,000 years and that his portraits nurtured dreams of liberty during the American and French revolutions.

But for almost as long Livy has been subject to criticism as an historian, though from a wildly assorted group of critics. The emperor Caligula, the mad great-grandson of Livy's friend Augustus, called him verbose and sloppy. In modern times critics have praised his style and narrative skill, while questioning his historical ability. Nineteenth-century positivist scholars criticized him as uncritical of his sources and insufficiently committed to truth. The distinguished philosopher of history R.G. Collingwood is particularly scathing on Livy's schematic approach and his inability to appreciate historical change. Hence Livy was seen as a kind of pleasant romancer who told wonderful stories, but who contributed no original insight to his study of the past.

The accusations are many. Livy included geographical and chronological errors, topographical anachronisms, projections of later political struggles into early Rome, internal contradictions and mistranslations from the Greek. He did not consult all available texts, and instead took the easy road of following a single source for each section. But while there are indeed errors, they seem relatively few for the size and scope of the book. Livy is patriotic but not fiercely chauvinistic; he does not use *nos* and *nostri*, as the annalists did, to refer to the Roman armies. He is trying to be impartial, and he achieves a higher level of fairness than any of his Roman predecessors.

Some critics inappropriately apply modern standards of historical writing to Livy; others misunderstand his goals. For those critics he is merely an *exornator rerum* – an elegant storyteller – who does not tell them what they really would like to know. They treat him as a source, not as a writer whose goal was to give pleasure while recreating the past. Recent scholars have been more sympathetic in attempting to delineate Livy's aims and to judge his achievements by standards appropriate to ancient times. First among those aims was to carry moral conviction by being persuasive and giving pleasure. Pleasure was not only to be derived from a felicity of style, but most importantly from the content, which traced the development of the Roman People. He spent his long working life reading and writing in order to trace the moral purpose of Rome's history. While specific factual certainty was less important to Livy than the overall evolutionary process, he was certainly determined to write both a more accurate, as well as a more literary, history than any of his Roman predecessors. That he succeeded in both is clear; he fulfilled Cicero's goal of oratorical history and his work soon displaced all earlier Roman annalists. His history preserved much material on archaic Rome that surely would have otherwise perished. He was recognized by Quintilian as the Roman Herodotus, and his speeches were particularly praised:

> I should not hesitate to match Sallust against Thucydides, nor would Herodotus resent Livy being placed on the same level as himself. For the latter has a wonderful charm and transparency in narrative, while his speeches are eloquent beyond description; so admirably adapted is all that is said both to the circumstances and the speaker; and as regards the emotions, especially the more pleasing of them, I may sum him up by saying that no historian has ever depicted them to greater perfection.
>
> (*Ins. Or.* 10, 1, 101, tr. Butler (Loeb))

Archaeology and epigraphy have, perhaps unexpectedly, also lent Livy greater credibility. Excavations of the Roman Forum attest early burials of a mixed population that reflect Latin and Sabine condominium, giving a historical framework for the Rape of the Sabine Women. The Forum was paved over about the time Livy places Tarquin's program of urbanization, and names of several Etruscan kings survive in inscriptions and tomb paintings. A careful study of Polybius shows that Livy's speeches may be embellished, but the content follows his Greek source.

Livy saw the past through contemporary spectacles, and he also saw the present as shaped by the past. His history is indeed concerned with historical change, and the patterns he sees in history reinforce the links between past and present. He understood that while some core element in Roman character was present even in remote times, the evolution of Roman institutions and values was primarily the result of historical processes. So Livy gave historical weight to stories from the monarchy, since he saw that they helped shape later Roman consciousness. So too he recorded prodigies that he openly disbelieved, because they too shed light on the evolution of Roman attitudes. His book is not a collection of random stories; it is an immense undertaking to explain the unfolding of the remarkable people who had come to dominate the world. The author traces the growth of empire and frankly describes the costs of imperialism: civil war, corruption, social dislocation, and the loss of freedom. His story is told with moral passion and brings its characters to life.

Livy was recognized as a classic in his own time. When a younger contemporary praised his *eloquentia et fides*, it was no idle compliment. Livy had produced over more than forty years a masterpiece of Latin prose, and he had also read countless dry historical annals, ransacked archives, and even visited some sites to produce the most accurate account possible of the broad sweep of Roman history. It is little wonder that he had admirers across the Roman world. The younger Pliny tells a famous story that makes the historian into a popular icon:

> Did you ever read the story of a man from Cadiz who was so moved by the name and reputation of Livy that he came from the very edge of the earth just to see him, and when he saw him, immediately went home again.
>
> (*Epistulae* 2, 3, 8)

4

TACITUS

Cornelius Tacitus (*c*. 55–*c*. 117 CE) was the greatest historian that the Roman world produced. His achievements were recognized immediately: his senatorial colleague Pliny wrote to his friend "Your histories will be immortal" (*Epistles* 7, 3). And so they are, but it was a very close call. Tacitus was deeply unpopular among the Christians of late antiquity and virtually unknown in the Middle Ages. His *Annals* and *Histories* – among the greatest works of Latin literature – each owe their survival to a single medieval manuscript! But after Tacitus was rediscovered in the Renaissance his works had an enormous impact. Their extraordinary influence across the last five centuries derives not (as Livy's does) from the uplifting matter of the story, for Tacitus' account of the loss of freedom under the Julio-Claudian and Flavian emperors is grim and depressing. However, he brought to that story psychological penetration, acute political analysis, moral grandeur, and a literary genius that have dazzled the most sophisticated readers. They have been enormously impressed by the author's cleverness and remain in awe of the remarkable power of his history. As Thomas Jefferson wrote to his granddaughter, "Tacitus I consider the first writer in the world without a single exception. His book is a compound of history and morality of which we have no other example." But some have also heaped insults upon him: liar, anti-Christian, immoral, anti-Semitic, and an enemy of kings. Napoleon attacked him on several occasions as a mere pamphleteer and slanderer. Even scholars have had trouble deciding if he is a very good, or a very bad, historian. It is the lavishness of the praise and the fury of the condemnations that are astonishing. Few readers, even after 1,900 years, remain unaffected by the provocative style and disturbing content of his books.

Life and career

Cornelius Tacitus was born about 55 CE into a prominent family in
southern Gaul – an area by then so Romanized that a contemporary
thought it to be "more truly Italy than a province." His father was a
financial official of equestrian rank, an important distinction but
still a large step below the senatorial order. Our information about
Tacitus' career derives largely from his own biography of his father-
in-law Agricola; we do not even know his first name (Gaius and
Publius are both mentioned) nor the precise dates of his birth and
death. During his adolescence, while the Roman world was
convulsed by civil war, Tacitus pursued the study of rhetoric and
eagerly apprenticed himself to leading orators. He first came to
public notice through the law courts and, when he married the
daughter of the influential Gallic senator and leading general,
Julius Agricola, he obtained connections at court.

He received his first public office under Vespasian (69–79 CE),
and under Titus (79–81 CE) he was elected quaestor and entered the
Senate. The emperor Domitian (81–96 CE) made Tacitus praetor and
he served as a senior provincial official from 89 to 93. We know
nothing of his activity during Domitian's reign of terror of 93–6,
but he reached the consulship in 97, perhaps even nominated by
Domitian before his assassination. It was an extraordinarily successful
career for a young Gallo-Roman of equestrian background, and he
mentions his offices to provide validation of his inside knowledge of
imperial politics. Thus we are more surprised by his claim that
fifteen years of life had been blotted out by the terror of Domitian.

> In the capital there were yet worse horrors. Nobility,
> wealth, the refusal or the acceptance of office, were grounds
> for accusation, and virtue ensured destruction. The rewards
> of the informers were no less odious than their crimes; for
> while some seized on consulships and priestly offices as their
> share of the spoil, others on procuratorships, and posts of
> more confidential authority, they robbed and ruined in
> every direction amid universal hatred and terror. Slaves were
> bribed to turn against their masters, and freedmen to
> betray their patrons; and those who had not an enemy were
> destroyed by friends.
>
> (*Historiae* 1, 2)[1]

He had served Domitian loyally and had been rewarded generously; we cannot tell if he bore the guilt of a collaborator or the shame of a survivor. His relations with Domitian shape his view of earlier emperors' relations with the Senate: collaboration, resentment, hatred. He recognizes the complicity of the Senate, and his histories are in large part an exorcism of his own responsibility.

On the death of Domitian, a series of "good emperors" began with the brief reign of the elderly Nerva (96–8 CE) followed by the long and happy rule of Trajan (98–117 CE):

> Now at last our spirit is returning. And yet, though at the dawn of a most happy age, Nerva Caesar blended things once irreconcilable – sovereignty and freedom – though Trajan is now daily augmenting the prosperity of the time.
>
> (*Agricola* 3)

In 112 CE Tacitus served as proconsular governor of the province of Asia, perhaps the highest distinction for a senator. His date of death is uncertain but 117 CE is most likely.

Historical writings

The orator and senator first turned to history as an escape from the terrible last years of Domitian. Like Polybius, he believed that history should be written by experienced politicians, who could assess motivations and evaluate documents. Tacitus did not wish to entertain, but as a successful orator he knew how to seduce an audience. His goal was twofold: utilitarian and commemorative. Like Thucydides, he thought that his history could be useful to future generations since he believed that history could intimidate tyrants by subjecting them to the judgment of posterity. He also believed deeply in the commemorative function of history: virtue should be rewarded, if only by consigning it to the collective memory. This is a duty that all civilized people owe to the virtuous men and women who have preceded them.

In 98 he published a brief, admiring biography of his father-in-law Agricola, who was a long-time governor of the province of Britain. That book, containing speeches and digressions, constituted the historian's apprenticeship. It will be discussed in the treatment of Roman biography in Chapter 7.

Germania

Soon after the *Agricola*, Tacitus produced his essay *On the Origin and Land of the Germans* (usually called *Germania*), the only purely ethnographic monograph that survives from antiquity. For centuries historians had inserted into their books material on the geography, local customs, political organization, and religious beliefs of various peoples. This continued the popular tradition of tales of remote societies, sometimes historical like Herodotus on Egypt and Scythia, and sometimes fabulous like Homer's Cyclopes and Lotus Eaters. The appearance of pseudo-ethnography in the stories of Alexander's conquest and in Greek romances shows the widespread interest in the customs of exotic peoples.

The first half of the *Germania* describes the geography and customs of Germany. One famous assertion, which has had a long and influential afterlife, is that the Germans are a "pure race," unmixed with other peoples (4). The second half of the book describes the individual German tribes. There is no evidence that Tacitus ever visited Germany; he relied almost totally on earlier books by Caesar and the elder Pliny, though he may have added some more current material gleaned from soldiers and merchants. Like other ancient writers, Tacitus sometimes generalized about barbarian peoples and transferred characteristics from one to another, but much in his book has been confirmed in general terms by archaeology – though archaeology itself has sometimes been distorted by attempts to correlate too closely surviving artifacts with Tacitus' tribal description.

The *Germania* is more than a monograph written to inform the Romans about Germany and its peoples. An important function of ancient ethnography was to provide a contrast with one's own society, another perspective from which the writer could examine his own state and customs. Hence even utopian or fictitious societies could provide interesting material for social and political speculation, as Lilliput did for Jonathan Swift or science fiction does today. While Tacitus certainly wished to alert the Romans to the threat to the Empire that the Germans would pose in the future, his central purpose was not to praise Germany so much as to criticize Roman morality and political life through the implied comparison.

Tacitus' anger at the fashionable immorality of contemporary Rome led him to idealize German life in a far more flattering description than his later treatment of the Germans in the *Histories*. Their avoidance of unnecessary display, as in the practicality of their wedding gifts, manifests a seriousness clearly opposed to the frivolity of Roman society. Marriage is taken seriously and "no one there laughs at vice" (19). Young Germans are eager to prove their valor in battle, not in seduction. The idealization is not so complete, however, as to omit the Germans' drunkenness, cruelty, and laziness.

The *Germania* also emphasizes the political freedom of the Germans who, unlike the Romans, make the most important decisions collectively: the power of kings is neither absolute nor arbitrary. There is a blunt though unspoken suggestion that, despite the trappings of a constitution, Rome is in fact an absolute monarchy. Tacitus also delivers a forthright warning for the future: if the Germans were to unite, Rome might not be able to resist them. This is not fatalism, but a challenge to the new emperor Trajan who had been campaigning on the northern frontier. Tacitus is urging Trajan to return to Julius Caesar's aggressively expansionist foreign policy.

Since its rediscovery in the fifteenth century, some Germans have viewed this monograph as an affirmation of their noble past and national independence. During the Reformation, the contrast between pure Germans and corrupt Romans was transferred to the religious sphere, where German reformers were attempting to purge the Christian Church of "Roman" (that is, papal) corruption. The propagandists of the Nazi era saw Tacitus' ancient and racially unmixed Germans and Richard Wagner's hero Siegfried as chaste and heroic supermen – prototypes of the "master race." Looking back on World War II, the great Italian Jewish historian Arnaldo Momigliano concluded that the *Germania* was among the "most dangerous books ever written."

Historiae

During the decade after the appearance of his two monographs, Tacitus was hard at work on a major narrative history of the Flavian emperors, Vespasian, Titus, and Domitian. He completed it about 109. This was a history of his own times, and he had held office under all three of the Flavians. He promised in the preface to move on to the reigns of Nerva and Trajan, if he were to live long enough – a promise Tacitus never fulfilled. The *Historiae* (or *Histories*), a name attached by a later editor, covered the period from 69 CE to the death of Domitian in 96 CE in twelve books. Only four complete books and part of a fifth survive in a single medieval manuscript – about a third of the entire work – which covers only two of the twenty-eight years. Following an annalistic structure, Tacitus begins a bit abruptly on January 1, 69 when Galba had already replaced Nero as emperor. The complex events of 69 CE, with its four emperors and continuous civil war, take more than three books and constitute the most detailed narrative we have in all of Greek and Roman historiography.

In the preface to his first great historical work, Tacitus makes explicit why he believed it was now both possible and desirable to write the history of the Flavians:

I begin my work with the time when Servius Galba was consul for the second time with Titus Vinius for his colleague [69 CE]. Of the former period, the 820 years dating from the founding of the city, many authors have treated; and while they had to record the transactions of the Roman people, they wrote with equal eloquence and freedom. After the conflict at Actium, and when it became essential to peace, that all power should be centered in one man, these great intellects passed away. Then too the truthfulness of history was impaired in many ways; at first, through men's ignorance of public affairs, which were now wholly strange to them, then, through their passion for flattery, or, on the other hand, their hatred of their masters. And so, between the enmity of the one and the servility of the other, neither had any regard for posterity. But while we instinctively shrink from a writer's adulation, we lend a ready ear to detraction and spite, because flattery involves the shameful imputation of servility, whereas malignity wears the false appearance of honesty. I myself knew nothing of Galba, of Otho, or of Vitellius, either from benefits or from injuries. I would not deny that my elevation was begun by Vespasian, augmented by Titus, and still further advanced by Domitian; but those who profess inviolable truthfulness must speak of all without partiality and without hatred. I have reserved as an employment for my old age, and should my life be long enough, a subject at once more fruitful and less anxious in the reign of the Deified Nerva and the empire of Trajan, enjoying the rare happiness of times, where we may think what we please, and express what we think.

(*Historiae* 1, 1)

Book 1   The aged emperor Galba adopts Piso, but both are soon murdered. The praetorians in Rome replace him with Otho, a survivor of Nero's court. The German legions meanwhile proclaim their commander Vitellius as emperor (January–March, 69 CE).

Book 2   In the East, the general Vespasian continues to put down the Jewish revolt. Vitellius' legions march into Italy where they confront the armies of Otho. After the defeat and death of Otho, Vitellius takes Rome. The eastern legions proclaim Vespasian as emperor, and the Danube legions join them (March–August, 69 CE).

Book 3   The Flavian armies invade Italy. Fighting between the troops, from northern Italy to Rome itself, where Tacitus provides a poetic account of the burning of the Capitol. The book ends with the cowardly death of Vitellius (September–December, 69 CE).

Book 4   Flavian domination in Rome, while Vespasian and his son Titus remain in Judaea. A revolt of northern German tribes is led by Civilis and appeals to the Gauls for support (early 70 CE).

Book 5   The book opens with a hostile, and very inaccurate, description of the Jews, their history, and their customs. The book breaks off with the impending defeat of the rebel Civilis (70 CE).

The pace of the early books of the *Histories* is remarkable. The compressed style contributes to the swift progress of the story, and dramatic vignettes, character sketches, and literary digressions enliven the march of the armies. This is public history, with many crowd scenes of armies, mobs, and provincials being addressed by generals, emperors, and rebel leaders. Only later would Tacitus turn to secret history in the *Annals*.

The Civil War sets a somber tone, only occasionally relieved by an act of heroism or an example of unexpected virtue. Though Tacitus acknowledges that some Flavians acted from noble motives in embarking on Civil War, he regards the entire episode as the result of an uncontrollable lust for power and the greatest evil ever to befall the Roman people. It destroyed military discipline and allowed the provinces to rebel; it ensured that scoundrels would come to power; and it resulted in the terrible sacrilege of the burning of the temple of Jupiter on the Capitol.

In the *Histories* Tacitus shows for the first time his impressive command of political theory and political reality. Whether in epigrams or in more theoretical speeches, he displays the mastery of the secrets of power (*arcana imperii*) with which his name has been linked through the centuries. He identifies the greatest "secret" to be that no constitution can ensure the peaceful transfer of power if the army chooses to ignore it. Tacitus, writing under Trajan, who had been adopted by Nerva, regards the adoptive monarchy as a means of avoiding hereditary despots, and he implants such ideas in the speech that Galba gives on his adoption of Piso.

The *Histories* is a masterpiece by a mature historian. Within the conventional structure of speeches and debates, Tacitus has forged a swift and powerful narrative as well as an individual style. But his contribution goes beyond style and structure. Tacitus here analyzes the political institutions of the Roman state, and he first presents his own ideology of Empire. Our loss of the last seven books of the *Histories* is indeed bitter; in them we would have been able to see Tacitus write the history of the reign of Domitian, which he had witnessed at first hand.

Annales

In the decade from the *Histories* to the *Annals* (Latin: *Annales*) Tacitus progressed further, from public to private history, from excellence to genius. He does not tell us' why he abandons his promise to write a history of his own time – the reign of Trajan – but it is most likely that he saw the origins of the Domitianic tyranny in Julio-Claudian times. So he moved backward rather than forward. The *Annals* is a penetrating exposé of imperial politics that represents the pinnacle of Roman historical writing. It survives in two separate blocks (1–6 and 11–16) which give most of the reign of Tiberius (14–37 CE), about half of that of Claudius (41–54 CE), and most of the principate of Nero (54–68 CE). The treatment of Caligula (37–41 CE) is completely lost. Tacitus probably intended to conclude the *Annals* in eighteen books at the end of 68 CE, since the *Histories* begins on January 1, 69 CE. We cannot be certain, however, that the work was in fact completed.

Books 1–2 (14–19 CE) Death of Augustus and the accession of Tiberius. The legions along the Danube and the Rhine mutiny, but the emperor's adopted son Germanicus restores the peace. War against the German leader Arminius. Germanicus dies in the East.

Books 3–4 (19–28 CE) Prosecution of Piso for death of Germanicus.

Rise of Sejanus. Death of Drusus; persecutions widen as Tiberius withdraws to Capri.

Book 5 (29–31 CE) Only a short fragment. The fall of Sejanus occurs in the lost pages.

Book 6 (32–7 CE) Prosecutions for treason. Death of Tiberius.

Books 7–10 (37–46 CE) These are lost. They contained the brief reign of Caligula and the first years of Claudius.

Books 11–12 (47–54 CE) Reign of Claudius. Conspiracy and death of the empress Messalina. Choice of Agrippina, mother of Nero, as new empress. Rebellion in Britain. Death of Claudius.

Books 13–14 (54–62 CE) Accession of Nero. War against Parthia. Murder of Agrippina and exile of Octavia. Marriage of Nero and Poppaea.

Books 15–16 (62–6 CE) War in the East. Great Fire at Rome. Persecution of Christians. Conspiracy of Piso and suicide of Seneca. Death of Thrasea and Petronius.

Books 17–18 (66–8 CE) These are lost. They contained the fall of Nero's regime.

Tacitus composed the *Annals* in three hexads, which form the basic structure of the work. The first six books cover the reign of Tiberius, and the hexad is divided by the first appearance of the evil praetorian prefect Sejanus at the beginning of Book 4. The opening of the second hexad is lost, but it also closes with the death of an emperor, Claudius. The third hexad opens with the accession of Nero, with a clear reminiscence of the accession of Tiberius: "The first death of the new regime..." (13, 1) recalls "The first crime of the new regime was the murder of Postumus Agrippa" (1, 6). The parallel between these regimes extends to implied comparisons of the domineering imperial mothers, Livia and Agrippina. Tacitus clearly divides the reigns of Tiberius and Nero into positive and negative phases, and he probably follows the ancient convention of doing the same for Caligula. Tacitus' structure may not be only a literary conceit, since many rulers do indeed come to power amidst high hopes and later crush those expectations.

The *Annals* does not begin with a formal prologue setting out the goals of the author, such as we find in the *Histories*. The first two words, *urbem Romam* ("The city of Rome"), signal the restricted perspective of Tacitus in the *Annals*: the city of Rome and its government. Wars and mutinies in the provinces are recounted primarily to shed light on the emperors and their court. In the fifth century St Jerome referred to Tacitus' book as *The Lives of the Caesars*. Though Tacitus did not write biographies, Jerome was perceptive in seeing that Tacitus' interest never wandered very far from the imperial palace.

After a few densely packed remarks on the decline of the Republic and the triumph of Augustus, Tacitus makes a brief comment on the inadequate historical treatment of the Julio-Claudian emperors:

> But the successes and reverses of the old Roman people have been recorded by famous historians; and fine intellects were not wanting to describe the times of Augustus, till growing sycophancy scared them away. The histories of Tiberius, Gaius Caligula, Claudius, and Nero, while they were in power, were falsified through terror, and after their death were written under the irritation of a recent hatred. Hence my purpose is to relate a few facts about Augustus – more particularly his last acts – then the reign of Tiberius, and all which follows, without either bitterness or partiality, from any motives to which I am far removed.
>
> *(Annales* 1, 1)

Tacitus then glances back to the reign of Augustus where the Roman people truly lost their collective political innocence: "Augustus seduced the people with food, the soldiers with bonuses, and everyone with the sweetness of peace" (1, 2). Though Tacitus deploys his literary skills to give an impression of duplicity and dynastic intrigue, he still admits that Augustus had restored peace after nearly a century of civil conflict and that the provincials were much better off than they had been under the senatorial rule of the Republic. At the funeral of Augustus, Tacitus uses the rhetorical device of having groups of spectators speak for or against the public and private life of the dead emperor. By adopting Tiberius as his successor, they conclude, Augustus hoped to ensure his own future glory by invidious comparison. In these few pages on Augustus, Tacitus provides a grim backdrop for Tiberius' entrance.

The gloomy, anti-social Tiberius is the most complex character in

Tacitus, perhaps in all of Latin literature. His natural diffidence is presented as dissimulation, his shyness as haughtiness, and his acts of generosity as hypocrisy. Yet, despite these innuendoes and even though Tacitus strongly disapproves of Tiberius' decision to follow the non-expansionist policy which Augustus established after his defeat in Germany, the historian does acknowledge that the Empire was well administered and the laws enforced until the ascendancy of the praetorian prefect Sejanus in 23 CE. After the emperor retires to Capri a few years later, Tacitus paints a picture of paranoid politics and moral depravity, but he also allows us to see Tiberius as a wounded husband, a bullied son, and a friendless and lonely old man. Tiberius gave his trust to Sejanus, who had once saved his life in a cave-in, but he chose badly since Sejanus had the emperor's son Drusus murdered in order to advance his own imperial ambitions. Tiberius' pre-emptive strike against Sejanus occurs in the lost section of Book 5, but Tacitus' account of the aftermath amply displays the increased bitterness and distrust felt by the aging emperor.

After a lacuna in the texts of Books 7–10 covering ten years, Books 11 and 12 treat the last seven years of the reign of Claudius. Perhaps Tacitus followed his usual practice and presented a more positive image of Claudius in the early years of his reign when he conquered Britain. By 47 CE, however, the emperor is displayed as controlled by his freedmen and his women. Messalina and the younger Agrippina step confidently into the imperial spotlight. Messalina treated imperial power as a toy to be used to satisfy her lust and her whims, but Agrippina was more dangerous: she used her sexuality to increase her power. The traditionalist Tacitus certainly believes that a man must keep his wife under control, and his contempt for Claudius is withering. There is little of the wit or charm of Suetonius' Claudius in Tacitus' pathetic account of his final years before his murder by Agrippina.

The last four surviving books of the *Annals* cover the twelve years from the accession of Nero through the matricide of Agrippina, the great fire of Rome, and the conspiracy of Piso, with the death of the emperor's tutor, the Stoic philosopher Seneca. Here Tacitus is much less concerned with political debate than in the Tiberian books; the focus is on Nero's increasingly bizarre behavior and Rome's foreign wars. The young emperor's accession was promising, with Seneca guiding his political and intellectual development. But Tacitus soon turns to tales of Nero's sexual abandon matched by the degradation of his performing on the stage, and bloody cruelty soon follows: Book 14 begins with Nero murdering his mother and ends with the death of his wife Octavia. Even his tutor Seneca, having retired with the emperor's kisses, was forced to commit suicide in a stirring and dramatic scene. Our text ends with Nero's reign of terror against the Senate; we must regret that the missing last two books contained the emperor's ludicrous singing tour of Greek festivals, the revolts in Judaea and Gaul, the final pathetic death of Nero, and the outbreak of civil war.

The *Annals* is far more than narrative history; Tacitus provides an analytical framework through several central themes: the growth of tyranny; the decline of Roman morality; and the misuse of language. The recurring pattern of imperial tyranny and senatorial cowardice are repeatedly contrasted with the courage of Rome's barbarian enemies, who fight and die to preserve their freedom. The German Arminius, the Gaul Sacrovir, and the British queen Boudicca are all given defiant speeches against Roman domination. When Roman senators do plot against Nero, the results are hardly heroic, since the captured conspirators quickly betray family and friends. Tyranny is accompanied by informers, manipulative freedmen, and universal paranoia. Despotism, sycophancy, and treachery form the web that ties together the whole of the *Annals*.

Closely linked to the rise of tyranny is the moral decline that pervades the Senate, the armies, and the entire Roman people. Tiberius was initially austere in his personal life, and he inspired fear when he reproached luxury, but his later orgies at Capri provided a model for his successors. Tacitus also sees moral weakness in Roman unwillingness to expand their imperial dominion. This unwillingness to fight abroad led to civil wars in which ambitious generals fruitlessly wasted Roman wealth and Roman lives, while Republican generals had once achieved their reputations by bringing treasure to Rome. The passive military policy of Augustus and Tiberius is for Tacitus a clear indication of moral weakness.

Tacitus was fascinated by language and was particularly sensitive to its misuse. Language creates illusions to conceal political realities and the historian was eager to expose the lies that form the basis of imperial rule. "The titles of the officials remained the same," says Tacitus, but he makes it clear that their actual powers had changed. He was almost obsessed with censorship and the repression of writers, since he knew as well as any Roman the connection between word, thought, and power, and those links lie at the heart of his masterpiece.

In the *Annals* Tacitus is at the peak of his stylistic powers. The force of the work lies in its compact style, which has a jackhammer quality. It is less smooth and more concentrated than the *Histories* – even the speeches are shorter and more intense – and the author strives to avoid triteness through surprising turns of phrase. Tacitus is a master of the epigram and he does not lack a sense of humor, though his jokes are bitter and ironic. The historian has created a very personal style, which delivers his message with great energy and precision. The abrasiveness of this bold work perfectly suits its unsettling content. Style, subject, and temperament come together to create a masterpiece.

Here Tacitus reflects more profoundly than before on his role as an historian, and makes clear his belief in the moral function of history. The recording of virtuous and evil acts will not only teach future generations; it will also reward and punish, and thereby encourage the good and deter the bad. Beneath the conventional application of moral judgments we should see the *Annals* as a brilliant and creative expression of deep personal suffering and political frustration.

The historian's method

Tacitus stood among those ancient historians who combined literary artistry, intellectual coherence, and research. While for a modern historian originality of research may be primary, Tacitus' primary goal was to understand the past and to convey his ideas effectively. Though he recognized the power of Fortune in human life, Tacitus believed that the past can be made to form a comprehensible pattern from which he and his reader can learn:

> Before I begin my project, it seems best to consider the condition of Rome, the feelings of the army, the attitude of the provinces, and the strengths and weaknesses of the entire Empire. Thus we can learn not only events and consequences (which are often determined by chance) but the underlying logic and causes as well.
>
> (*Historiae* 1, 4)

If research is the consultation and evaluation of sources, there can be little doubt that Tacitus engaged in serious research, even if it is not often apparent in the smooth flow of his narrative. He consulted both obvious and obscure sources, though like other ancient writers he thought that personal research was more important for the history of recent times. In a closed society where decisions were often taken secretly in the imperial palace, sources could sometimes be difficult to find. In his quest for first-hand accounts of important events, he consulted Verginius Rufus and Spurinna, both active in the Civil War of 69 CE. He also asked his friend Pliny for his eyewitness account of the eruption of Mount Vesuvius, which destroyed Pompeii and Herculaneum in 69 CE and which the teenage Pliny had observed from across the Bay of Naples. Pliny's lengthy report survives in a letter to Tacitus (*Ep.* 6, 16); it is unfortunate that Tacitus' own version was contained in the lost portion of the *Histories*, so that we cannot see what use he made of this primary document.

Tacitus' research was hardly restricted to asking living contemporaries for their accounts; there is evidence that he diligently read histories, reminiscences, biographies, autobiographies, letters, speeches, and even collections of deathbed thoughts of famous men, as well as the Acts of the Senate. This archival research is especially evident in the early books of the *Annals*, and it may have been a significant innovation in the historical writing of the time. Some of this material, like the senatorial decree on the trial of Piso, was engraved on bronze and set up in public; otherwise he sought it out in public or private archives. Then, as now, princes and politicians tried to control their future reputation through autobiographies and memoirs. Tacitus would surely have read the autobiographies of Augustus, Tiberius, and Claudius, but he referred specifically only to the memoirs of the general Corbulo and those of the empress Agrippina. He also seems to have implicitly used, and responded to, the *Res Gestae* of Augustus. As Tacitus says, after mentioning several sources for the life of Nero:

> When the sources are unanimous, I will follow them; when they provide different versions, I will record them with attribution.
>
> (*Annales* 13, 20)

Despite the absence of specific references, it is evident that the Tiberian and Claudian books of the *Annals* also rely on a wide range of primary and secondary sources. Tacitus would find our need to identify every source unnecessary and even tiresome; he judged them privately and freely reorganized their material without troubling his readers with such details. The ancient reader looked for political intelligence and stylistic polish in an historical text; he did not expect the writer to justify himself with evidence of research. But the absence of extended discussion of sources did not preclude the careful collection and thoughtful analysis of them. Tacitus had done both; he used the sources of political history well. Nor did he believe everything he read. He points out that the bigamous marriage celebration of the empress Messalina, while her husband Claudius was in Ostia for the day, seems to defy belief. But he tells us that he checked further and confirms that it did happen.

Outside the realm of politics, however, Tacitus was less well informed and much less scrupulous. He was sometimes weak on geography (as most Romans are) and military tactics, especially on the northern frontier and in his confusing account of the campaigns of Germanicus. Theodor Mommsen called him "the most unmilitary of historians." For a man who had served as governor of Asia, his knowledge of Jews and Christians was woefully (and unnecessarily) confused. The Jewish historian Josephus lived in Rome and frequented the court during the Flavian era; there is no excuse for Tacitus' use of garbled nonsense (Jews came from Crete) and anti-Semitic clichés (their lasciviousness). On the other hand, he sometimes condemned them for what we might find admirable: "They consider it a crime to kill an unwanted child" (*Hist.* 5, 5). Confusion between Christians and Jews may have been understand-able in the time of Nero, but Tacitus was writing in the early second century when many government officials such as his good friend Pliny had learned the clear differences between them. We can only attribute this blind spot to Tacitus' contempt for all easterners, Greeks, Jews, and Egyptians alike; he clearly thought them unworthy of the curiosity and research he lavished on court intrigues.

If the speeches in Tacitus' histories reflect the historian's own trenchant and analytical tone, he does not necessarily misrepresent the attitudes of the speakers. Like all ancient historians Tacitus tried to make his speeches rhetorically plausible, and so Tiberius' combi-nation of canniness and common sense appears in his speeches. (Tacitus tells us that Nero was the first emperor to use "ghost-writers" for his speeches.) We can particularly see Tacitus' method in the speech of Claudius on the admission of Gallic nobles to the Senate. It is the only ancient speech that survives both on an official bronze copy (found in Lyons) as well as in an historian's literary version. The original reminds us of the woolly-minded Claudius depicted by Suetonius: digressions laced with historical pedantry. Though the beginning and other sections of the speech are missing, we can easily compare the first half of Claudius' rambling oration with the first few sentences of Tacitus' version, which describe similar historical precedents:

And indeed, looking to the very first and foremost impression in the minds of the public, which I foresee will meet me at the very outset, I beg of you not to be startled at my proposal, as at the introduction of a new precedent, but much rather to reflect how many new precedents have taken their place in our constitution, and into how many forms and phases from the first origin of our city our republic has been made to fit.

There was a time when kings possessed this city, without however being able to hand it down to successors within their own families. Others took their place from other families and even from other nations. Thus Numa succeeded Romulus, imported from the Sabines, a neighbor it is true, but of a foreign stock. Thus Priscus Tarquinius succeeded Ancus Martius. The former, born at Tarquinii, of Demaratus, a Corinthian, and a high-born mother of that city...poor she must have been, to be compelled to marry such a husband...he, I say, being precluded through the taint of his blood from obtaining honors in his own home, migrated to Rome and obtained the position of king. Between him again and his son or grandson, for on this point our authorities disagree, there intervened Servius Tullius, sprung, if we believe our own historians, from a captive woman named Ocresia. According to Tuscan writers, I may remind you, he was once the loyal and devoted retainer of Caelius Vivenna, whose every fortune he shared, and when by changing fortune he was driven to leave Etruria with all that was left of the army of Caelius, he occupied the Caelian Mount, giving it this name from his leader Caelius, and changing his own name from the Tuscan form, Mastarna, assumed that by which we know him. At any rate, as I have said, he obtained the position of king, with the greatest advantage to the State. Later on, when the habits of Tarquinius Superbus and no less of his sons, became hateful to our State, the minds of the people grew weary of the kingship, and the administration of the republic was transferred to the annual magistrates whom we call consuls.

(Dessau, *Inscriptiones Latinae Selectae* 212, tr. E.G. Hardy)

Tacitus downplays the personal idiosyncrasies of Claudius; the speech is briefer and the arguments are much more cogently presented. The historian has generously placed his own rhetorical skill at the service of an emperor whom he despised to present a powerful statement on behalf of the inclusion of provincials in the Senate. While some scholars believe Tacitus has almost ignored Claudius' speech, by his own lights Tacitus is faithful to Claudius' arguments and to the occasion, retaining just a touch of pedantry: where Claudius refers to a speech in Livy, Tacitus consults the speech directly and uses it. Any modern desire for verbal exactitude would have seemed to him "antiquarian" and unworthy of the literary artistry expected in serious historical writing. Here is the beginning of Tacitus' version:

> "My ancestors, the most ancient of whom was made at once a citizen and a noble of Rome, encourage me to govern by the same policy of transferring to this city all conspicuous merit, wherever found. And indeed I know, as facts, that the Julii came from Alba, the Coruncanii from Camerium, the Porcii from Tusculum, and not to inquire too minutely into the past, that new members have been brought into the Senate from Etruria and Lucania and the whole of Italy, that Italy itself was at last extended to the Alps, to the end that not only single persons but entire countries and tribes might be united under our name. We had unshaken peace at home; we prospered in all our foreign relations, in the days when Italy beyond the Po was admitted to share our citizenship, and when, enrolling in our ranks the most vigorous of the provincials, under color of settling our legions throughout the world, we recruited our exhausted empire. Are we sorry that the Balbi came to us from Spain, and other men not less illustrious from southern Gaul? Their descendants are still among us, and do not yield to us in patriotism."
>
> (*Annales* 11, 24)

The most difficult issue may be that of accuracy or, since no historian is completely accurate, the desire for accuracy. The third-century Christian apologist Tertullian called Tacitus "the most articulate of liars" (*Apologeticus* 16). The historian says on several occasions that he is not motivated by partiality or bias toward the emperors, so that he can write without the favor of the flatterers or the hatred of the persecuted. Of course, despite these avowals, Tacitus had very strong feelings, which are expressed in his books to the detriment of strict impartiality. He might avoid direct accusation, but he attributed thoughts and motives where he could not possibly have evidence for them. These unsubstantiated insinuations would be criticized in modern historical writings, but even they confirm Tacitus' basic honesty, since he retains inconveniently contradictory evidence that, to a perceptive reader, undermines the general impression. When the "cruel" Tiberius is upset by his son Drusus' excessive enthusiasm for blood sports, and even boycotts some games to show his displeasure, Tacitus criticizes him for exposing his son to criticism. Even the skillful administrator can be found lurking in the details of the account of the bumbling Claudius. Tacitus' passionate opinions should not obscure the fact that he is the most accurate of all Roman historians.

One can, however, be factually accurate and still deceive. In modern times, writers and politicians often deceive through statistics – "Lies, damn lies, and statistics!" – while the ancient writer used instead his rhetorical training. In some instances, it is a case of different priorities. A recently discovered bronze text sheds some light on this. This senatorial decree, set up around the Empire to announce the suicide and condemnation of Piso in 20 CE, shows several things about Tacitus' narrative. One is that the decree was intended to squelch precisely the rumors – that Piso might have been murdered – that Tacitus includes by innuendo. That is fair enough; the publication of official edicts rarely stops rumors. A more serious point is that Tacitus seems to have moved the trial from December to the previous spring. If that reconstruction is correct, he presumably did it for the sake of a better narrative. He would regard the precise date of an event as of no great importance to an historian who seeks to convey moral truth through a persuasive narrative.

In Tacitus' writings there are occasional contradictions between the facts reported and the impression the reader gets from the narration. The author may state briefly that the provincials were better off under the Empire than under the rapacious governors and tax-collectors of the Republic, but that statement is submerged under a prevailing impression of imperial tyranny and cruelty. Despite the persistent rumors and innuendo, Tiberius was accused of few direct crimes before the rise of Sejanus and the reign of terror. Despite the fact that he sarcastically dismissed the earliest of such charges, the emperor is linked to the treason trials. Tacitus suggests that Tiberius hypocritically masked his secret hatreds, but how could Tacitus (or his sources) penetrate the inmost emotions of so enigmatic an emperor?

The notorious treason trials under Tiberius give the impression of a horrifically repressive regime:

I realize that most writers omit the trials and punishment
of many men. They tire of the repetition, fearing what they
found tedious and depressing would produce a similar revulsion in their readers. But I have found much worth knowing,
even if unrecorded by others.

(*Annales* 6, 7)

At one point, near the end of Tiberius' reign, Tacitus refers to
"continual slaughter," but in fact the killings amount to a handful
of judicial executions and seven suicides in a three-year period. That
is unpleasant, but trivial compared to the reigns of Caligula and
Nero, not to speak of the Wars of Religion, or modern revolutions
or tyrannies. Tacitus records fewer than a hundred treason trials in
the twenty-three years of Tiberius' reign. Some defendants were
acquitted and some were admittedly guilty – this hardly constitutes
"continual slaughter." The psychology of the tabloid press is not far
from Tacitus' manipulation of his readers' sensibilities. The historian knew that Tiberius was far less cruel than his successors, but he
also realized that the repression of his own senatorial class first
began under Tiberius, who thus bore a special responsibility. He also
believed that the trials pitting senator against senator began the
path to the civil wars that saw Roman fighting Roman in the streets
of the capital. Tacitus remained scrupulous about factual details,
but presented them in a way that inevitably creates a false impression. Does this confirm Tertullian's charge that Tacitus is a liar?
Hardly. Tacitus sincerely believed that the sane and competent
Tiberius had started the Empire on the terrible road to political
persecution and made possible the horrors of his unstable successors
Caligula, Nero, and Domitian. The rhetoric may certainly seem
overheated, but Tacitus presented a factual basis for his view. This
perception of Tiberius, especially the late Tiberius, was hardly
unique to Tacitus; it also appears in Suetonius' *Life of Tiberius* and in
the later historian Dio's portrayal of the emperor. Tacitus' portrait
went further; with his literary art he has crafted the impression of a
desperate, lonely, misanthropic old man who has become one of the
most vivid characters in Latin literature.

The historian as moralist

Tacitus continued the Roman tradition of moral history, but he
transformed it into something more profound. He avoided the
shallow moralizing to be found in the early annalists and goes

beyond the easygoing chauvinism of Livy to show that, in an age of absolute rulers, political virtue consisted in something more complex than fighting to the death to defend the state against a foreign enemy. Of course Tacitus told stories of traditional *virtus*, but a central theme of his history is to relate the loss of *virtus* to the loss of political freedom at Rome. Hence Tacitus saw moral courage as needed in the political arena more than on the battlefield, and if Livy's heroes are Horatius and Camillus, Tacitus' are senators like Thrasea and Helvidius who suffered martyrdom for their political beliefs, and his own contemporaries who endured the terror of Domitian. Courage in the face of hopelessness is the *virtus* of the subjects of tyrants:

> Yet the age was not so barren in noble qualities, as not also to exhibit examples of virtue. Mothers accompanied the flight of their sons; wives followed their husbands into exile; there were brave kinsmen and faithful sons-in-law; there were slaves whose fidelity defied even torture; there were illustrious men driven to the last necessity, and enduring it with fortitude; there were closing scenes that equaled the famous deaths of antiquity.
>
> (*Historiae* 1, 3)

The morality of Tacitus did not derive from traditional Roman religion, toward all forms of which he was skeptical. If Tacitus hated Christians and despised Jews, he also had little use for the Roman cult of emperors or for astrology. He admired individual Stoic philosophers, but he distrusted the pretensions of philosophical charlatans. For him, as for most Romans, the bedrock of the Roman moral system was the noble deeds of past Romans. In their achievements and values he found the only reliable guide to public or private conduct. Thus he presented exemplars of personal courage in the face of death, devotion to intellectual freedom, and dignity in suicide. Likewise, on the dark side, we find negative examples in paranoid leaders, ambitious henchmen, sycophantic flatterers, informers, traitors, and executioners. These moral vignettes are his legacy.

Tacitus saw political change as deeply affecting moral values. One could no longer trust the personal compacts like *amicitia* (friendship) that formed the basis of political life in the Republic; now flattery toward those in power had corrupted all relationships. He displayed the xenophobia prevalent during the Republic, and was revolted by the trappings of Greek culture – actors, eunuchs, gymnasia, astrologers – and the sexual license of the imperial court, such as Tiberius' orgies on Capri, Messalina's promiscuity, and Nero's bisexuality. Tacitus cites with sympathy anonymous critics of Neronian corruption:

> Traditional morality, gradually slipping away, was entirely undermined by imported laxity so that whatever corrupts or can be corrupted would be seen in Rome, and foreign taste would reduce our youth to a bunch of gymnasts, loafers, and perverts. The emperor and the Senate are at fault; they not only allow these vices, but even force Roman nobles to debase themselves by declaiming or singing on stage. What remained, save to strip naked, put on gloves, and practice boxing instead of serving in the army.
>
> (*Annales* 14, 20)

In fact, Tacitus was much less concerned with sexual depravity than with political ambition, arrogance, and hypocrisy. Debauchery is primarily used to link the moral failings of the imperial family to the decline of freedom at Rome. He was not interested in private morality for its own sake, but for the light it sheds on public actions. Where private vices do not affect public life, he passed over them in silence. The depraved private life of Petronius, the "Arbiter of Elegance" at Nero's court, does not prevent Tacitus from praising his governorship and consulate. For Petronius – and this is always important for Tacitus – died well. When falsely implicated in a conspiracy against the emperor, he faced death with nobility while avoiding, perhaps even parodying, the sanctimonious suicide of Seneca. Petronius also had the last laugh on Nero, and we can perhaps catch our serious historian in a wry smile:

> Yet he did not fling his life away with precipitate haste, but having made an incision in his veins and then, according to his humor, bound them up, he again opened them, while he conversed with his friends, not in a serious strain or on topics that might win for him the glory of courage. And he listened to them as they repeated, not thoughts on the immortality of the soul or on the theories of philosophers, but light poetry and playful verses...
>
> Even in his will he did not, as did many in their last moments, flatter Nero or Tigellinus or any other of the

men in power. On the contrary, he described fully the prince's shameful excesses, with the names of his male and female lovers and their novelties in debauchery, and sent the account under seal to Nero...Nero was puzzled how the nature of his nocturnal activities had become known.

(*Annales* 16, 19–20)

It is a death worthy of an Oscar Wilde.

Earlier Roman historians had idealized the Roman people and army of the Republic. Tacitus agrees, but believes both had been corrupted in the Empire. The Roman crowds who watched their own armies fighting in the streets during the civil war enjoyed the bloodshed as much as if it were a festival in the Coliseum. This was no longer the Roman People, but a contemptible mob who had forgotten their ancestors. Likewise army mutinies arose from the conscription into the army of the lazy and self-indulgent urban rabble. The traditional Roman connection between morality and social station could not be more clearly displayed than when Tacitus condescendingly describes the loathsome Sejanus as a "small-town adulterer."

At the beginning of each of his historical works, Tacitus suggests that traditional Roman virtues have become dangerous. Emperors felt threatened by examples of old-fashioned virtue and preferred to surround themselves with fawning creatures as despots have through the ages. It was not only the emperors who were distrustful of the virtuous; the army, the mob, and even many senators dreaded the accession of an incorruptible emperor. The integrity and austerity of Galba quickly led to his downfall, when the army demanded its bonus. Ancient virtue was much praised, Tacitus would say, but few were eager to see its return.

Tacitus, however, understands full well that even the virtuous might be corrupted by the concentration of power, since he believes the love of power is a universal drive. Lord Acton was hardly the first to realize that absolute power corrupted absolutely. Tacitus has a senator say that Tiberius was "transformed and perverted by absolute power despite his experience in public affairs" (*Annals* 6, 48). He highlights the decline of virtue among the Romans by contrasting it with the natural morality of Britons, Gauls, and Germans, both in their chastity and especially in their fierce love of liberty as they fought and rebelled against Roman domination.

Other Roman writers described political decline and moral decay, but Tacitus' dark meditation raises political and moral failure to an existential level of despair. There is a pervasive physical darkness in the *Histories* and the *Annals* that matches Tacitus' vision of an age bereft of morality. Of course this melancholic vision is closely related to Tacitus' own biography in which moral, political, and psychological motives intertwine. Could Tacitus have remained so genuinely bitter through two decades of Trajan's benevolent rule, or do we see instead a lawyer and orator presenting his greatest case with posterity as the jury? Was his pessimism heartfelt, or was it a rhetorical *tour-de-force* to prevent the Romans from returning to the autocracy of a Nero or a Domitian? Whatever his motives, of all ancient writers, perhaps only St Augustine goes further than Tacitus in his concentration on evil. The pagan historian provided a model for the Christian philosopher.

Political analysis

Tacitus was a politician long before he became an historian; his political passions drove him to history. During the preceding two centuries Republican government had first collapsed and then been replaced by the emperors and their courtiers. Once-powerful senators were reduced to docile administrators or court sycophants. There is no doubt that Tacitus loathed the Julio-Claudian and Flavian emperors; in the words of the great English poet John Milton, he was "the greatest Enemy to Tyrants" (*Defense of the People of England*). But what did Tacitus want to replace them with? Was Tacitus only opposed to tyrannical emperors, or to the principate itself?

There is no easy answer, and through the centuries Tacitus has been variously interpreted as a Machiavellian who taught rulers how to maintain power and courtiers how to flatter well, or as a revolutionary who incited resistance to those same rulers. He was popular both with some Italian princes and with French and American republicans; he was quoted in support of absolute monarchy, and by the English regicides. How can his text be open to such a range of interpretation?

There are several reasons. As Tacitus researched and wrote his histories, his attitude toward tyranny inevitably evolved. In addition, since he tempered his deep hostility to the emperors with realism and resignation, his pithy aphorisms lend themselves to quotation out of context for contradictory purposes. Most importantly, however, was Tacitus' own ambivalence toward imperial power. He might be called a "sentimental republican" in his heart, but his mind accepted the principate as a realistic necessity to maintain peace and stability over the Empire. Yet he detested individual emperors and, while proud of the Senate's historical role, he also despised the groveling senators of his own time almost as much as he scorned anything resembling democracy.

Hence Tacitus provided no coherent theory of an ideal state; he was rather an astute critic of the realities of political life. He recognized, for example, that power in the Roman Empire rested upon secrecy and deception. In our own age of "disinformation" and "official secrets," this may hardly seem extraordinary but it was a departure from senatorial government in which state business was public knowledge. Emperors and courtiers traded in secrets, but Tacitus recognized the unspoken "secret" on which the entire imperial system was built. With the Civil War of 68–70 CE, it became obvious that emperors derived power not from law or tradition, not from votes by the Senate or the people, but through naked military force. The shrewder emperors disguised this fact, not least from the armies themselves and their ambitious generals, but even in the reign of Augustus the army had stood quietly behind the throne. Later all could see that it not only protected emperors but created and destroyed them as well.

The antidote to a culture of official secrecy is freedom of speech. At the beginning of his reign, Tiberius tolerated criticism and even scurrilous lampoons. Tacitus does not report it, but Suetonius recounts that the emperor would often say, "There should be free speech and free thought in a free country"(Suetonius, *Tib.* 28). Tacitus begins his earliest work with an account of philosophers' books burned in the Forum to "destroy the voice of the Roman people, the freedom of the Senate, and the accumulated knowledge of the human race" (*Agr.* 2). But the most famous case of freedom of speech in Tacitus concerns an historian, Cremutius Cordus, who was prosecuted for having praised Brutus and Cassius in his history. He had determined to commit suicide, so he put up a strong defense and pointed out the willingness of both Julius Caesar and Augustus to tolerate dissent. After he committed suicide by self-starvation, the Senate decreed that his books be burned. Tacitus concludes the episode with words of universal resonance:

> And so one is all the more inclined to laugh at the stupidity of men who suppose that the despotism of the present can actually efface the remembrances of the next generation. On the contrary, the persecution of genius fosters its influence; foreign tyrants, and all who have

imitated their oppression, have merely procured infamy for
themselves and glory for their victims.

(Annales 4, 35)

It is precisely that disrepute and the victims' renown which Tacitus
achieves so brilliantly in his history.

It is clear that Tacitus was no revolutionary. He preached the
virtues of political moderation and greatly admires the quiet sub-
mission of his revered father-in-law Agricola. He also presents other
senators who manage that most difficult task, survival with integrity:

> This Lepidus, I am convinced, was for that age a wise and
> high-principled man. Many a cruel suggestion made by the
> flattery of others he changed for the better, and yet he did
> not want tact, seeing that he always enjoyed a uniform
> prestige, and also the favor of Tiberius.
>
> *(Annales* 4, 20)

From his positive allusions to Trajan, it is clear that Tacitus was
prepared to accept as the best possible form of government rule by a
benevolent emperor. Yet he felt anger and contempt for the century
of imperial rule in which tyrants had empowered freedmen above
their senatorial betters. His other favorite target was the corruption
of language. The historian relished the exposure of official lies and
the misuse of language as when Augustus retained the republican
titles for his magistrates, even though they had none of their former
authority. Galba called his stinginess "economy," and his cruelty
"severity." For those who have read George Orwell or observed a
modern political campaign, all this is hardly surprising. Still,
Tacitus was an innovator in exposing the debasement of language in
the service of politics. He gave his most famous example to the
British chieftain Calgacus who, stirring his forces to fight for their
freedom, says of the Romans:

> Neither East nor West has satisfied them...To robbery, to
> slaughter, and to theft they give the false name of "Empire";
> where they create desolation, they call it "Peace."
>
> *(Agricola* 30)

Tacitus remained an imperialist, and believed that foreign wars and
conquests were to the moral advantage of the Roman people. He
respected resistance rather than docile compliance – hence his

sympathy for the Britons and Germans, and his contempt for the Greeks – but he had no illusions about the "benefits" of Roman rule. He offered ringing calls to fight for freedom, which seems to contradict his own admiration for the "moderate" course of Romans like Agricola. But this contradiction stems in part from a fatalism about the possibility of change. The Romans were fortunate to be ruled by Trajan, but what would insure that another Nero would not appear? For all his political perceptiveness, Tacitus could not suggest a viable alternative to the present political system.

The historian as psychologist

A good part of Tacitus' effectiveness as a political historian is due to his skill as a psychologist for, in an authoritarian political system where policy depends on the personality of the ruler and his entourage, political analysis and psychology must go hand in hand. In the words of Thomas Macaulay, "In the delineation of character, Tacitus is unrivaled among historians, and has few superiors among dramatists and novelists." Modern historians, trying for objectivity, prefer to describe the personality of a historical figure without moral judgment. For Tacitus, a character sketch would include both the intellectual and moral qualities of his subject. Though most Romans believed the human personality is fixed at birth and is essentially static, Tacitus was less deterministic and accepted the possibility of change. He believed power further corrupted Tiberius – though he felt he was evil from the start – while it improved Vespasian. We must always be aware, however, that Tacitus used psychology as a tool in his rhetorical arsenal. He was not a modern social scientist who prizes consistency; Tacitus was by training an advocate and a politician, preferring persuasiveness to consistency.

While Cato, Sallust, and Livy all rejected Greek detachment and wrote morally and politically committed history, Tacitus took this subjectivity still further into an internal, psychological drama. Like Rome's greatest poet, Virgil, and philosopher, Augustine, its greatest historian partakes of the characteristic introspection that is the central original feature of Latin literature. While Virgil was pre-eminent in examining human emotions, Tacitus linked public action to private thoughts, feelings, and moods. At first sight, Tacitus' characters might seem to fall into the familiar ancient stereotypes learned in the rhetorical schools: tyrant, collaborator, noble barbarian, philosophical martyr, etc. These "characters" have been described by essayists, and similar character-types (boastful general, cunning slave) have been used by comedians from Menander and Plautus to Charlie Chaplin. Tacitus certainly uses the philosophical and rhetorical tradition, but his imagination allows him to transform these stereotypes; for example, Tiberius and Nero are quite different as tyrants. Messalina and Agrippina are both treacherous imperial wives, but they have little in common psychologically, since there is an enormous difference between the flighty, spoiled, and lascivious Messalina and the cold, cunning Agrippina. Tacitus does not merely use character-types; he builds on them, just as he transformed the earlier literary character of Sallust's Catiline into his corrupt and bloodthirsty Sejanus.

Tacitus was not interested in physical appearance or lurid anecdotes; moral physiognomy is more important than baldness, acne, or sexual aberrations. He does not care about warts or body odor (as the biographer Suetonius sometimes does), but prefers to assess the psychological and moral qualities of a character. His greatest portrait is that of Tiberius. It seems likely that his personal animosity toward Domitian, who admired Tiberius, drove Tacitus to seek the roots of Domitian's treason trials in the reign of his predecessor. The emperor both intrigued and repelled the historian. Tacitus provides evidence that Tiberius, after an exemplary early military career, became tormented by the fact that his mother Livia and stepfather Augustus used him for their own political aims. He was forced to divorce a beloved wife to marry the emperor's promiscuous daughter Julia, whose scandalous behavior must have made him the laughing-stock of Roman society and finally drove him to seek voluntary exile in Rhodes. Though Tacitus regards Tiberius' moodiness as an innate flaw, he also makes clear that the man had been cruelly mistreated. His accession to the imperial throne at the age of fifty-five could hardly erase decades of humiliation. This desperately lonely man placed in Sejanus an understandable, if unwarranted, confidence. When he was betrayed by Sejanus, his bitterness overwhelmed him. A modern psychologist would regard him as a human tragedy – a creation of his family and his circumstances. Though Tacitus provides all this information, his obituary of Tiberius is unforgiving:

> And so died Tiberius, in the seventy-eighth year of his age. Nero was his father, and he was on both sides descended from the Claudian house, though his mother passed by adoption, first into the Livian, then into the Julian family. From earliest infancy, perilous vicissitudes were his lot. Himself an exile, he was the companion of a proscribed father,

and on being admitted as a stepson into the house of Augustus, he had to struggle with many rivals, so long as Marcellus and Agrippa and, subsequently, Gaius and Lucius Caesar were in their glory. Again his brother Drusus enjoyed in a greater degree the affection of the citizens. But he was more than ever on dangerous ground after his marriage with Julia, whether he tolerated or escaped from his wife's profligacy. On his return from Rhodes he ruled the emperor's now heirless house for twelve years, and the Roman world, with absolute sway, for about twenty-three. His character too had its distinct periods. It was a bright time in his life and reputation, while under Augustus he was a private citizen or held high offices; a time of reserve and crafty assumption of virtue, as long as Germanicus and Drusus were alive. Again, while his mother lived, he was a compound of good and evil; he was infamous for his cruelty, though he veiled his debaucheries, while he loved or feared Sejanus. Finally, he plunged into every wickedness and disgrace, when fear and shame being cast off, he simply indulged his own inclinations.

(Annales 6, 51)

The *a priori* nature of the judgment is clear; Tiberius' many accomplishments and reasonable decisions are attributed to hypocrisy and a complex character is reduced to a few sentences. Tacitus' narrative provides a far more convincing picture of Tiberius than his capsule summary. It illustrates the danger of taking brief Tacitean judgments out of their narrative context.

Tacitus' Nero is a far simpler character than Tiberius, and more comprehensible to the modern reader. Nero's aesthetic pretensions may have baffled contemporary senators, but there is little psychological complexity in the presentation of his personality. Tacitus traces the development of this budding monster from his gilded youth to a cruelty that far exceeded that of Tiberius. His murder of his mother Agrippina seems understandable, even inevitable, in the context of Nero's petulant, willful hedonism. Whatever his flaws, Tiberius was struggling to ensure his own power and that of his successors; Nero merely sought pleasure and applause. He is a shallower tyrant, unworthy of innuendo or complex analysis; he is merely the object of satire and contempt.

Tacitus was less interested in the virtuous than the vicious. His Germanicus and elder Agrippina are clearly to be admired, but neither is an example of Republican virtues. Germanicus is an affable contrast to Tiberius, but he is too emotional for a Roman leader and has suspicious eastern interests. Agrippina is too headstrong and arrogant for a Roman matron; she may indeed have a great deal of courage but her confrontations with the emperor destroyed most of her family. Elsewhere Tacitus says, "Weeping is for women; men must remember" (*Ger. 27*). Germanicus and Agrippina are flawed heroes. Only in Agricola do we find a truly exceptional Roman depicted with affection and attention. This pragmatic patriot embodies the values Tacitus would like others to see in himself.

The psychological historian has much material to occupy him in the imperial court. The emperors and courtiers alike practiced dissimulation; senators nurtured resentment deep within them; and fear was universal in a way that foreshadows the methods of the modern police state:

> Never was Rome more distracted and terror-stricken. Meetings, conversations, the ear of friend and stranger were alike shunned; even things mute and lifeless, the very roofs and walls, were eyed with suspicion.
>
> (*Annales* 4, 69)

Tacitus was adept at group psychology, especially the irresponsibility of a mob: "As happens in a panic, all give orders; no one obeys" (*Hist.* 3, 73). When a crowd switches from misery to joy, he says "the crowd is unrestrained in either emotion" (*Hist.* 2, 29). Despite his idealization of the Senate and Roman People of the Republic, Tacitus has no sympathy for the people acting collectively under the emperors. The possibility of disorder terrified him.

Tacitus was a strong-willed moral and political judge of character, but he did not have the twentieth century's vocabulary for psychological analysis. Since he could not easily explain ambiguities, they are expressed as contradictions. Hence Tacitus' love of freedom for senators, and contempt for the people; his admiration and scorn for self-appointed martyrs. His psychological understanding was on an emotional rather than an analytical level, but in the days before professional psychology he was an important source for Francis Bacon and Michel de Montaigne, when they began four centuries ago to develop the language of introspection.

The historian as literary artist

In the reign of Nero, when Tacitus was beginning his education, the Romans regarded rhetorical training as the basis of all literary and intellectual activity. Neronian poetry, philosophy, drama, and even Petronius' sprawling comic novel, the *Satyricon*, all display the rhetorician's hand. Quintilian, who during Tacitus' youth became the first official professor of rhetoric at Rome, regarded history as a subdivision of oratory "nearest to the poets and may be regarded as a prose poem" (*Inst. Or.* 10, 1, 31). In this environment Tacitus grew to maturity as a self-described devotee who followed orators around the city.

Though Tacitus chose to forswear his oratorical career at the age of forty, he could hardly expunge the very basis of his intellectual formation. His rhetorical training informs every page of his histories, but it is most obvious in his reliance on speeches to shape the historical narrative. Even Rome's enemies are granted an opportunity to speak, and to speak more effectively than they ever actually did on the battlefields of Britain or Germany. Many speeches in the *Histories* have the leisurely amplitude and the ringing patriotism of Livy. Others mark out important political positions in the time of turmoil. For example, Galba spoke (*Hist.* 1, 16) in favor of an adoptive monarchy, a policy that failed for Galba but produced a peaceful transition from Nerva to Trajan in Tacitus' own time. Cerialis' speech to the Gauls (*Hist.* 4, 72) is perhaps the most effective surviving defense of Roman imperialism. The speeches in the *Annals* mirror Tacitus' own developing voice: trenchant, analytical, and self-confident. Yet, as we have seen in the case of Claudius, he does not misrepresent the attitudes of the speakers.

The structure of Tacitus' historical narrative is informed by a wide range of literary devices like digressions, strands of narrative, and parallels. Digressions range from an exotic anecdote on the Egyptian phoenix to various historiographical issues. Their purpose is usually evident as are the strands of narrative – trials, corruption, mutinies – that link together the text. Parallels are perhaps more interesting. Some parallels are quite explicit: dynastic intrigue in Rome and Parthia; Germanicus compared to Alexander the Great; a death by treachery for both Germanicus and Arminius. There is an obvious parallel between Nero and Tiberius (sometimes even called by his cognomen "Nero"). Both were dominated by imperious mothers and manipulated by murderous praetorian prefects. In Tacitus' day all acknowledged the viciousness of Nero and the murderous immorality of Agrippina, but Tiberius and Livia were another matter. Through overt and subtle parallels between the couples, Tacitus casts a deadly pall over Tiberius from the very day of his succession.

Like Charles Dickens, Tacitus created characters who demand to be transported to the theater. Ben Jonson and Racine put them in plays, Claudio Monteverdi put Nero and Poppaea on the operatic stage, and in our own time the BBC mini-series of Robert Graves' novel, *I, Claudius*, brought them to television. Though no dramas survive from Tacitus' own maturity, he lived in a theatrical age and brought drama into his history. Individual books of the *Annals* often begin or end like the acts of a play. Book 2 closed with the death of Germanicus, Book 6 with the death of Tiberius, Book 11 with the execution of Messalina and Book 14 with the death of Nero's wife Octavia (after having opened with the murder of his mother). The deaths of the philosophers Seneca and Thrasea are highly theatrical, and Nero introduced two-edged drama when he paraded himself in costume and sang arias from Greek tragedy. Tacitus understood better than any other ancient writer the theatrical fantasies of political life. It is understandable that his picture of Tiberius, through the mediation of Thomas More and Holinshead, helped flesh out other theatrical villains, Shakespeare's Richard III and Pushkin's Boris Gudonov.

In addition to the larger dramas of Tiberius, Germanicus, and Nero, Tacitus was a master of the vignette that captures in a few pages or a few lines that essence of drama, the sudden reversal of fortune. Hence the senator Haterius, falling to his knees to beg pardon for an offensive comment, accidentally trips the emperor and is almost killed by the nervous bodyguards. The historian includes devices familiar from Greek tragedy, like the dramatic use of silence, omens, and portents, though the Olympian gods have no place in such a skeptical writer.

Tacitus' gift for drama was matched by his interest in investing his narrative with vivid tableaux. Scenes reminiscent of the historical paintings of the Renaissance led Racine to call Tacitus "the greatest painter of antiquity," and Napoleon continued the metaphor when he complained that Tacitus "painted" everything black. He was less interested in actual physical appearances, though he added colorful details at crucial moments to enliven the picture: the weeping emperor Vitellius lifting his small son to the crowd, a banquet given on a lavishly decorated raft floating in a lake, or Nero's hypocritical embrace of his old tutor Seneca as he prepares to drive him to suicide.

The most extraordinary of the Tacitean tableaux is his account of the mutinies in Book 1 of the *Annals*. For almost twenty pages Tacitus provides a cinematic drama in which individual scenes and characters are brilliantly interwoven. Amid the grand movements and emotions of the crowds of angry soldiers, Tacitus, like the director of a great historical film – Griffith or Eisenstein or Lean – shifts his focus from the panorama of the faceless mob to glimpses of individuals: an eloquent mutineer rouses the troops; aged veterans strip to show their scars and shove Germanicus' fingers onto their toothless gums; greedy centurions are humiliated by the troops; and Germanicus melodramatically threatens to commit suicide until a cynical soldier offers his "sharper sword."

Tacitus rejected the smooth and flowing prose of Livy and looked rather to Sallust for an intense and acerbic style suitable to his subject and his temperament. Rhetoric can embellish and conceal; Tacitus produced a rhetoric of exposure as his fierce syntax combines with a richness of diction to produce the most politically charged Latin ever written. The reader is disoriented by shifts of syntax, as Tacitus seeks to vary trite expressions and pursues a surprising turn of phrase. That asymmetrical style also reflects the changes of mood: here a narration at breakneck speed and there an extended portrayal of a static scene. When he wishes to strive for grandeur, he resorts to a more poetic diction. Thus the historian has created in his intense and probing style an extraordinary instrument of description and analysis. His delight in his verbal skill is that of a poet; one leader is called "more devious, not better" (*Hist.* 2, 38) while another "played the slave to become the master" (*Hist.* 1, 36). Historian or poet, Tacitus' ideas are inextricably intertwined with his style. There is compression of thought as well as words when he says of the unfortunate Galba, *capax imperii nisi imperasset* ("thought to be capable of ruling, if he had never ruled") (*Hist.* 1, 49). But no translation can do justice to the irony of Tacitus' Latin, which Paul Plass compares to Freud's famous quip, "He has a great future behind him." So too did Galba, and Tacitus knew how best to express with startling brevity that complex thought.

Voltaire, who did not like Tacitus, called him "a fanatic with flashes of wit." But it is no small thing to be regarded by Voltaire as being witty, even if only occasionally. Of Caligula's fawning on the aging Tiberius, he quotes the epigram of Passienus, "There had never been a better slave or a worse master" (*Ann.* 6, 20). Some of those *bons mots* were the product of senatorial wits, but many must have been the author's creation. When Otho and Vitellius accuse each other of debauchery, Tacitus dryly observes, "neither was lying" (*Hist.* 1, 74). Tacitus wrote in an age of epigrams and he provided them in abundance. Several have been adapted and survive in English. His saying that the British chiefs "fight separately and are conquered together" (*Agr.* 12) lies behind Benjamin Franklin's call to the colonial leaders "to hang together or be hanged separately." In his description of the funeral in 22 CE of the aged Junia, sister of Brutus and wife of Cassius, who had together assassinated Julius Caesar sixty-five years earlier, Tacitus points out that among the effigies of ancestors carried in the funeral procession, "Brutus and Cassius were the most conspicuous, precisely because their portraits were not on view" (*Ann.* 3, 76). A nineteenth-century English politician converted this to "conspicuous by their absence" and it has remained an evocative phrase ever since.

A century ago the Latin scholar Friedrich Leo pronounced Tacitus "one of the few great poets of the Roman people." The echoes of Virgil and Lucan are evident, especially in the *Histories*, when the burning of Rome during the Civil War conjures up the burning of Troy in Virgil's *Aeneid*. Tacitus is the tragic poet of lost liberty, and the *Annals* is the finest literary achievement of post-Augustan Rome. One could question whether so much literary artistry can be good history. But thus we return to the nature and purpose of history for the Romans. The ideal of history is the revivification of the past, and in that Tacitus is an unquestioned success. He used his literary powers and personal experience to create the most vivid historical tableau that has come down to us from antiquity. It is both poetry and history, for his imagination has recreated historical truth.

Conclusion

European and American thinkers from the Renaissance through the American and French Revolutions accorded Tacitus a central role in shaping the Western intellectual tradition. In sixteenth-century Italy, he was studied to learn how to prosper at court under the rule of tyrants, and his sayings were collected into handbooks for courtiers. On a political level, he was viewed as an enemy of tyrants, and appealed to Montaigne and John Milton, John Adams and Thomas Jefferson as much as he displeased James I of England, Philip II of Spain, and Napoleon. But his views were more complex. His bitter and ironic appraisal of man's political and moral fate in the greatest age of the Roman Empire marked him as an historian of the dark side of human nature. He understood the inevitability of human suffering and the unlikelihood that virtue would prevail. But victory for Tacitus is not the only outcome of a battle; even the defeated may retain their honor and achieve eternal glory. He elevated mere pessimism to an intellectual grandeur that led Gibbon to call him "the most philosophical of historians."

Tacitus claims to write for moral and political reasons, and so he does. But in a man so driven we might wish to look below the conscious to his own guilt as a survivor of Domitian's persecutions. Feelings of guilt might be present in his passionate, but ambivalent, reactions to those who stood up to tyranny. What are we to make of the passage in which the historian says: "Soon our hands dragged Helvidius to prison; the reproachful looks of Mauricus and Rusticus shame us and we were stained with Senecio's innocent blood" (Agr. 45). He makes it clear that a part of Domitian's torture is for the senators, including Tacitus, to see themselves as cowards. That shame and guilt drove him to write history and inspired his historical imagination.

Tacitus, through his mind and his heart, translates his experience into the most powerful evocation of tyranny – tyranny as both a political condition and a psychological state. Thus he provides influential analyses of issues that remain centrally important in our own time: political paranoia, freedom of speech, and the corruption of power. It is true that he does not give a balanced appraisal of emperors who brought peace to Rome after decades of civil war. He lacks the long view of history, that in the long run peace and prosperity may be seen as worth a few dozen executions. He gives powerful expression to the short view, the howl of the victim for recognition, for remembrance, and for vengeance. He saw the need for memory, the role of the historian to commemorate suffering. It is important that, in our quest for a carefully balanced interpretation, we ignore the emotional power and political insight expressed by a writer and thinker like Tacitus.

5

AMMIANUS
MARCELLINUS

At the end of the fourth century CE, the last great pagan writer of the ancient world provided what in retrospect is a grand farewell to the values of the Greco-Roman tradition. A pagan living in an increasingly intolerant Christian Empire, Ammianus Marcellinus (c. 330–95 CE) chose to take up the weighty mantle of Tacitus and write the bitter-sweet history of Rome in the second, third, and fourth centuries of the Christian era. As a native of Syria, he had a provincial's admiration and idealization of Roman institutions and the civilizing mission of the Roman Empire. He had a corresponding contempt for those Romans who demeaned their own ancestral greatness. This remarkable man was courageous, original, intelligent, learned, and fair – an ideal combination of virtues for the last great historian of Rome and one who has been too often overlooked. Ammianus created a masterpiece, in its way as extraordinary an historiographical achievement as the work of Livy and Tacitus. It is the only surviving large-scale contemporary history in Latin. The extant part of his work serves as a beacon through the political, diplomatic, and administrative complexities of his own time. Edward Gibbon, though he was sometimes exasperated with Ammianus' post-classical style, recognized the immeasurable value of the man and his work. When he reaches 378 CE, the eighteenth-century English historian of Rome's decline and fall pays admiring tribute to what has been his indispensable source:

> It is not without the most sincere regret that I must now take leave of an accurate and faithful guide, who has composed the history of his own times without indulging the prejudices and passions which usually affect the mind of a contemporary. Ammianus Marcellinus, who terminates his useful work with the defeat and death of Valens, recom-

mends the more glorious subject of the ensuing reign to the youthful vigor and eloquence of the rising generation. The rising generation was not disposed to accept his advice or imitate his example.

(Gibbon, *Decline and Fall of the Roman Empire*
III, 122 (ed. Bury))

Life and works

Ammianus was probably born about 330 CE, to a prosperous Greek-speaking family in the great cosmopolitan capital of Antioch in Syria. His education encompassed both Greek and Latin literary and rhetorical studies – this last is not surprising when we recall that Libanius, the greatest Greek professor in Antioch at that time, complained about the success of Latin rhetoricians with students ambitious for a government or military career. Soon after 350 CE Ammianus joined an elite regiment of guards (*protectores domestici*) and was assigned to serve under Ursicinus, the master of the cavalry, to whom Ammianus remained devotedly loyal.

After 353 CE we can follow Ammianus' military career through the pages of his history, since he appears more in his own writings than any other Roman historical writer except Julius Caesar. He served with Ursicinus in northern Italy, Gaul, Germany, and Illyria. It was in Gaul in 355 CE that Ammianus first served under Julian, posthumously called "The Apostate," who was at that time Caesar, or junior emperor, and who would later play such an important role in Ammianus' history. With his patron Ursicinus he was transferred to the eastern front threatened by the Persians. In 359 CE Ammianus fought against the Persian siege of Amida. As the city was falling, after a siege of seventy days, Ammianus escaped by a postern gate and describes his desperate flight before the enemy to the safety of Antioch.

Ursicinus was blamed for the capture of Amida and was dismissed from office; we know nothing about Ammianus' activities until he reappears in 363 CE serving in the army of Julian who had by then become sole emperor. He accompanied him on the ill-fated expedition deep into Persian territory and witnessed the emperor's death in battle. For the next fifteen years Ammianus lived in Antioch and occupied himself in reading and historical research, but he tells little of himself after he drops out of his history with the death of Julian. His report of the treason trials in Antioch in 371 CE shows his own fears, and perhaps he is telling us of the destruction of his own books:

Young and old were indiscriminately deprived of their property without any opportunity of defense, although they were quite guiltless, and after suffering wholesale torture were taken off in litters to execution. The result was that throughout the eastern provinces whole libraries were burnt by their owners for fear of a similar fate; such was the terror which seized all hearts. In a word, we all crept around at that time in a Cimmerian darkness.

(29, 2)[1]

The echo of Homer in "Cimmerian darkness" is precisely the sort of literary allusion with which Ammianus fills his history. He traveled throughout the eastern Mediterranean where his visits to Egypt, Greece, and the Black Sea region, in addition to his earlier campaigns in Europe and Mesopotamia, made him the best-traveled historian of antiquity, even including Herodotus. Ammianus returned to Rome sometime after 380 CE and continued his historical research among the eyewitnesses of the reigns of Constantius and Julian. In that period he became more familiar with the senatorial elite and began to give public readings in the capital. He published his histories early in the 390s and probably died about 395 CE or soon after. His proud, and touching, conclusion to his book was probably written not long before his death:

This is the history of events from the reign of the emperor Nerva to the death of Valens, which I, a former soldier and a Greek, have composed to the best of my ability. It claims to be the truth, which I have never ventured to pervert either by silence or a lie. The rest I leave to be written by better men whose abilities are in their prime. But if they choose to undertake the task I advise them to cast what they have to say in the grand style.

(31, 16)

For the 250 years since Tacitus, serious historical writing had virtually disappeared in Latin. It was held in such low esteem that the emperor Tacitus (275–6), who claimed descent from the historian, ordered that ten copies of his ancestor's books be made annually "lest they perish from the neglect of readers." While Appian, Arrian, Dio, Herodian, Dexippus, and many others wrote in Greek, Latin historical writing was reduced to biographies and the ever-popular brief histories or summaries of earlier writers like Livy.

Ammianus' ambitious goal was to begin his history with the reign of Nerva in 96 CE, where Tacitus' *Histories* ended, and proceed until his own day. His initial plan was to conclude with the death of Jovian in 364 CE, since that was when Ammianus left the army and began to do his research. It would not do to write about living emperors, especially such cruel men as Valentinian (364–75 CE) and Valens (364–78 CE). His plan was completed in twenty-five books, though the first thirteen (96–353 CE) are now lost, and had already been lost by the sixth century. The author's original preface has been lost, but he wrote a second preface to Book 15 as he began the history of his own time in 355 CE:

> Using my best efforts to find out the truth, I have set out, in the order in which they occurred, events which I was able to observe myself or discover by thorough questioning of contemporaries who took part in them. The rest, which will occupy the pages that follow, I shall execute to the best of my ability in a more polished style, and I shall pay no heed to the criticism which some make of a work which they think too long. Brevity is only desirable when it cuts short tedious irrelevance without subtracting from our knowledge of the past.
>
> (15, 1)

The historian's announcement that he is writing no brief history is very appropriate. To this point Ammianus had covered 258 years in fourteen books; the next eleven books, largely dealing with his hero Julian, will cover a meager ten years. With the popular reception of these twenty-five books in 391 CE, Ammianus decided that it was now safe enough to take his story down to the death of Valens and the terrible defeat at Adrianople in 378 CE, and so he begins Book 26 with a third preface:

> Having spared no pains in relating the course of events up to the beginning of the present epoch I had thought it best to steer clear of more familiar matters, partly to escape the dangers that can always attend on truth, and partly to avoid carping criticism of my work by those who feel injured by the omission of significant detail, such things, for example, as the emperor's table-talk or the reason for the public punishment of soldiers. Such folk also complain if in a wide-ranging geographical description some small strongholds are

not mentioned, or if one does not give the names of all who attended the inauguration of the urban prefect, or passes over a number of similar details which are beneath the dignity of history. The task of history is to deal with prominent events, not to delve into trivial minutiae...

(26, 1)

Here Ammianus responds to the sort of exasperating queries he must have been asked at his public readings (though we know from Libanius how popular these were), but he is also preparing his reader for a less full account of the fourteen years contained in the final six books. During those years the historian was doing research; he was neither at the court nor on campaign, and so had little first-hand information to contribute. In addition, he was less emotionally engaged in that depressing era than he had been in the exciting campaigns and reign of Julian. Hence, of his thirty-one books, we have Books 14 to 31 covering the years 353 to 378 CE. Thanks to Ammianus, those twenty-five years are the best attested since the first century CE.

Books 1–13 (96–353)   These are lost.

Book 14   The life and death of the Caesar Gallus. Ammianus provides a lengthy critique of the Roman senators and Roman people. (353–4 CE).

Book 15   Rebellion of Silvanus and appointment of Julian as Caesar. (355 CE).

Books 16–18   Julian campaigns in Gaul and Germany, with great victory over the Germans at Strasbourg. The emperor Constantius campaigns on the Danube. After failed negotiations, King Sapor of Persia invades Mesopotamia. (356–8 CE).

Book 19   Siege of Amida and treason trials in Rome. (359 CE).

Book 20   Julian acclaimed Augustus; Constantius campaigns in the East. (360 CE).

Books 21–22   Death of Constantius; preparation for war with Persia. (361–2 CE).

Books 23–24   Advance of Julian through Mesopotamia. (363 CE).

Book 25   Death of Julian and evaluation. Brief reign of Jovian. (363–4 CE).

Books 26–27   Valentinian and Valens as emperors. (365–9 CE).

Books 28–29   Treason trials at Rome and in the East. The corruption of Roman society. Invasion of Pannonia. (370–3 CE).

Book 30   Armenian and Persian affairs. Death of Valentinian. (373–5 CE).

Book 31   Invasion of Goths. Death of Valens at Adrianople. (376–8 CE).

Ammianus' historical method

Ammianus looked back to Cornelius Tacitus as the only great historian of the Roman Empire. Even though Ammianus does not refer directly to Tacitus in the extant books, the shadow of his predecessor falls over much of the work: the proclamation of dispassionate objectivity; the alternation between foreign affairs and political intrigues at Rome; the moralizing evaluation of emperors; and above all the deep seriousness about the task of the historian. Both men feel that it is their patriotic duty to leave for future generations the history of Rome and, especially, of their own times. These are not historians who write for fame, or money, or political advancement, but as a genuine vocation. Though Ammianus excels his master on military and diplomatic matters and his character sketches are more balanced, Tacitus' political insight and literary ability continue to make him the greatest of all Roman historians.

Much of the material contained in Ammianus' history recalls his predecessors, but the world of late antiquity has introduced new characters and new themes: Christian bishops and palace eunuchs, Germans serving in the Roman army, and religious bigotry. Perhaps the most unfamiliar aspect is the shift in balance from the capital to the frontiers and even beyond the frontiers. The emperors themselves spend little time in Rome; they move from Trier to Milan, from Sirmium to Constantinople, and much of the court accompanies them. That frees the historian from the traditional focus on Rome. In addition, as an easterner himself, Ammianus becomes the first Roman historian to approach a universal history. Though many peoples beyond the frontiers are described only in the extensive digressions, within the Empire the historian treats Asians, Europeans, and Africans with generosity and respect, and thus stretches the emotional reach of Roman historical writing.

We have a very distorted picture of Ammianus' sources, since only his writings dealing with his own lifetime have survived. He did use the lost imperial history called the "Kaisergeschichte" consulted by other late writers including St Jerome, as well as several Greek writers on Julian's Persian expedition: Eunapius, Oribasius, and Magnus. But his most important sources for this period were his personal knowledge and the eyewitnesses whom he interviewed. The lively portraits of his commanders Ursicinus and Julian and the engaging narratives of battles in which Ammianus took part demonstrate the importance of personal experience. We sometimes forget that most ancient historians wrote contemporary history and relied heavily on oral tradition, personal testimony, and autopsy. Though Ammianus did consult some public records, he also complains when he cannot read a document or letter preserved in the imperial archives. For his last six books (364–78 CE), no histories had been published and he himself was not present at court or in the army. Hence he had to create the historical narrative solely on the basis of personal testimony.

Who were his sources? Four men, who had each held the prefectureship of Rome and lived in the city after 380 CE, are highly praised by Ammianus: Eupraxis of Mauretania (prefect, 374 CE); Hypatius of Antioch (prefect, 379 CE), related by marriage to Constantius II; Praetextatus (prefect, 368 CE); and the African Aurelius Victor (prefect, 389 CE), who was himself an historian and served with Ammianus under Julian in Persia. These men, outsiders to Rome and/or committed pagans, are the most likely sources for the reigns of Constantius II and Valentinian, since Ammianus characterizes each of them as reliable, honest, fearless, etc. A more surprising source may be the Armenian eunuch Eutherius, once chamberlain to Constantius II and Julian, whose loyalty and moderation are highly praised:

> Hence it came about that when he afterward retired to Rome, where he fixed his residence in old age, he carried a clear conscience about with him and was cherished and loved by peoples of all classes, whereas in general men of his kind look out for a secret retreat in which to enjoy their

ill-gotten wealth, and hide like creatures who hate the light from the eyes of the multitude of those whom they have wronged. Turning over the records of the past, I have not found any eunuch with whom I could compare him.

(16, 7)

Ammianus is not exaggerating; Eutherius is a rare eunuch who has escaped the torrent of abuse levied by ancient writers on virtually every other eunuch in Roman times.

In adopting Tacitus as his model, Ammianus was rejecting the long tradition of Suetonian biography. He expresses scorn for senators who read only Marius Maximus, the continuator of Suetonius, implying that such a writer was only read for entertainment. And yet, even if Ammianus is a true historian rather than a biographer, he has learned literary techniques from Suetonian biography, such as the physical descriptions of emperors he includes in their obituaries. Those lengthy obituaries, which sum up their virtues and vices, are among the most effective in all antiquity. However unpleasant the emperor, Ammianus seems to be able to form a balanced and detailed opinion. The final obituary is that of Valens; here is a sample of the good qualities and character flaws:

> He was a faithful and reliable friend, and repressed ambitious intrigues with severity. He maintained strict discipline in the army and civil service, and took particular care that no one should gain preferment on the score of kinship with himself. He was extremely slow both to appoint and to remove officials. In his dealings with the provinces he showed great fairness, protecting each of them from injury as he would his own house. He was especially concerned to lighten the burden of tribute, and allowed no increases in taxation...
>
> He was insatiable in the pursuit of wealth and unwilling to endure fatigue, though he affected enormous toughness. He had a cruel streak, and was something of a boor, with little skill in the arts of either war or peace. He was quite willing to gain advantages for himself from the sufferings of others, and his behavior was particularly intolerable when he construed ordinary offenses as *lèse-majesté*. Then his rage could only be satisfied by blood.

(31, 14)

The long evaluation of Julian was so detailed that Ammianus categorized his positive character traits according to the traditional philosophical virtues of self-control, wisdom, justice, and courage, each of which is given an extended treatment.

While Ammianus both professes, and seems to have achieved, fair-mindedness in his evaluations, it does seem that his own loyalties enter into his judgments. His first patron was Ursicinus, and when the master of cavalry was replaced after the fall of Amida, Ammianus tries hard to defend him, even if he is not very persuasive. Ursicinus was himself capable of base treachery, and hardly seems worthy of such unquestioning devotion. Though Ammianus was also loyal to Julian, he was in no way blind to the flaws that are made very explicit in his obituary. On the other side, there seem to be no individuals against whom Ammianus shows unreasonable prejudice. He certainly has strong hostility to Germans, corrupt and ignorant senators, the urban mob, and lawyers, but he also provides considerable evidence that all these groups were pursuing their selfish interests to the detriment of the state. On the whole, he shows remarkable detachment.

Ammianus obviously takes pride in his accuracy, and few of his facts can be disproved from other sources. His attention to detail is impressive, and wherever his accuracy can be checked against Greek, Latin, or even a Syriac source on Armenian history, Ammianus is confirmed. Sir Ronald Syme paid him no small tribute when he called him "an honest man in an age of fraud and fanaticism." He even, uniquely among Latin historians, has an interest in and knowledge of geography. But if dishonesty and sloppiness play no role, forgetfulness befalls even the most scrupulous. There are some topographical inaccuracies in his account of the siege of Amida, but there he relied on his faulty memory of events thirty years earlier. That is of small consequence; Ammianus is almost always reliable on facts. But if the facts are accurate, a trained rhetorician may well color a passage to convey his own attitudes.

Political and religious attitudes

As the poet Simonides says, if a man is to live a life of perfect happiness he above all needs a country of which he can be proud.

(14, 6)

A Syrian Greek, Ammianus was enormously proud to be a Roman citizen, and he always remained devoted to the dignity of the Roman state and the history of its Empire. But his pragmatism allowed him to differentiate between the imperial ideal and the actual behavior of emperors. He relishes the justifiable pomp with which the soldiers first acclaimed Julian as emperor, but can be scathing toward the cruelty and tyranny practiced by individual emperors like Valens:

> How much might have been put right in those dark days if Valens had been taught by wisdom the lesson of the philosophers that sovereign power is nothing if it does not care for the welfare of others, and that it is the task of a good ruler to keep his power in check, to resist the passions of unbridled desire and implacable rage, and to realize that, as the dictator Caesar used to say, the recollection of past cruelty is a wretched provision for old age.
>
> (29, 2)

Ammianus believes deeply in the legitimacy of the principate, and he thus expects that emperors should be fair, dignified, and tolerant, and exercise self-control. They must respect ancient institutions like the Senate, and themselves observe the laws. Though he found most emperors of his own day wanting, Ammianus, like the good soldier that he was, is deeply loyal to every emperor. It is not the grudging loyalty of a Tacitus, but a passionate loyalty to the state even if there was a personal disappointment that bad emperors were themselves a blot on the glorious history of Rome.

He held the capital itself in the highest regard. While in his own day the emperors rarely visited Rome and his own contemporaries often neglected its glorious past, Ammianus is determined that his own history will evoke its noble mission and reminiscences of its past:

> If any foreigner should happen to read this work, I suppose he may wonder why, when it has occasion to speak of events at Rome, it should confine itself to riots and taverns and similar sordid subjects.
>
> (14, 6)

Ammianus does not wish Rome merely to be the site of urban unrest and senatorial corruption, so he keeps the city before his reader by devoting perhaps undue attention to the often inconsequential activities of the urban prefect who was charged with the administration of the capital. The spectacular description of the first visit to Rome by Constantius II in 357 CE – perhaps inspired by the next imperial visit, that of Theodosius I in 389, when Ammianus was actually in the city – provided an opportunity for a rhetorical set-piece on the glories of the capital. Emperors may avoid Rome, but Ammianus moved to the city to write his book and remained there until his death. He deeply appreciated its symbolic value for the Empire as *caput mundi* ("head of the world").

Ammianus displays his devotion to Rome's long history by the frequent use of historical parallels, or *exempla*. These may be good, bad, or mixed. Augustus had brought obelisks from Egypt as Constantius II was to do (17, 3), and the overwhelming Roman defeat at Adrianople had not been seen since Hannibal's extermination of the Romans at Cannae almost six centuries earlier (31, 13). The good and evil imperial brothers, Julian and Gallus, are shown as having antecedents three centuries earlier in Titus and Domitian (14, 11). But the most important continuing parallel is that of Julian with the virtuous emperors of the past, especially Marcus Aurelius, who shared his philosophical proclivities.

The same Julian is the focus of the surviving portion of Ammianus' history. It is certainly extraordinary that an emperor who ruled for only two years should be the subject of ten books, fully a third of the original thirty-one books which covered 282 years. Though Ammianus served under Julian both in Europe and Asia, that alone cannot explain the devotion which begins with a lyrical panegyric:

> My narrative, which is not a tissue of clever falsehoods but an absolutely truthful account based on clear evidence, will not fall far short of panegyric, because it seems that the life of this young man was guided by some principle which raised him above the ordinary and accompanied him from his illustrious cradle to his last breath. By a series of rapid steps he attained such distinction both at home and abroad that in sagacity he was reckoned the reincarnation of Titus the son of Vespasian, in the glorious outcome of his campaigns very like Trajan, as merciful as Antoninus, and in his striving after truth and perfection the equal of Marcus Aurelius, on whom he endeavored to model his own actions and character.
>
> (16, 1)

There are certainly many aspects of Julian's character that the historian can point to with admiration: his military leadership, which incites or restrains his troops as appropriate to the moment; his desire to reduce taxes and reform administration; the emperor's very un-Roman chastity in rejecting all sexual contact after his wife's death, even refusing Persian captives of remarkable beauty. And yet there are elements of Julian's character and personality, especially after his accession to the throne, that Ammianus criticizes both in his narrative and in his obituary: too great a liking for blood sacrifices; too much superstition toward divination and omens; impulsiveness and stubbornness; and an undignified need to be popular with everyone. Though he was himself a pagan, Ammianus also condemns Julian's intolerance toward the Christians during his final years. If the historian had such a balanced view of Julian's strengths and failings, why is his overall tone one of panegyric? It is perhaps that Julian represents for Ammianus his only genuine link with the ancient Roman virtues and through him Ammianus could believe that such virtue could still survive in the debased age of contemporary Rome.

Like his predecessors Livy and Tacitus, Ammianus had grown up in the provinces in awe of the history and traditions of Rome. That conservative respect for institutions like the Senate led him to scorn the snobbish, self-important and corrupt men who made up that august body in his own time. We cannot be certain how well Ammianus knew individual senators, but he certainly knew the breed well enough to devote two long passages to their failings (14, 6 and 28, 4). It is the examples of preposterous extravagance that make the best satire, as when he depicts Roman nobles galloping through the city with armies of slaves and eunuchs ostentatiously following them. But Ammianus is also wounded by the anti-intellectualism of senators, who study singing rather than philosophy, and are more interested in theater than literature: "The libraries are like tombs, permanently shut" (14, 6). He tells, with personal outrage, of the expulsion of foreign intellectuals from Rome in the expectation of a famine:

> No respite whatever was granted to professors of the liberal arts, though very few in number, while at the same time the hangers-on of actresses and those who posed as such for the occasion, together with three thousand dancers with their choruses and the same number of dancing instructors, were allowed to remain.
>
> (14, 6)

These senators are said to "despise anyone born outside the walls," and we see Ammianus chafing at the prejudice and condescension on the part of vapid senators who in his view have no idea what it means to be a true Roman.

Another privileged group in the capital who enrage Ammianus are the advocates who throng the courts and public areas of the city. His contempt for lawyers has a long lineage, and many of his criticisms may well be derived from ancient diatribes against advocates, like the conventional "lawyer-jokes" of our own day:

> The profession of forensic oratory is defined by the great Plato as a "counterfeit branch of the art of government" or as "the fourth kind of pandering." Epicurus too calls it a "bad skill" and regards it as a mischievous activity.
>
> (30, 4)

He accuses lawyers of stirring up conflict between friends or relatives, as well as offering their expertise to protect the guilty. In fact, relying on their lawyers for protection, many commit crimes with impunity. Their greed, hypocrisy, and ill-temper are all depicted, as is their corruption of judges. Only at the end of this long digression does Ammianus show a small degree of sympathy for lawyers, when he admits that many judges themselves demand bribes and every client who loses a case, however weak, blames his advocate.

Each of Ammianus' long digressions on the failure of the senatorial class concludes with a much briefer criticism of the urban proletariat. The complaints are traditional: the poor are lazy, addicted to drink, gambling, the theater, and especially the chariot races:

> Those who have drained life to the dregs and whose age gives them influence often swear by their white hair and wrinkles that the country will go to the dogs if in some coming race the driver they fancy fails to take the lead from the start, or makes too wide a turn round the post with his unlucky team. Such is the general decay of manners that on the longed-for day of the races they rush headlong to the course before the first glimmering of dawn as if they would outstrip the competing teams.
>
> (28, 4)

The periodic riots in Rome are often caused by, for Ammianus, trivial reasons, like a rumored shortage of wine or the arrest of a popular charioteer. Others were the result of famine or factional struggles among the Christians. Some prefects repress such outbreaks with violence; others argue their case to the masses. Ammianus only reports a single urban riot outside of Rome, when the Christians lynched their own bishop Georgius in Alexandria. In that case Julian decided there should only be a weak reprimand.

Though Ammianus was a pagan, we have seen that he criticized Julian for an excess of religious zeal in sacrifices and divination. Ammianus sometimes uses the language of Neoplatonism, and his religious interests are more philosophical than ritual. He often refers to Fate, Fortune, and Nemesis, but there does not seem to be any coherent philosophical system underlying these comments. Likewise, his treatment of Christianity is quite tolerant; he does not criticize Christians for their belief, only for their behavior. Religious tolerance, for which he praised Valentinian (30, 9), came easily to him and he does not believe negative rumors about the Christians. On the other hand, his first-hand knowledge of Christianity is limited and the religion plays a surprisingly small role in his history. For example, he says nothing about the serious doctrinal disputes between Arians and orthodox Christians that raged throughout the fourth century, nor does he report the decisions, or even the existence, of important Church councils of the time. He does, however, refer to such controversies when he writes that "no wild beasts are such dangerous enemies to man as Christians are to one another" (22, 5).

Ammianus did know enough about the Christian ethic of poverty to satirize greedy and ambitious bishops. In Alexandria Athanasius was expelled by the synod, and another bishop, Georgius, was attacked and killed in the street. In Rome itself Christian mobs took to the streets in 366 CE in support of two rival candidates for the papacy, and 137 murdered corpses were found in one basilica on a single day. Yet, despite his strictures on the metropolitan bishops, Ammianus recognizes much virtue in the Christian hierarchy:

> [The Roman bishops] might be truly happy if they would pay no regard to the greatness of the city, which they make a cloak for their vices, and follow the example of some provincial bishops, whose extreme frugality in food and drink, simple attire, and downcast eyes demonstrate to the supreme god and his true worshippers the purity and modesty of their lives.
>
> (27, 3)

Religious partisans often use their opponents as scapegoats in the aftermath of disaster, but Ammianus does not blame Christianity for the catastrophe at Adrianople. Of course, we must consider the effect of a Christian emperor on an historian. Valentinian may have been even-handed, and even Theodosius (379–95 CE) at first appointed pagan officials. So, in the period up to 392 CE, when Ammianus was working on his first twenty-five books, Theodosius was relatively lenient on religious issues. But in his last three years, with the ascendancy of Bishop Ambrose of Milan, imperial religious policy became much more rigorous and resulted in the dismissal of most pagan officials. During those years Ammianus composed his final six books, and it can hardly be chance that nowhere in those books does he mention his own pagan beliefs. In fact, religious topics almost disappear from his history. Hence, if Ammianus was so careful in his final books, we might surmise that even in the earlier books he moderated his views on Christianity to the prevailing religious ideology. How much he did so, we can never know.

Barbarians play an important role in Ammianus' narrative, both the Germans beyond the Rhine and Danube frontiers and the Persians beyond the Euphrates. Since the historian is an easterner himself, it is understandable that the Persians are depicted with respect. But the intensity of the normally equitable Ammianus' hatred for the Germans is unexpected. That he calls them, but not the Persians, *barbari* is comprehensible in cultural terms, but his willingness to see them slaughtered is not. He as strongly opposes subsidies paid to German tribes as he condemns the appointment of German commanders in the Roman army. He is especially exercised when Julian appoints to the consulship the barbarian Nevitta, described as "uncultivated, rather boorish and, what was even less tolerable, cruel" (21, 10). Barbarism is for Ammianus quite simply the enemy of all that holds together civilized society. He sees only animal savagery when he looks at barbarian armies and has little compassion even for those who had served Rome faithfully. The final pages of the history concern the Goths, who fought under Roman commanders and were stationed throughout Asia. After Adrianople, Roman commanders feared they might join with the Gothic armies victorious at Adrianople:

> The Goths were to be collected quite unsuspecting outside
> the walls in the expectation of receiving the pay that they
> had been promised, and at a given signal all put to death

124

on one and the same day. This wise plan was carried out
without fuss or delay, and the provinces of the East saved
from serious danger.

(31, 16)

Thus Ammianus devotes just a few words to the murderous
treachery that ends his history. We can only conclude that the years
fighting on the Rhine frontier must have so hardened him against
the Germans that even such brutal treatment seemed to him inconsequential. It is a blind spot in Ammianus – both in his lack of
humanity toward the Germans and in his lack of understanding of
their central role in the defense of the Empire.

Rome may be for Ammianus the "eternal city," but he also recognizes that the state is in decline. The decline was not an inevitable
decree of fate; it was the result of human weakness. In the great
tradition of Roman historiography, Ammianus found the cause of
the decline in moral failure, in this case of emperors, senators, and
the urban masses. So, like Sallust, Livy, and Tacitus, Ammianus
presents a somewhat pessimistic picture. Yet all was far from lost,
since Rome's future survival or future greatness depends for him on
the moral determination and military energy with which her leaders
confront the state's problems and its enemies. John Matthews
concludes his masterful treatment of Ammianus with these
thoughts:

> Nowhere is Ammianus more Classical in his perspective
> than in so connecting the eternity of Rome with human
> will and human effort. Ammianus' career, his morality and
> his history alike express the conviction that, whatever the
> crisis and whatever the scope of accident, something can be
> done, and that it is in the nature of man to attempt it.
> (Matthews, *The Roman Empire of Ammianus Marcellinus*, 472)

We have seen that Ammianus boasted in his final words that he has
never perverted the truth either by silence or a lie. But his silence
concerning religious matters in the last six books seems to belie that
claim. We cannot, however, be too severe. From the reigns of
Diocletian and Constantine, the citizens of the Roman Empire had
to live under tighter central control, with official spies and eager
informers ready to report any deviation. Ammianus reports frequent
treason trials at Rome and Antioch that must have terrified him.
Are there other topics that he might have passed over or distorted

from fear? One notable absence in his history was the death of the general Theodosius, father of the emperor Theodosius I. Though Ammianus provides generous praise for the elder Theodosius, he never reports his execution in 377 CE, which is reported by Jerome and Orosius. (In fact Ammianus tells us nothing about events in the West between 375 and 378 CE, a fact that once led scholars to posit a lost book.) There seems to be a conspiracy of silence. Ammianus praises the general, though his actual narrative shows him to be cruel. Soon after his death, the emperor Gratian appointed both his brother and son to high positions. The only conclusion is that the elder Theodosius was executed for justifiable reasons that did not involve members of his family. Yet Ammianus, with his son on the imperial throne, takes such a wide berth of the fall of Theodosius that he simply omits several years of western history. Ammianus is fair and accurate, but he also finds it prudent to avoid provoking the master of the Roman Empire. He seems not to be quite as courageous or principled as he boasts, but perhaps we must not expect too much from one writing in such an uncertain age.

The literary art of Ammianus

Ammianus was a Greek and was certainly proud of his heritage, but he chose to write in Latin – the first major Latin history since Tacitus and the last secular history of Rome to be written in the city's own language. He does not tell us why he did so, but there were probably both literary and political reasons. The obvious literary reason was to continue the work of Tacitus, while the political reason was to write in what the contemporary Greek rhetorician Themistius called τὴν διαλέκτον κρατοῦσαν ("the language of our rulers"). Unlike the courtier Themistius, Ammianus was not trying to curry imperial favor, but he was deeply committed to Rome and its political heritage. His pride in his Roman citizenship is evident throughout his history.

So Ammianus chose to write in Latin, and he did it remarkably well: only occasional Grecisms can be found in his work. He chose to write in an elaborate and elevated style, which is unsurprising for one writing in a second language. His range of reading in Latin literature was extraordinary, and he echoes two dozen Latin authors in addition to topical allusions to Greek writers like Herodotus, Polybius, and especially Homer. Though he imitates some Tacitean usages and preserves the dark atmosphere of his predecessor, the spare style of Sallust or Tacitus does not attract Ammianus. It is rather Cicero who is the paramount stylistic reference, though a Cicero transformed through a prism of the poetic vocabulary, the epic pictorialism, and the emotional intensity so congenial to late antiquity. There are also more explicit references to Cicero than to any other author. For his description of battles Ammianus draws on Virgil and Homer, but when he wishes to attack the degenerate nobility and urban plebs he looks back to Juvenal. This gives his Latin a richly ornate quality. It should be clear that this is not schoolbook knowledge quickly learned by an ordinary soldier; Ammianus was a well-educated superior officer who was deeply imbued with the literary culture of his adopted language.

By classical standards, however, the style is overripe. Edward Gibbon repeatedly criticizes Ammianus' writing: "unnatural vehemence of expression" (II 249 n. 18); "affected language" (II 399 n. 7); "superfluous labor" (II 415 n. 43); "bad taste of Ammianus" (III 69 n. 1); "superfluous prolixity" (III 96 n. 67); and "turgid metaphors" (III 104 n. 83). But Gibbon weighs the vices and virtues of the historian much as Ammianus himself judges the emperors in his obituaries:

> We might censure the vices of his style, the disorder and perplexity of his narrative; but we must now take leave of this impartial historian, and reproach is silenced by our regret for such an irreparable loss.
> (Gibbon, *Decline and Fall of the Roman Empire* III 111 n. 93)

If Gibbon seems harsh, the literary critic Erich Auerbach even further suggests that his highly rhetorical style is gruesomely sensory and its crude realism approaches the grotesque and the macabre (*Mimesis* 50–60). Ammianus' style is admittedly mannered, but it was also effective in his depiction of character and the dramatic scenes of siege and battle. If the historian includes grotesque scenes, it is largely because of the monstrous cruelty actually present in the war and political persecutions of his time.

Many of these literary "defects" are merely the historian's adoption of the taste of his time. Ammianus largely avoids the greatest defect of late antique prose, the overuse of panegyric. Nor should we overlook the remarkable eye of the historian, as he brings a genuine visual texture to his description of battles, political spectacle, and landscape. His style is in many ways far removed from the historians of the early Empire nearly three centuries earlier, but that is only natural. The gap between Tacitus and Ammianus is longer than that between the elegant periods of Edward Gibbon and the prose of the present day.

Like other ancient historians, Ammianus generally avoids documents and rewrites speeches to capture the substance of the original. (The letters between Julian and Constantius were also recomposed by the historian.) This is no deception; Ammianus makes it quite clear that the speeches are in his own words. Despite his rhetorical training, there are no more than a dozen lengthy speeches. In many earlier historians, notably Thucydides and Livy, speeches form part of the democratic deliberative process and might actually be regarded as an aspect of the action. For Tacitus and Ammianus, living in times of imperial despotism, speeches often seem merely to be a decorative interruption in the narrative. In Ammianus, they play a much smaller role than in Tacitus, and, for a rhetorical author, they are unusually restrained.

Perhaps the most literary element in Ammianus' history is his prodigal use of digressions. Though digressions were used by all ancient historians, Ammianus goes further in including an extraordinary range: ethnography, geography, and zoological oddities like geese flying with stones in their beaks to avoid alerting eagles of their proximity, or the fact that the lion population in Mesopotamia is only controlled by gnats. Many scholars find that Ammianus has gone too far, especially in his books on Julian where digressions comprise almost half of the text. But for his contemporary audience of listeners and readers, the digressions were paramount examples of the historian's art and an opportunity to deploy his rhetorical technique. They provided interesting information; they served a dramatic function in the structure of the history; and they could delight the audience in the same way that a rhetorician's epideictic oration on why Helen of Troy was a virtuous woman could attract a crowd of listeners. Like a saxophonist's riff in jazz, or a stand-up comedian's monologue, or an operatic cabaletta, a digression could be a virtuoso display to be enjoyed for its own sake. Though a modern reader tends to regard these as superfluous interruptions in the narrative, we should not be blind to their intrinsic appeal. And many of Ammianus' digressions include material of interest. Here, for example, is a portion of his description of the Chinese:

> Beyond these lands of both the Scythians, the summits of lofty walls form a circle and enclose the Seres [Chinese], remarkable for the richness and extent of their country...

The Seres themselves live a peaceful life, for ever unac-
quainted with arms and warfare; and since to gentle and
quiet folk ease is pleasurable, they are troublesome to none
of their neighbors. Their climate is agreeable and healthful,
the sky is clear, the winds gentle and very pleasant. There
is an abundance of well-lighted woods, the trees of which
produce a substance which they work with frequent
sprinkling, like a kind of fleece; then from the wool-like
material, mixed with water, they draw out very fine
threads, spin the fabric, and make silk, formerly for the use
of the nobility, but nowadays available even to the lowest
without distinction.

(23, 6, 64; 67, tr. J.C. Rolfe (Loeb))

Narrative is the staple of the historian's craft and Ammianus writes
very vivid narration. We can best see the speed and energy of his narrative powers in his accounts of his own personal experience of the siege
and fall of Amida to the Persians. The episode is not only of intrinsic
interest, but it allows Ammianus to place himself at the scene:

For a long time the outcome of this bloody fight hung in
the balance. The unremitting courage of the besieged set
death at defiance, and the strife had reached a stage when
only some unavoidable accident could decide the issue.
Suddenly our mound, on which we had spent so much
labor, fell forward as if struck by an earthquake; it filled the
gap that yawned between the wall and the ramp outside
like a causeway or a bridge, and presented the enemy with
a level surface over which they could pass unhindered. Most
of our men were thrown down and crushed or gave up the
struggle from exhaustion. Nevertheless there was a general
rush to avert the danger caused by this sudden catastrophe,
but in their haste men got in each other's way, whereas the
spirit of the enemy rose with their success. The king called
up all his forces to take part in the sack; hand-to-hand
fighting ensued and torrents of blood were spilt on both
sides. The trenches were filled with corpses, which
provided a broader front for the attack, and when the
furious onrush of the enemy's troops filled the city all hope
of defense or escape was gone, and soldiers and civilians
were slaughtered like sheep without distinction of sex.

(19, 8)

But even when Ammianus was far from the scene, as in Constantius' first visit to Rome in 357 CE, the historian captures the emperor's awe at seeing the monuments of the capital:

> But when he came to the Forum of Trajan, a creation which in my view has no like under the cope of heaven and which even the gods themselves must agree to admire, he stood transfixed with astonishment, surveying the gigantic fabric around him; its grandeur defies description and can never again be approached by mortal men. So he abandoned all hope of attempting anything like it, and declared that he would simply imitate Trajan's horse, which stands in the middle of the court with the emperor on its back...
>
> The emperor then, after viewing many sights with awe and amazement, complained of the weakness or malice of common report, which tends to exaggerate everything, but is feeble in its description of the wonders of Rome.
>
> (16, 10)

Conclusion

This last great pagan writer has given us a remarkable history. What remains is a detailed history of twenty-five years of his own time – an account which in its breadth of interest, its personal knowledge, and its innate fairness cannot be equaled in ancient historical writing. While it is true that Ammianus' acute intelligence does not attain the political perception of Thucydides or Tacitus, who could discern the reality beneath the surface of the historical narrative, few political historians of any age measure up to that standard. Unlike either of his predecessors, Ammianus was never close to the center of political power and never held high office. He was one of the few great historians of antiquity who was a social outsider. In that context, his political discernment is noteworthy.

Ammianus compensates with his wider interest in military and provincial affairs, foreign diplomacy, the bureaucracy, and even cultural issues. Though impressed by the glorious history of "eternal Rome," he is by nature a pragmatist and does not allow Rome's past to blind him to its present catastrophes. Yet he puts these disasters into context through his frequent use of historical parallels or *exempla*. Great Romans of the past had confronted and overcome foreign enemies and civil wars; to do so again was always possible. Ammianus put his reliance on the courage of his fellow-citizens and their sheer willingness to devote energy to the heroic task of preserving Rome's greatness. While he may not be optimistic about the future, at least this last great historian of Greco-Roman antiquity holds out to his contemporaries the hope of preserving a millennium of civilization. That in itself is an act of exceptional courage.

6

ROMAN BIOGRAPHY

Greek antecedents of Roman biography

Biography, or the writing of a life (Greek: *bios*), gradually became an important literary form in the Greek and Roman world, and it has remained so until our own time. Despite its popularity across the centuries, intellectuals and literary critics have regarded it as a genre inferior to history. Since the earliest biographers were principally concerned with the development of moral character, biography was regarded as primarily ethical and rhetorical, while the writing of history demanded research and analysis. In some eras biography and history might approach each other, and authors like Xenophon and Tacitus wrote in both genres, but with the rise of modern historical scholarship during the nineteenth century biography came to be regarded as a dilettantish avocation for gentlemen rather than scholars. The distinguished philosopher of history R.G. Collingwood called biography "anti-historical." During the last fifty years, however, there has been a growing similarity and, though the Pulitzer Prize Committee maintains separate categories for History and Biography, many scholarly biographies are almost indistinguishable from history and both forms are often written by the same scholars. Scholars, of course, remain scornful of popular biography, but they would be equally scornful of popularized history if it was published in equal measure. It is not, since the book-buying public much prefers biography to history, which encourages many historians to write in a mixed genre – for example, *Woodrow Wilson and his Times* – to reach a wider audience. In the words of Arnaldo Momigliano, "Biography has never been so popular, so respected, so uncontroversial, among scholars as it is now." Those words, written a quarter of a century ago, are even more true today.

In biography, as in most other forms of literature, Rome owed much to Greece, though perhaps not as much as it might seem at first glance. Plutarch, whose *Parallel Lives* make him the greatest of all ancient biographers, was a Greek, but he lived under the Roman Empire and was a contemporary of the two finest Roman biographers, Suetonius and Tacitus. Thus his work can hardly be regarded as a model for Roman writers. In fact, there is no specific model for Roman biographers, or for Plutarch himself, only a range of Greek biographical writing with quite different purposes and forms. Some scholars would even trace biography back to the *Odyssey*, which recounted the adventures of Odysseus. When Alexander the Great visited the site of ancient Troy, he lamented that he, unlike Achilles, had no poet like Homer to commemorate his deeds, and thus he seemed to regard the *Iliad* as a biography. By the fifth century BCE, the eulogistic songs sung at banquets and funerals in praise of aristocratic achievements were given a literary form by Pindar and other poets who sketched the lives of mythical or historical personalities in their victory odes. At the same time, historians like Herodotus and Thucydides provided brief portraits of Croesus, Themistocles, and Pericles.

It was in the fourth century BCE that Greek biographical writing burst forth in monographs, dialogues, and what we might today call historical novels. These different forms reflected the different goals of the authors. The best known are Plato's *Dialogues* and Xenophon's *Memorabilia*, which intended to preserve the personality and ideas of their teacher, Socrates. (It is not relevant for our purpose to address what of the philosophy in the *Dialogues* is due to Socrates and what to Plato.) In addition to such philosophical tributes, Xenophon's *Anabasis* includes short lives of dead generals, which Samuel Johnson considered the earliest Greek biographies:

> He apprehended that the delineation of *characters* in the end of the first Book of the *Retreat of the Ten Thousand* was the first instance of the kind that was known.
>
> (Boswell, *Life of Johnson* IV 31, 32)

Monographs by Xenophon (*Agesilaus*) and the orator Isocrates (*Euagoras*) are prose encomia detailing the achievements and virtues of their subjects, modeled perhaps on the poems of Pindar. Isocrates boasted that his treatment of the Cypriot ruler Euagoras in 365 BCE was the first to eulogize a living person. When Xenophon wrote his *Agesilaus* a few years later, he included more factual material and thus brought it closer to biography. While all these works attempted to keep alive the memory of a notable Greek, Xenophon's *Education of Cyrus (Cyropaedia)* was a novelistic treatment of the training of a Persian prince intended to provide a model for aristocratic education. These various forms were used and combined in the histories, biographies, and historical fiction inspired by the extraordinary life and achievements of Alexander, which flourished across much of Europe and Asia for centuries as the "Alexander Romance."

Later in the fourth century, Aristotle and future generations at the Lyceum, the school of what were called the Peripatetic philosophers, developed the theory that an individual's character is fixed, though it might only be gradually revealed during one's life. Thus came the Peripatetic school of biography which sought to identify the character traits present in a given personality and derive moral lessons from them. Aristotle's successor as director of the Lyceum, Theophrastus, even wrote a book (*Characters*) which presented brief sketches of different personality types, while others wrote actual lives in which character was revealed through action. For such a biography, a treatment of the entire life would be unnecessary, so the biographer might select only those anecdotes necessary to illuminate the character and thus illustrate the moral lesson. These writers were erudite researchers who collected material from many sources. Some of their books were mere collections of sayings or anecdotes, which later became a popular literary form in the ancient world. But in other cases they wove this material into a learned life. There was particular interest in the lives of philosophers, in which the ideas of the thinker, his sayings, and anecdotes from his life might be brought together. Collections of such lives, containing generations of teachers and students, became the earliest form of intellectual history among the Greeks. There was less interest in writing the moral biography of men of action: that seemed the province of history proper or a rhetorical encomium like Polybius' lost *Life of Philopoemen*. Polybius says that he had in that monograph described Philopoemen's family and his training as a boy, but he spells out the quite different purpose of his *History*:

> It is evident that in the present narrative my proper course is to omit details concerning his early training and the ambitions of his youth, but to add detail to the summary account I gave of the achievements of his riper years, in order that the proper character of each work may be preserved. For just as the former work, being in the form of an encomium, demanded a summary and somewhat exag-

gerated account of his achievements, so the present history, which distributes praise and blame impartially, demands a strictly true account and one which states the ground on which either praise or blame is based.

(*Hist.* 10, 21, 7–8, tr. Paton (Loeb))

No early Peripatetic biographies survive; we know them only from ancient references. But Plutarch of Chaeronea, who wrote much later (about 100 CE), incorporated two of the most important elements of that tradition: research and a moral purpose. His approach was different – not Aristotelian, but Stoic – but an ethical concern lay at the heart of his writing. Shaped by the Stoic tradition, he reoriented Peripatetic biography toward men of action: founders, statesmen, and generals. Since he wrote parallel lives of Greeks and Romans with moralizing comparisons appended, he had to select and highlight elements in the lives that lent themselves to such a comparison. Though he organized his material into a chronological framework not unlike history, he made it clear that biography gave him a freedom that history would not:

I shall make no other preface than to entreat my readers, in case I do not tell of all the famous actions of these men, nor even speak exhaustively at all in each particular case, but in epitome for the most part, not to complain. For it is not History I am writing, but Lives; and in the most illustrious deeds there is not always a manifestation of virtue or vice, nay, a slight thing like a phrase or a jest often makes a greater revelation of character than battles where thousands fall, or the greatest armaments, or sieges of cities. Accordingly, just as painters get the likeness in their portraits from the face and the expression of the eyes, wherein the character shows itself, but make very little account of the other parts of the body, so I must be allowed to give my more particular attention to the marks and indications of the souls of men, and while I endeavor by these to portray their lives, may be free to leave more weighty matters and great battles to be treated by others.

(Plutarch, *Life of Alexander* 1, tr. Perrin (Loeb))

In addition to the encomium and the Peripatetic moral biography, scholars at the Museion, the great research institute at Alexandria, developed a third form of biography that had no political or moral purpose. Such lives were first written to be included in the scholars' new editions of famous Greek poets. Unlike the previous forms, they were written for purely utilitarian reasons and had little literary merit. The biographer assembled material on a poet's life and works, with anecdotes on his education, travels, etc. The material, which was uncovered through research or deduced from the author's writings, was organized in categories, rather than chronologically. Since the biographers had no rhetorical pretensions, they might quote actual documents rather than rewrite them. These biographies were not intended for the education of statesmen or the literary edification of the sophisticated, but as scholarly collections for those interested in learning the facts quickly and painlessly. With the exception of a papyrus fragment of Satyrus' *Life of Euripides,* only the names of biographers and the titles of their books survive, but some material reaches us through inclusion in later lives of poets.

Greek ideas of biography reached Rome in two ways: directly through the reading of written Greek lives, and indirectly through the schools of rhetoric. The schools provided training, first entirely in Greek and by the first century BCE in Latin as well, in epideictic, or display, oratory through a series of graduated exercises. The exercise for describing the "external excellence" of a character included much of a biographical nature: a character's noble birth and ancestry, native city and family, education and friends, public achievements and the nature of his death. Hence, even before there was written biography in Latin, orators like Cicero were trained to use biography in their speeches. Since no proper biographies survive from the Roman Republic, the long passages in Cicero's speeches that describe his client's background may be regarded as the earliest extant Roman biographical writing.

Rome did not completely depend on Greek models of biography; we have seen that there were independent traditions of funeral orations (*laudationes funebres*), banquet songs, and commemorative inscriptions preserved by aristocratic families. A funeral oration would not only include the decedent's career, but it would rehearse the offices and achievements of his or her notable predecessors. In his funeral oration for his nephew and son-in-law Marcellus, Augustus traced the family back to the third century BCE, as Julius Caesar had done in his oration at the funeral of his aunt Julia, the widow of Marius. These orations depended, to a greater degree than the generalized Greek encomia, on the actual details of the subject's career. There may have been some relation between these biographical orations and the popularity of realistic portraiture during the late Republic; Plutarch himself links biography with portraiture in the passage from the *Life of Alexander* cited above. While the Greeks preferred more idealized images in stone as in words, the Romans tended to present their ancestors with a greater degree of reality.

The earliest known Roman biography, the eulogistic treatment of Tiberius Gracchus by his brother, Gaius Gracchus, does not survive. After the death of the younger Cato in 46 BCE, Brutus wrote a *Cato*. That this was a political tract rather than a genuine biography is demonstrated by the fact that Caesar himself responded sharply with a pamphlet called *Anti-Cato*. These works, like that of Gracchus and of a later life of Brutus, were in fact political pamphlets. While this form of ideological expression had important consequences in the hagiography of Stoic "martyrs" under the Empire, they were not truly biographies. Nor was Tiro's *Cicero*, an encomiastic life of his master which focused on personal and literary matters rather than politics. According to St Jerome, the first person to write biography at Rome was the learned polymath Marcus Terentius Varro. In addition to brief Alexandrian-style biographies of the Roman poets, he published an enormous work called *Imagines*, which contained the portraits of 700 distinguished Greeks and Romans – poets, philosophers, statesmen, and performers – each accompanied by a brief epigram and explanatory prose material. Whether biography or not, none of these works survives, and the Roman Republic ended without leaving us a single extant biography. It was only during the triumviral period (43–31 BCE) that the earliest surviving Latin biographies were written.

Cornelius Nepos' *Lives of Famous Men*

Cornelius Nepos (*c.* 100–24 BCE), born to a wealthy non-senatorial family in Cisalpine Gaul, wrote the earliest surviving lives. Though he came to Rome by 65 and lived there for forty years, Nepos studiously avoided involvement in the political life of the capital. He was a particular friend and admirer of another political neutral of the age, Atticus, at whose villa he would have met Cicero and Varro. Though the letters between Nepos and Cicero have not survived, they seem to have been concerned with literary matters. He lived through the civil wars and died in old age in 24 BCE.

Nepos realized that, as Rome became more involved with the Greek world, it was important that Romans be better acquainted with Greek history. Highly educated men like Cicero, who had studied in Greece and read Greek easily, could use Greek historical parallels, but Romans who read only Latin had almost no written material available on foreign peoples and so fell back on the crudest caricatures. Nepos was determined to bring a certain awareness of cultural relativism to Rome:

> I doubt not, Atticus, that many readers will look upon this kind of writing as trivial and unworthy of the parts played by great men, when they find that I have told who taught Epaminondas music or see it mentioned among his titles to fame that he was a graceful dancer and a skilled performer on the flute. But such critics will for the most part be men unfamiliar with Greek letters, who will think no conduct proper which does not conform to their own habits. If these men can be made to understand that not all peoples look upon the same acts as honorable or base, but that they judge them all in the light of the usage of their forefathers, they will not be surprised that I, in giving an account of the merits of the Greeks, have borne in mind the usage of that nation.
>
> (Nepos, *De Duc. Illust.* Preface 1–3)[1]

As the first step in this program of introducing Romans to international culture, Nepos prepared a universal history in three books called *Chronica* – a synchronization of the chronologies of Greece and Rome already mentioned in Chapter 1. Though Nepos' book was soon supplanted by a superior single volume by his friend Atticus (*Liber Annalis*), we should not overlook that Nepos first brought comparative history to a wider audience at Rome. It is this book that his friend Catullus playfully invokes when he dedicates his own first book of poetry to Cornelius Nepos:

> Who am I giving this smart little book to,
> new, and just polished up with dry pumice?
> Cornelius, you; because you already
> reckoned my scribblings really were something
> when you, alone of Italians, boldly
> unfolded all history in three volumes –
> the effort, my God! and the erudition!
> So have this little book, such as it may be...
>
> (Catullus 1, tr. T.P. Wiseman)

Though some have read these lines as containing biting irony or parody directed toward Nepos, this is probably no more than affectionate teasing between good friends from the same region of northeast Italy.

Lives of Famous Men was a collection of biographies comparing foreigners and Romans in various categories; the foreigners are usually Greek, with an occasional Persian or Carthaginian. Nepos organized the work, which was dedicated to Atticus, in sixteen books, with Roman and foreign kings, generals, lawgivers, orators, philosophers, poets, historians, and grammarians. There were perhaps four hundred lives in all, though only twenty-four survive: the book on foreign generals (including Alcibiades and Hannibal) as well as the lives of Cato and Atticus from the book of Roman historians.

Nepos had no intention of writing history; his goal was to introduce his readers to foreign notables and draw moral lessons from their lives. But he was well aware that the ignorance of his readers, whom he refers to as the *vulgus* (crowd), demanded that he provide a certain amount of historical and cultural background.

> Pelopidas, the Theban, is better known to historians than to the general public (*vulgus*). I am in doubt how to give an account of his merits; for I fear that if I undertake to tell of his deeds, I shall seem to be writing a history rather than a biography; but if I merely touch upon the high points, I am afraid that to those unfamiliar with Greek literature it will not be perfectly clear how great a man he was. Therefore I shall meet both difficulties as well as I can, having regard both for the weariness and the lack of information of my readers.
>
> (Nepos, *Pelopidas* 1)

These first political biographies to survive from the ancient world are quite varied in size, form, and approach. Most are Peripatetic biographies with a moral message, though some shorter lives (e.g. *Iphicrates; Conon; Cimon*) are more purely factual in the Alexandrian style. Nepos even uses the encomiastic mode in his *Alcibiades* and *Atticus*. Some lives are mere sketches, but several come alive as the author is engaged by the personality. One such is the life of *Eumenes*, the only Greek general among the Macedonian inner circle of Philip and Alexander and the successor of Alexander who fought the most loyally to preserve his kingdom for his son. Nepos was touched by that loyalty and his warmth toward Eumenes is palpable. In this biography the author has to explain Eumenes' high position as secretary to Philip II, since at Rome "scribes are considered hirelings."

The most vibrant of the Greek lives is certainly that of *Alcibiades*. Though Nepos usually distrusts strongly individualistic behavior, he is entranced by Alcibiades, of whom he said: "In this man Nature seems to have tried to see what she could accomplish" (1). He provides a wealth of detail on Alcibiades' beauty, intelligence, and charm, though he omits the usual story of his seduction of the wife of the Spartan king. He does not conclude this tempestuous life with a moral – which would have been easy – but continues the eulogistic tone to the very end: "He was held in the first rank wherever he lived, as well as being greatly beloved" (11).

The brief life of Cato, which was included in the book of Roman historians, refers to a much longer life, now lost, which Nepos wrote at the request of Atticus. Since his long life of Cicero is also lost, we must turn to his life of Atticus for the only surviving example of a contemporary biography. This eulogistic life is a fitting commemoration of the friend to whom the entire book was dedicated. Despite a highly rhetorical approach, personal knowledge and obvious sympathy make this by far the best of Nepos' lives. It was published before the death of Atticus in 32 BCE, though Nepos issued a revised version not long before his own death. Much of the material was based on Nepos' own observation as well as conversations with mutual friends, so here Nepos becomes an important primary source for life during the waning decades of the Roman Republic.

Atticus is best known as the friend and correspondent of Cicero, but he was also a friend of Nepos and most of the Roman political leadership for a half-century. What is extraordinary is his success at remaining neutral in civil conflict while keeping up friendly relations with nearly all the combatants: the younger Marius; Sulla; Pompey; Caesar; Cicero; Brutus; Antony; and finally Augustus. This wealthy businessman and scholar retreated to Athens for two decades; when he returned in 65 BCE he remained loyal to his friends as individuals, but refused to be tempted by political office or alliances. Since most of our sources concern political intrigues and grabs for power, the survival of this equestrian at the very center of political life but detached from it provides a fascinating look at the ties that bind the Roman elite even in the midst of civil war. Nepos reports that Atticus lived to see his one-year-old granddaughter, Vipsania, become engaged to the future emperor Tiberius.

The biography provides a wonderful window on late Republican Rome, and it demonstrates that Nepos could, when interested and knowledgeable, write a very interesting biography.

There is little question that Nepos found Atticus so attractive because he too was a scholar rather than a politician. If there is a recurrent theme through Nepos' lives, it is the horror of civil strife and the many vices it encourages, especially greed and profligacy. He introduces the theme of freedom into some lives, like that of the Sicilian general Timoleon, where that theme is absent in Plutarch's version. The civic virtues of freedom, obedience, and communal harmony are given an important role by an author who preferred the quiet, orderly life of the study to the turmoil of the Senate or the Forum. Perhaps the clearest expression of Nepos' anxiety is his frequent return to the role of Fortune in human affairs. As he says of Dion,

> This success, so great and so unexpected, was followed by a sudden change, since Fortune, with her usual fickleness, proceeded to bring down the man whom she had shortly before exalted.
>
> (*Dion* 6)

For one who lived through the last five tumultuous decades of the Republic and two decades of civil war, Nepos' resigned acceptance of Fortune's power is understandable.

Since Nepos wrote relatively clearly in short sentences and because of his high moral tone, his lives used to be read in beginning Latin courses and so constituted the introduction to Greek history for generations of German and British schoolchildren. Yet scholars have been critical of his many inadequacies: he confuses the two Miltiades (uncle and nephew); his chronology (as in the case of Xerxes' invasion) is sometimes garbled in his Greek lives; his haste or carelessness leads on occasion to internal contradictions; and there is a gross mistranslation from a Greek source. He does not seem to have any great critical ability in using sources and, in fact, it is far from clear whether Nepos actually used all the sources he mentions. At the beginning of the century a German scholar pronounced Nepos "neither an artist nor a scholar," while he has more recently been dismissed, in Nicholas Horsfall's much quoted phrase, as "an intellectual pygmy."

These judgments are harsh. Nepos was the first Roman to attempt Greek historical subjects, the first to write political biography, the first to write biographies of intellectuals, and the first to write biographies of his contemporaries. He did this without even a reliable history of early Rome – Livy's first books were published about the time of Nepos' death – so he had to use the very problematic annalists. Without reference works to synchronize the various calendars – based on Roman consuls, Athenian archons, Olympiads, regnal dates of Hellenistic kings – he had to undertake that work himself in his earlier *Chronica*. While Nepos' product is far from perfect, the task he set himself in writing four hundred biographies was nothing short of monumental.

On the other hand, Nepos is no better than a mediocre stylist in Latin. He is no Cicero, nor Caesar, whom his Latin more closely resembles. Nepos can write clear and pleasant, if rather dull, Latin as long as he keeps his sentences short and syntax simple; in longer sentences the style sometimes becomes contorted and the syntax confused. At times he unleashes a rhetorical flourish that is almost embarrassing, as when he compliments Cicero's letters in these terms: "There is nothing that they do not make clear, and it may readily appear that Cicero's foresight was almost divination" (*Atticus* 16). This absurd exaggeration would be humorous if Cicero's final political misjudgments had not cost him his life.

Nepos' literary failings were probably less important to his audience. He simplified things for his readers in a number of ways: foreign offices are expressed in Roman terms, so that Hannibal is called a king (*rex*) at Carthage and the Spartan *gerousia* is called the Senate. Likewise he refers to a cult of Minerva in Greece instead of Athena, and has Hannibal sacrifice to Jupiter Optimus Maximus in Carthage in what was a cult of Baal. It was perhaps also his non-aristocratic readers that made Nepos sexually prudish. Not only does he omit the sexual adventures of Alcibiades, but Epaminondas' creation of a fighting force of homosexual lovers, successful enough to defeat Sparta, is passed over, with only a few allusions to the fact that he had no wife and children (*Ep.* 5, 10). Similarly, the implications of a homosexual relationship between Hamilcar and his son-in-law Hasdrubal are brushed aside with the suggestion that all great men are slandered (*Has.* 3).

Nepos attributes much to Fortune in his lives, and it is indeed through fortune that his work has survived. Some critics say that he writes like a schoolmaster and barely deserves to be read. But if his good anecdotes and usually agreeable Latin are not sufficient, there are several more important reasons to read him. Firstly, when he writes the history of his own time, as in the *Atticus*, he shows himself to be a fair-minded critic and an important source. Secondly, it was Nepos' comparative lives that stood as a model behind the more important book of Plutarch over a century later. Finally, Nepos' biographies shed light on the concerns of the non-political classes during the civil war. His repeated yearning for freedom is included in many lives, and his hostility to the selfish and egotistical behavior of the political leaders of the late Republic provides a different perspective from the writings of Cicero, Caesar, and Sallust. Our understanding of the age is enriched by the survival of these biographies.

Tacitus' *Agricola*

With the fall of Domitian, as Tacitus turned his mind toward historical writing, he published a brief, laudatory biography of his father-in-law, Cn. Julius Agricola, long-time governor of Britain and one of the most successful generals of the Flavian era. With the publication of the *Agricola* in 98 CE, Tacitus fulfilled several purposes: he paid sincere tribute to Agricola; he opened the political critique on the repression of the Flavian era; and he announced the emergence of a great historian. There are many aspects to this encomiastic work, but it is above all a biography; Tacitus in fact uses the same phrase as Nepos (1, 4: *narrare vitam*) for the writing of a life history.

Some have suggested that the *Agricola* is a written version of the traditional funeral oration (*laudatio*) that Roman aristocrats delivered to praise the achievements of the deceased, and glorify the deeds of their ancestors. In the Empire such tributes often had a political edge, and Tacitus tells us that the published eulogies of the victims of Nero and the Flavians were burned in the Forum by the public executioners. Yet the *Agricola*, while it begins and ends as a eulogy, is much more. Actual funeral orations were quite short, highly rhetorical and emotional, and less concerned with actual achievements than with the reflected glory of the ancestors. Here Tacitus gives us a public life in its political context, framed by a few rhetorical commonplaces. Though it respects the spirit of the funeral speech, it is a biography − the first great biography from Rome.

Yet this brief but ambitious book goes well beyond the usual confines of ancient biography; it contains geography and ethnography, as well as historical narrative and formal speeches. In the form of biography, Tacitus has produced an embryonic version of his

complex historical masterpieces: the political agenda, the humiliation and resentment, and the literary strategies are already apparent.
Like the *Histories* and the *Annals*, it begins with a prologue linking
the present with the past. In the *Agricola* we see the genesis of the
historian's moral, political, and psychological ideas.

There was a long tradition among Greek and Roman historians
of including ethnographic material within larger historical works.
Within its biographical framework, the *Agricola* contains the basic
elements of ancient ethnography: discussions of geography, local
customs, and political institutions. His famous description of the
climate remains apt today: "The sky is covered by clouds and
frequent rain, but the cold is not severe" (12). He comments both
on agriculture and the mining of precious metals, and he compares
the British pearl-fishers with those of the Indian Ocean. There is
much – such as a discussion of the Druid religion – that is missing,
but we must be grateful for what Tacitus provides. It is unreasonable to expect that a few pages of ethnography within a biography
would satisfy our curiosity about barbarian Britain.

The large central historical section of the *Agricola* (10–38)
provided Tacitus with an opportunity to try his hand at narration
and speeches. In Agricola's campaigns on Anglesey and in Scotland,
Tacitus subordinates details of tactics to the visual and psychological sweep. Exceptionally in a biography, the author writes speeches
both for the hero and for his antagonist, the rebel chieftain
Calgacus. Though Calgacus is otherwise unknown, Tacitus projects
Roman attitudes and rhetoric into his speech to his 30,000 troops
and thus makes him an opponent worthy of Agricola. The speech
echoes accusations, familiar from Sallust, of Rome's greed, cruelty,
and love of power, and contains the most famous denunciation of
Roman imperialism:

> To robbery, to slaughter, and to theft, they give the false
> name of "Empire"; where they create desolation, they call it
> "peace."
>
> (*Agricola* 30)

Agricola's briefer speech also recalls an earlier text: Livy's account of
Scipio and Hannibal addressing their troops. Tacitus used both
rhetorical and historical skills in these first speeches that he wrote
for others' voices.

Though Agricola is not the most detailed character in Tacitus'
writing, there is a better balance here between the public and

private man, and the general appears as more credible (and more normal) than the characters of the *Histories* and the *Annals*. Tacitus devotes scant attention to Agricola's physical appearance; it is always the inner man that interests him. Thus we read of Agricola's Stoic endurance at the murder of his mother and the early death of his only son, and his continuing devotion to his wife and daughter. With the ring of authenticity, Tacitus emphasizes his father-in-law's amiability, openness, and modesty, and registers his annoyance at skepticism that such a famous man could be truly modest. Agricola's modesty seems more like excessive shyness – his arrival at Rome by night to avoid publicity and never meeting with more than one or two friends – but the loyal Tacitus represents it as the only way to combine achievement with survival under the rule of a tyrant.

Tacitus maintains here the serious tone that one expects in Roman historical writing, though not necessarily in biography. It becomes clear that at Rome political biography required some political analysis and was thus closer to the genre of history. Casual conversations, trivial details, and coarse anecdotes are absent, and Tacitus avoids the jokes found in Plutarch, not to mention the scandal of Suetonius. The severity is relieved only by the story of the barbarian Usipi who were sold as slaves and later became famous for telling their adventures. Although there are occasional examples of the irony he would develop in his mature style, the *Agricola* already contains the elevated tone, the brevity, and the descriptive power of Tacitus' later histories.

The *Agricola* contains several political themes later developed in greater detail: the connection of censorship with the loss of political freedom; the insidious workings of imperial freedmen; and the corruption of values under an autocratic regime, so that a good reputation might be more dangerous than a bad one. The central theme is one that lies at the heart of Tacitus' political philosophy: "even under bad emperors men can be great" (42). Like Agricola, one should avoid the inflammatory setting of the Senate and fight for Rome in the provinces, since there honor is still attainable. In Rome itself, the compromise (*moderatio*) of an Agricola serves Rome better than the dramatic resistance of a self-appointed martyr. It is a political apologia, but for whom? Do we sense Tacitus' own guilt and self-justification in his desire to distinguish compromise from collaboration? Whatever its origin, the theme would recur throughout his writings.

Although Domitian's despotism left Tacitus a bitter and angry man, he has only warmth and benevolence for Agricola. That the work is neither a political pamphlet nor a history is clear in the concluding chapters where Tacitus directly addresses Agricola. The address abounds with rhetorical commonplaces, but Tacitus invests them with a sincerity that lifts the conclusion from cliché to a powerful, personal farewell:

> If there is any dwelling-place for the spirits of the just; if, as the wise believe, noble souls do not perish with the body, rest thou in peace; and call us, thy family, from weak regrets and womanish laments to the contemplation of thy virtues, for which we must not weep nor beat the breast. Let us honor thee not so much with transitory praises as with our reverence, and, if our powers permit us, with our emulation...
>
> Whatever we loved, whatever we admired in Agricola, survives, and will survive in the hearts of men, in the succession of the ages, in the fame that waits on noble deeds. Over many indeed, of those who have gone before, as over the inglorious and ignoble, the waves of oblivion will roll; Agricola, made known to posterity by history and tradition, will live for ever.
>
> (*Agricola* 46)

Tacitus could not know the irony of his words when he asserts the achievements of Agricola would live forever. From the scant texts that survive we would know almost nothing of Agricola were it not for Tacitus. His military victories and his political courage survive only in this biography, written as an act of piety.

Gaius Suetonius Tranquillus
Lives of the Twelve Caesars

Life and works

The most important work of Latin biography is the twelve imperial lives written by the scholar-bureaucrat C. Suetonius Tranquillus (*c.* 70–130 CE). Little is known of his life. There are several internal references, five letters of the younger Pliny, an inscription from Hippo in North Africa, and several less certain references in later sources like the *Historia Augusta* and the Byzantine encyclopedia called the *Suda*. Even the dates of his birth and death can only be inferred. Yet, because his *Lives of the Caesars* is so unlike any other ancient book, it is important to consider how his shadowy life and career might have affected his writings.

Suetonius was probably born about 70 CE in north Africa to an equestrian father who had served as a military tribune at the battle of Bedriacum. His cognomen, Tranquillus, is attributed to his father's relief at peace established after the terrible civil wars of 69 CE. From the beginning he seems to have forgone any political or military ambitions in favor of intellectual pursuits. He was studying rhetoric in Rome by 88 CE, and a decade later he asked Pliny to seek a postponement of a law case he was trying. (Suetonius says he has been frightened by a bad dream, and has lost his confidence.) His lack of self-confidence and his unrhetorical temperament must have made him a mediocre advocate, and he directed his interests to scholarship. Pliny secured a military position for Suetonius, but he preferred to pass it on to a kinsman, and Pliny obliged. Pliny called his friend *probissimus honestissimus eruditissimus* – "honest, distinguished, and a fine scholar" – when he wrote to Trajan to secure for the childless Suetonius the honorary "right of three children"; the emperor wrote back to grant the request. It must have been Pliny's influence with the emperor Trajan that secured Suetonius the position *a studiis* where he did research for the emperor and also *a bibliotheca* (imperial librarian). The honorific inscription shows that Suetonius was later *ab epistulis* (private secretary to the emperor in charge of appointments) to Hadrian and probably traveled with that restless emperor. It was also through Pliny that he became close to Septicius Clarus, praetorian prefect under Hadrian to whom Suetonius dedicated the *Lives of the Caesars*. (Pliny also dedicated the first book of his *Letters* to Septicius.) In 122 CE the emperor dismissed both his prefect and Suetonius for, according to the *Historia Augusta*, disrespectful behavior toward the empress Sabina. Whatever the truth of this story, nothing more is known of Suetonius' life, though an allusion in his biography of Titus shows that he lived to 130 CE.

Suetonius wrote a wide range of books on linguistic, antiquarian, and biographical subjects, though for most only the titles survive. He was obviously a scholar of great range, since he wrote books on such diverse topics as the Roman year, the calendar, the names of seas, and the lives of famous prostitutes. The most frequently cited was his work on Greek and Roman games, including dancing, chariot-racing, theatrical performances, and gladiatorial combat. It must have been one of those early books that Suetonius was so loath to release in 105 CE that Pliny had to write him a politely scolding letter: "You outdo even my doubts and hesitations. So, bestir yourself, or else beware lest I drag those books out of you!" (*Ep.* 5, 10). But it was in biography that Suetonius had his greatest impact. His largest biographical collection was *Lives of Illustrious Men*, five books devoted to lives of intellectuals, with sections on poets, orators, historians, philosophers, and teachers of literature. There were perhaps one hundred lives in all. Unfortunately, the surviving section is from the book concerning teachers, divided into grammarians and rhetoricians – perhaps the least interesting portion of the work. In addition to thirty brief lives of teachers, longer surviving lives of Horace, Terence, Lucan, and (perhaps) Virgil came from Suetonius' collection. This collection required a great deal of reading and probably appeared between 110 and 120 CE. Jerome used it as the model for his lives of Christian authors.

The *Lives of the Caesars* was published in eight books. Each of the first six contained the life of a single ruler from Julius Caesar to Nero, the seventh book contained three emperors of 69, and the eighth covered the three Flavian emperors. Moral biography in the style of the Peripatetics held no attraction for Suetonius, whose imperial lives developed rather from the antiquarian lives of poets and grammarians he had already written. He thus adapts the Alexandrian tradition of scholarly biographies of intellectuals to lives of the emperors, and avoids the moral approach adopted by Nepos and by his own contemporaries Plutarch and Tacitus.

The Suetonian lives are notable in turning from a chronological to a largely thematic organization. Each life begins with a brief account of birth and family background and concludes with a record of the emperor's death, but the bulk of the biography is organized by categories like appearance, style of life, intellectual interests, entertainments provided, virtues and vices.

> Having given as it were a summary of his life, I shall now take up its various phases one by one, not in chronological order, but by classes, to make the account clearer and more intelligible.
>
> (*Life of Augustus* 9)[2]

This is a well-known rhetorical device, "division into parts," used for the purposes of clarity in an oration, but the actual categories may vary from one life to another. For example, the physical description of Claudius is included among his vices, while that of Nero is given after his death. The essential element is that the topical arrangement allows greater emphasis on the individual emperor's private life and character rather than the chronological progression of his reign.

Biography versus history

It is important that we judge the *Lives* on Suetonius' own terms as biography and not regard them as an inferior form of history. His purposes, methods, and results were all quite different from the literary and moral aims of an historian. The genre of history at Rome had a chronological, usually annalistic, structure, a highly elevated rhetorical and poetic style, and a focus on such public subjects as political and military affairs. Suetonius uses a non-chronological organization to make it clear that he is not writing history, his style is workmanlike, and he prefers to treat private life rather than state business. Most of all, the writing of history was a moral act, while Suetonius merely presents the data and allows, or pretends to allow, the reader to form a personal judgment. Unlike the historians of antiquity, Suetonius is not primarily a literary artist; he is the ancestor of the modern scholar.

The popular image of Suetonius as a crude scandalmonger obscures his formidable research skills which far surpassed those of his contemporaries. As we read Suetonius, we can see him at work on his card index (or its Roman equivalent), sorting anecdotes according to theme. (It is not at all clear how ancient scholars did such research and retrieved relevant information, but it is certain that memory played a far greater role than it does today.) He drew on a wide range of materials: archives, acts of the Senate, pamphlets, histories, monuments, inscriptions, and oral tradition, including his father's experiences in Otho's army. We can see his scholarly delight in handling original evidence, as when he comments that he has had proof for Augustus' original cognomen of Thurinus (with which he was taunted by Marc Antony):

> That he was surnamed Thurinus I may assert on very trust-worthy evidence, since I once obtained a bronze statuette, representing him as a boy and inscribed with that name in letters almost illegible from age. This I presented to the emperor Hadrian, who cherishes it among the Lares of his bed-chamber.
>
> (*Life of Augustus* 8)

Likewise he boasts that he has seen Nero's own private notebooks:

> I have had in my possession notebooks and papers with
> some well-known verses of his, written in his own hand and
> in such wise that it was perfectly evident that they were not
> copied or taken down from dictation, but worked out
> exactly as one writes when thinking and creating; so many
> instances were there of words erased or struck through and
> written above the lines.
>
> (*Life of Nero* 52)

His greatest treasure was letters from that indefatigable correspondent, Augustus. He quotes from dozens of letters, not only in the life of Augustus but in later lives as well as his lives of Virgil and Horace. Some of Augustus' letters had been published, since both Tacitus and Pliny refer to them, but Suetonius must have found many autograph copies in the archives, since he comments on Augustus' peculiar way of squeezing material onto the end of a line as well as oddities of his spelling. Some letters deal with the most confidential family matters, like the problem of Livia's dribbling, stuttering, twitching, and limping grandson Claudius. Augustus writes to Livia (*Claudius* 4) that he is concerned that the crowd might laugh at the young prince if he sits in the imperial box at the games. In a later letter, the emperor offers, in Livia's absence, to dine each night with young Claudius to keep him from some undesirable friends. The letters shed touching light on a prominent family struggling to minimize the embarrassment of a problem child.

These letters and other source material made the lives of Julius Caesar and Augustus the richest, and longest, of the lives: about 45 and 65 modern pages. Lives of later Julio-Claudians (Tiberius, Caligula, Claudius, Nero) range between 30 and 42 pages, while Vespasian and Domitian (in whose reigns Suetonius lived) are only 15 and 18 pages each. The histories of other writers, like Livy and Tacitus, become longer and more detailed as they approach the lifetime; this pattern makes sense since there are both more abundant sources for, and greater interest in, the more recent past. Why then are Suetonius' lives of Julius and Augustus the fullest? There are several possible reasons, which are not mutually exclusive. It has often been suggested that after Suetonius was dismissed from his post he no longer had access to private letters in the imperial archives. That is a real possibility and may explain the absence of later correspondence, but it does not explain the huge disparity in the scope of the later lives. As we have seen from his discovery of Nero's notebook, Suetonius could find original materials on later reigns. Another possibility concerns his great contemporary, Tacitus. When Suetonius began working on the *Lives*, Tacitus had published his history of the Flavian era and was known among the circle of Pliny to be working on the emperors from Tiberius onwards. Hence Suetonius would have seen little or no competition on the early period. Finally, it is possible, or even probable, that Suetonius had a particular interest in the era of Julius and Augustus. It seems to be his main archival preoccupation in the earlier lives of poets, and references back to it recur in later imperial lives. Some combination of opportunity, motivation, and personal interest (or lack of it) caused Suetonius to produce briefer and less satisfying lives as he approached his own day.

How do we reconcile Suetonius the administrator with Suetonius the scholar? To the Romans of his era no gulf would be apparent, since librarians and archivists had for centuries been scholars. When Julius Caesar decided to establish Rome's first public library, he turned to Varro, the greatest scholar of the age. Suetonius' occupation and literary training not only provided access to research material, but also shaped his biographies. He gives us interesting material on the reading habits of the emperors since, for him, this was an important window on personality. And of course he has a deep interest in the emperors' correspondence, not only the letters themselves, but how they are dealt with: Julius read them at the games, while Vespasian dealt with some letters before dressing for the day. He even includes cases of misbehavior by imperial secretaries. Augustus punished a certain Thallus (by having his legs broken) for selling confidential information, while under Claudius the freedmen had a field day forging and amending documents for a price.

One clear indication that Suetonius is at heart a scholar is his habit of quoting verbatim, both in Latin and in Greek, rather than rewriting a text in his own style. His failure to do the artistically respectable thing provides a treasure of primary material that would otherwise have been lost, especially letters and quotations. Some famous sayings come to us from Suetonius, such as Julius Caesar's statement on crossing the Rubicon to invade Italy: *jacta alea est* (*Julius* 32, "The die is cast"). During his triumph over the king of Pontus, Suetonius reports that Caesar displayed on placards only three words to describe the war: *VENI–VIDI–VICI* (*Julius* 37, "I came, I saw, I conquered"). Quotations in Greek are very rare in

Latin literary texts, though we know from Cicero's letters that the elite peppered their correspondence (and probably conversation) with Greek as the eighteenth-century Russian aristocrats did with French. It is especially interesting to see that the last words both of Julius and Augustus were in Greek. Julius Caesar turned to his assassin and former protégé Marcus Brutus with the words καὶ σὺ τέκνον ("You too, my child?"). Fifty-seven years later, after Augustus asked his friends whether he had played his part well in the comedy of life, he quoted two lines from the close of a Greek comedy:

> "Since I've played my part well, all clap your hands
> And dismiss me from the stage with applause."
> *(Life of Augustus* 99)

The *Lives of the Caesars* is different in matter and manner from other Roman histories or biographies, because it is a book written by and for the equestrian, that is, for the administrative class. Suetonius and the equestrians shared the culture of the senators, but did not have the same interest in rhetoric or politics. The loss of freedom lamented by Tacitus and others was the political freedom of a few hundred members of the senatorial elite; the equestrians never had such freedom and preferred to judge the emperors on their effectiveness. They were basically sympathetic toward the principate, and preferred concrete data to ideological rhetoric when evaluating the performance of a particular emperor. It is important to know this to understand why Suetonius is much less interested in political issues than in building construction, the celebration of games, and financial policies. These matters, like the emperor's effectiveness with paperwork, are of paramount importance to the administrators of the Empire. Yet if Suetonius writes from an equestrian perspective, he does not display a parochial self-interest. Emperors who blatantly tried to promote the *equites* to the disadvantage of the Senate, as Nero did (*Nero* 37), did not merit praise. Suetonius believed that bad emperors like Caligula, Nero, and Domitian were hated by all elements of Roman society, just as the good were loved by all.

Suetonius wrote his lives of the Caesars neither to titillate, nor to mock the imperial system, though his writings have surely had such results with later readers. He wished primarily to provide in a scholarly way the material necessary for the reader to make his own judgment. Thus, for example, he devotes much space to the celebration of games. These were an important element in ensuring concord in the population of the capital and had a ritual role in the public contacts between rulers and ruled. Augustus boasts of his games in the *Res Gestae*, and Pliny mentions them in his panegyric oration to Trajan — games were an important element in judging the effectiveness of emperors. So Suetonius provides information about the games of each emperor; sometimes emperors who are otherwise detestable (Nero and Domitian) are commended for their entertainments. So too the biographer provides physical descriptions, sexual perversions, building programs, religious devotion — all to be taken into account by the reader in forming an individual judgment. He particularly records the growing Hellenization of the imperial court: music, homosexuality, gambling, dancing, and astrology. This empirical approach, with its superficial impartiality, contrasts sharply with Tacitus' moral pronouncements based primarily on political criteria. Suetonius believes his readers would rather read a list of virtues and vices than deduce them from a narrative. The very form of his book seems designed for administrators.

He avoids the elevated style of history, and writes the clear, businesslike Latin of a scholar. In fact, he writes better Latin than other technical writers of the early Empire like Vitruvius on architecture, Celsus on medicine, and Frontinus on aqueducts. He also had greater stylistic freedom than the historians were allowed. Not only can Suetonius use obscenities, but a range of earthy or merely banal details are not out of place here as they would be in rhetorical prose. Thus his physical description of Nero:

> He was about the average height, his body marked with spots and malodorous, his hair light blond, his features regular rather than attractive, his eyes blue and somewhat weak, his neck over-thick, his belly prominent, and his legs very slender.
>
> (*Life of Nero* 51)

While Suetonius does not really have the art to embellish a scene, his narrative ability is such that it can vigorously bring inherently dramatic scenes to life: the assassination of Julius Caesar; the accession of Claudius; the death of Nero. This last scene is Suetonius' greatest literary moment, though as always with Nero, much of the theatricality and melodrama come from the emperor himself:

> At last, while his companions one and all urged him to save himself as soon as possible from the indignities that threatened him, he bade them dig a grave in his presence,

proportioned to the size of his own person, collect any bits of marble that could be found, and at the same time bring water and wood for presently disposing of his body. As each of these things were done, he wept and said again and again: "What an artist the world is losing!"

While he hesitated, a letter was brought to Phaon by one of his couriers. Nero snatching it from his hand read that he had been pronounced a public enemy by the Senate, and that they were seeking to punish him in the ancient fashion; and he asked what manner of punishment that was. When he learned that the criminal was stripped, fastened by the neck in a fork and then beaten to death with rods, in mortal terror he seized two daggers which he had brought with him, and then, after trying the point of each, put them up again, pleading that the fated hour had not yet come. Now he would beg Sporus to begin to lament and wail, and now entreat someone to help him take his life by setting him the example; anon he reproached himself for his cowardice in such words as these: "To live is a scandal and shame – this does not become Nero, does not become him – one should be resolute at such times – come, rouse thyself."

(*Life of Nero* 49)

Conclusion

Suetonius is both the pre-eminent Latin biographer as well as an important source for the first century CE, especially for the periods for which Tacitus' text has not survived. Though he was once criticized as a salacious scandalmonger, scholarly criticism of his *Lives of the Caesars* is now directed either toward his weakness as a biographer or his inadequacy as a source. The latter criticisms are, of course, unfair, since Suetonius never intended to be a "source"; he only wished to write biographies. Therefore our dissatisfaction with his omission of political material like the crisis under Tiberius, his lack of interest in chronology, his refusal to synthesize an emperor's personality as a totality, and his unwillingness to enter into the thoughts of his characters all stem from our desire for Suetonius to behave like an historian. But he is not an historian and our demand that he behave like one is unfair.

On the other hand, some criticisms of his biographies may be justified. When he repeatedly refers to sources vaguely as "some say," we can expect better from a scrupulous scholar. He is also too quick to accept, or at least include, scandalous stories which even he does not believe. He writes of the death of Augustus' stepson Drusus:

> He made no secret of his intention of restoring the old-time form of government, whenever he should have the power. It is because of this, I think, that some have made bold to write that he was an object of suspicion to Augustus; that the emperor recalled him from his province, and when he did not obey at once, took him off by poison. This I have mentioned, rather not to pass it by, than that I think it true or even probable; for as a matter of fact Augustus loved him so dearly while he lived that he always named him joint-heir along with his sons, as he once declared in the Senate...
>
> *(Life of Claudius* 1)

Such innuendoes might be understandable in a rhetorical historian, but not in Suetonius. There is also sloppiness, as when he claims that Claudius was poisoned by mushrooms or by a drink (*Claudius* 44), but then in his life of Nero at one point blames the mushrooms (*Nero* 33) and elsewhere the drink (*Nero* 39). We might also expect a bit more psychological penetration from a biographer. Finally, the biographies of the Flavian emperors are woefully inadequate, though we have no idea for what reason Suetonius chose to make them so much skimpier than the early lives.

On the other hand, even as a source, Suetonius has much more to recommend him. His objectivity and indiscriminate approach to his material has preserved an enormous amount that any Roman historian would have jettisoned. One might compare him to an indiscriminate collector who gathers the books, pamphlets, newspapers and other ephemera of the time; a century later scholars are grateful that the collector did not discriminate since he has thus saved material that actual libraries would have thrown away. Moreover, the fact that Suetonius did not edit his material makes it more valuable than the elaborate speeches found in historians' texts.

On some occasions, Suetonius is quite impressive in his treatment of material. In his life of Julius Caesar, he provides critical reactions to Caesar's commentaries from Cicero, Hirtius, and Asinius Pollio (*Julius* 56). Then, rather than recounting the conquest of Gaul, he assumes his reader knows it and provides his own extended analysis (*Julius* 57–70) of the generalship of Caesar, including discussions of personality, tactics, strategy, and relations with his troops. If Caesar's own book had not survived, we would surely complain that Suetonius had not summarized it, but in the circumstances his treatment is more thoughtful and probing than we might expect of a biographer.

There are also several cases where the biographer seems determined to correct mistakes in Tacitus, though the historian is never named. In the life of Tiberius, Suetonius refers to "some" who have written that Augustus did not think well of Tiberius and only named him as his successor to please his wife, or so that he himself would seem better to posterity. This is a direct allusion to Tacitus' report of popular gossip at the funeral of Augustus (*Ann.* 1, 10). The biographer is explicitly critical:

> But after all I cannot be led to believe that an emperor of the utmost prudence and foresight acted without consideration, especially in a matter of so great moment. It is my opinion that after weighing the faults and the merits of Tiberius, he decided that the latter preponderated.
>
> (*Life of Tiberius* 21)

He then quotes passages from a half-dozen of Augustus' letters to prove his point. Another instance is Tacitus' brief comment (*Ann.* 14, 16) that Nero relied on others to provide him with poetic lines. Suetonius actually consulted Nero's manuscript notebook to ascertain that the poems were in his own handwriting, with crossings-out as if they were being worked out. A third case shows Suetonius rising to a level of critical analysis and substantiated argument rarely found in ancient historical writing. The biographer says he is responding to Pliny's assertion, based on an inscription, that Caligula was born in his father's military camp in Gaul, but the thoroughness of his discussion makes it likely that he was actually refuting Tacitus' passing comment on the same point. Suetonius first discounts the inscription – it could as well apply to the birth of Caligula's sister – and then produces a letter from Augustus as well as the *Acts of the Senate* that place the birth at Antium on the Italian coast. In these three instances Suetonius successfully uses research and documentation to rebut his more distinguished, but always unnamed, contemporary. It must have given him considerable satisfaction.

The *Lives of the Caesars* made such an impression that biography replaced narrative history as the preferred form of political narrative for over 250 years. Suetonius himself became the model for later biographers, both pagan and Christian. He was also important in the Carolingian era as the model for Einhard's very Suetonian *Life of Charlemagne*. It was inevitable that his portrayal of the outrageous behavior of the Roman emperors would find many readers in Renaissance Italy. Petrarch and Boccaccio were among the earliest to read him in manuscript and use him in their own writings. Only in the eighteenth century did the moral biographies of Plutarch replace Suetonius as the model for biography.

Suetonius created a unique literary form. Not only were his lives a marriage of Alexandrian intellectual biography and Roman features, but his was the first series of linked lives from the ancient world, anticipating the *Parallel Lives* of Plutarch. This scholar was not an historian, but he remains one of the two most important sources for the early Empire. His lives are particularly useful for Augustus, and for the reigns of Caligula and Claudius where Tacitus' text is totally or partially lost. His prodigious learning provides much that cannot be found elsewhere, especially information about literary, cultural, and scientific developments. The scattered data are the more valuable since they are presented with cool detachment rather than as part of an argument. If he is a lesser intellectual figure than his Greek contemporary Plutarch, he is in many ways a more valuable historical source.

Historia Augusta

One of the strangest literary texts from the ancient world is the series of biographies preserved in a ninth-century codex (from which all later copies derive), and for centuries it has infuriated scholars and delighted ordinary readers. The manuscript is entitled "Lives of Various Emperors and Pretenders from the Deified Hadrian to Numerianus Written by Different Authors" (*vitae diversorum principum et tyrannorum a divo Hadriano usque ad Numerianum diversis compositae*). In the seventeenth century, the editor Isaac Casaubon gave it the name *Historia Augusta*, since in a passing reference the text (*Life of Tacitus* 10, 3) refers to the emperor Tacitus as a descendant of the "author of the imperial history" (*scriptorem historiae Augustae*). That name has stuck down to the present day.

There are thirty biographies in all, though some contain lives of more than one ruler: four with two lives, two with three, one with four, and one collective biography called "The Thirty Tyrants" gives very brief accounts of various pretenders to imperial power in the third century CE. The entire collection covers the period from Hadrian to Numerianus, 117–284 CE, though there is a lacuna for the period between 244 and 259 CE. The lives, which include emperors, their heirs, and unsuccessful pretenders to the throne, are attributed to six different authors: Aelius Spartianus, Julius Capitolinus, Aelius Lampridius, Vulcacius Gallicanus, Trebellius Pollio, and Flavius Vopiscus. The authors evidently lived in the time of Diocletian (284–306 CE) and Constantine (306–37 CE), since many lives are dedicated to these emperors and the first four authors occasionally address them directly. Though Pollio and Vopiscus do not dedicate their biographies to the emperors, references within their writings indicate that they were contemporaries of the others.

As early scholars attempted to describe the characteristics of the individual authors, they began to find the attributions troubling. Even Edward Gibbon, who made much use of these biographies in the early chapters of *The Decline and Fall of the Roman Empire*, smelled a rat and came close to despair in the *Advertisement to the Notes*:

> But there is so much perplexity in the titles of the mss., and so many disputes have arisen among the critics concerning their number, their names, and their respective property, that for the most part I have quoted them without distinction, under the general and well-known title of *Augustan History*.
>
> (Gibbon, *Decline and Fall of the Roman Empire* I ix)

The biographies follow the model of Suetonius, beginning with the birth and early life, and closing with the death and posthumous honors or reputation. In the large central section of the biography, the material is divided into categories. Like Suetonius', these lives are filled with the gossip of tabloid journalism mixed with a large number of "documents" (letters, official decrees, senatorial acclamations, etc.), quotations from the emperors, and references to other ancient writers. Major lives may run to well over twenty modern pages, though some pretenders treated in "The Thirty Tyrants" may warrant as little as a paragraph.

The problems with the Historia Augusta

During the last two centuries scholars have identified a wide range of problems in this strange book. One is a seeming homogeneity of style in all the lives, a point that has recently been confirmed by computer analysis. This stylistic uniformity is accompanied by similarities of attitude and treatment: a pro-senatorial bias and polemics against hereditary monarchy and the imperial court, as well as similar kinds of digressions and puns on the names of emperors. Even more serious, scholars gradually proved that most of the 130 documents included range from the suspicious to the outrageously false. The earlier lives, which contain more reliable material that can be cross-checked against other sources, do not contain such documents, but they proliferate in the more suspicious lives. Likewise, many of the names and sources mentioned throughout are fabrications. There are also anachronisms, such as the mention of Pertinax as emperor in a speech by Marcus Aurelius, who died thirteen years before Pertinax became emperor (*Avidius Cass.* 8, 5). The most serious chronological problem is the material that comes from Aurelius Victor and Eutropius, whose books were published in 360 and 369 CE respectively, a half-century after the dates when the biographies were ostensibly written.

Another problem is that several of the authors claim that they have written lives of *all* the emperors:

> It is my purpose, Diocletian Augustus, greatest of a long line of rulers, to present to the knowledge of your Divine Majesty, not only those who have held as ruling emperors the high post which you maintain – I have done this as far as the Deified Hadrian – but also those who have borne the name of Caesar, though never hailed emperors or Augusti.
> (Aelius Spartianus in *Aelius* 1)[3]

> For I have undertaken, Diocletian Augustus, to set down in writing the lives of all who have held the imperial title whether rightfully or without right, in order that you may become acquainted with all the emperors that have ever worn the purple.
> (Vulcacius Gallicanus in *Avidius Cass.* 3, 3)

If several series of lives were written, who chose which ones to include in this collection? Is it possible that an editor rewrote the lives, thus producing the stylistic and methodological similarities?

What is the Historia Augusta?

In 1889 the distinguished Roman historian Hermann Dessau suggested that the entire *Historia Augusta* was written by a single author in 395 CE – from sixty years to one hundred years after it claimed to be. The next century produced a torrent of scholarly criticism, arguments, and hypotheses, culminating in the pronouncements of the greatest Roman historian of the recent past, Sir Ronald Syme (1903–89). Syme concluded that the authorship, date, dedication, and all the documents were fraudulent, though he agreed with Dessau that the work was written by a single author about 395 CE. Where does this mountain of scholarly controversy leave us?

The reason this dispute is so crucial is that the *Historia Augusta* is the most important source – or at least would be, if we can believe it – for the second and third centuries CE, the apogee of the Roman Empire and the beginning of its collapse. Even if the authors and the date are false, anything we may be able to deduce about them is valuable. There is much reliable history in the early lives, so an understanding of date, authorship, and purpose of the work might help us determine what else is reliable. Even the act of fabrication might tell us something about the time in which it was composed or compiled. Hence the historical stakes are high in trying to understand the origins and motivations of this extraordinary book.

The lives contain outrageous scandal mixed with a pretense of scholarship. In addition to casual cross-references to other bogus material in the collection, the authors refer repeatedly to otherwise unknown "sources." A certain Aelius Junius Cordus is referred to two dozen times, and is even criticized:

> For we do not think we need recount absurd and silly tales such as Junius Cordus has written concerning his domestic pleasures and petty matters of that sort. If any desire to know these things, let him read Cordus; Cordus tells what slaves each and every emperor had and what friends, how many mantles and how many cloaks.
>
> (*Gordiani* 21, 3–4)

Since Junius almost certainly never existed, these repeated references look like a prank or a private joke. So too does Flavius Vopiscus' beginning of his *Aurelian* (1–2), where he rides up to the Palatine with the prefect of the city in 303 CE, Junius Tiberianus, who offers to get special permission to see linen rolls with the emperor Aurelian's diary. The mention in the passage of the "fellow-biographer" Trebellius Pollio almost certainly clinches the fact that the entire scene is a fabrication. So too the following passage where the author's creative imagination conjures up ivory books:

And now, lest any one consider that I have rashly put faith in some Greek or Latin writer, there is in the Ulpian Library, in the sixth case, an ivory book in which is written out this decree of the Senate, signed by [the emperor] Tacitus in his own hand. For those decrees which pertained to the emperors were long inscribed in books of ivory.

(*Tacitus* 8, 1–2)

If the biographies are similar in style, there are certainly differences. The lives of important second-century emperors seem reasonably reliable and have virtually no suspicious documentation. But the later life of Severus Alexander (222–35 CE) reads like an historical novel whose protagonist greatly resembles an idealized picture of Julian, called the Apostate (360–3 CE). The lives of the later third century seem to deteriorate as the author becomes more inventive in creating documents and bolder in his falsification of history.

In recent decades the *Historia Augusta*, which was once seen merely as a mediocre collection of badly written biographies, has taken on a new interest; it has been called a hoax, a forgery, a history *à clef* for an inner circle, and even a spoof of imperial biography. No one any longer takes it at face value, and nearly all scholars believe it was written or rewritten by a single author. The most important issues now are when and why this fraud was constructed. Hypotheses have placed it at various dates between 337 and 500 CE, but in recent years scholars have come to agree that it was written about the last decade of the fourth century – somewhere around the date suggested by Dessau and Syme. The reasons are numerous, but one is the dependence of the *Historia Augusta* on Book 15 of Ammianus Marcellinus, first published in 392 CE.

The more difficult question is why. "*Cui bono?*" asked Theodor Mommsen: "Who profited from it?" There are actually two questions: why write a fraudulent book and why disguise its authorship? The second question is a bit easier. By projecting his work back to the reigns of Diocletian and Constantine, the author gave it increased credibility and greater authority. Whether he has a political or religious agenda, or just wanted to write a popular book, an earlier date increased his chance of success. Another possible reason for anonymity is to ensure his personal security. The pro-pagan, pro-senatorial bias was common enough among the aristocratic elite of the late fourth century, but the *Historia Augusta* also contains repeated criticisms of the imperial court and even sympathy for Republican views. For example, the Empire is shown as prospering in the six months in 275 CE between the death of Aurelian and the selection of Tacitus as his successor (*Tacitus* 1–2). Since the interregnum was actually about two months, the author lengthens it and thus emphasizes the advantages of senatorial control. He might prefer to attribute such views to a fictitious writer.

Why write such a book? The biases of the author have long been recognized, but it seems unlikely that the *Historia Augusta* was primarily written as a work of propaganda. It is simply too frivolous, and too scandalous, to be taken seriously in support of political or religious ideas. A passage at the end of the biography of the pretenders leaves little doubt that the author comes close to flaunting his hoax:

> Now bestow on anyone you wish this little book, written not with elegance but with fidelity to truth. Nor, in fact, do I seem to myself to have made any promise of literary style, but only of facts, for these little works which I have composed on the lives of the emperors I do not write down but only dictate, and I dictate them, indeed, with that speed, which, whether I promise aught of my own accord or you request it, you urge with such insistence that I have not even the opportunity of drawing breath.
>
> (*Thirty Tyrants* 33, 8)

We must imagine the author, surrounded by scattered papyrus copies of earlier sources, dictating to his slave. It would seem he decided to produce a series of lives, taking up where his great model Suetonius left off. He should have begun with the short-lived Nerva and the competent (but dull) general Trajan. He preferred to begin with the more colorful Hadrian – hence the first lie – and when he begins there are reasonably good sources available. Thus he need only mix in an occasional salacious story. But as he proceeds and the better sources fall away, he roguishly invents what he needs, more and more outrageously, as he moves from biography to fiction. There is little question that the author was humorous and irreverent, and that he immensely enjoyed the process of creating the hoax. Whether he was a lawyer, an historian, or a grammarian – all have been suggested – he added his own private jokes: elaborate references to his six fictional alter-egos, strange etymologies, and genuine quotations transferred from one emperor to another. More than one scholar has been reduced to fury by this behavior. But our author is no more a lunatic than those tabloid editors who boost circulation with Elvis re-sightings. He simply became so caught up with his own creation that his talent as a biographer was far exceeded by his genius as inventor of fiction.

The Historia Augusta *as an historical source*

Since historians cannot afford to cast aside any substantial source, it is necessary to analyze the lives carefully to see what may come from reliable earlier sources. Scholars have sometimes been overcritical: Veturius Macrinus, praetorian prefect in 193 CE, was dismissed as an invention until an inscription confirmed his existence. Even in this fabricated *Augustan History*, most of the life of Hadrian can be confirmed by other historical sources, like Cassius Dio, or by archaeological remains such as the brickwork of the Pantheon, Hadrian's Wall in Britain, and his villa in Tivoli. But we must always be aware that what is not otherwise confirmed may be a historical fact, an invention, or a joke. Those three possibilities must continuously be kept in mind.

Some of the author's sources are known, though few have survived. For the second century we have a set of biographies as far as Caracalla by an unnamed author – scholars imaginatively call him Ignotus – who seems to have been reasonably reliable, and another set of more gossipy ones by Marius Maximus (whom the *Historia Augusta* mentions almost thirty times). In imitation of Suetonius, Marius, who was consul in 197 and 223 CE, wrote twelve lives from Nerva to Heliogabalus. He was almost certainly the model our impish author was attempting to imitate or even supplant. Our author also used the Syrian Greek Herodian for 180–238 CE, the Athenian Dexippus down to 270 CE, and a lost imperial history (known as *Kaisergeschichte*) for the period after 260 CE, as well as surviving writers like Aurelius Victor and Eutropius.

Perhaps we should conclude the brief examination of this difficult text with the author's final words. Even at a distance of sixteen centuries we can tell that his tongue is firmly in his cheek:

> And now, my friend, accept this gift of mine, which, as I have often said, I have brought out to the light of day, not because of its elegance of style but because of its learned research, chiefly with this purpose in view, that if any gifted stylist should wish to reveal the deeds of the emperors, he might not lack the material, having, as he will, my little books

as ministers to his eloquence. I pray you, then, to be content and to contend that in this work I had the wish to write better than I had the power.

(*Carus* 21, 2–3)

7

AUTOBIOGRAPHY AT ROME

Greek antecedents

It has been said that autobiography was unknown to the ancient Greeks. This statement is true only if we restrict autobiography to that genre of personal self-revelation best known in St Augustine's *Confessions* and in writings of later writers like Jean-Jacques Rousseau. That genre, in which the author traces his or her educational and emotional development, was indeed unknown in Greece. Writing about oneself indeed flourished in Greek poetry – from Hesiod's story of his dispossession, Sappho's emotional attachments to her female students, and the early poet-philosophers' revealing aspects of their lives. But writing about oneself is not autobiography, which requires a historical dimension of writing about one's past life. Yet there is in fact a form of autobiography we find in Greece that is also popular today: the memoirs of a public figure. Figures like Henry Kissinger or Colin Powell may not tell us about their adolescent temptations and spiritual development, but they provide an "inside perspective" – usually in terms of an *apologia* for their actions – on important political or military affairs. Similar memoirs survive from the fourth century BCE, and there may have been even earlier ones.

The most famous Greek military memoir is the *Anabasis* ("The March Up-Country") by the Athenian Xenophon, who had enlisted as a mercenary under the Persian prince Cyrus in his attempt to wrest the throne from his brother. The book tells of the march of 10,000 Greek recruits to Mesopotamia, where disaster befell them in 400 BCE. With Cyrus dead on the battlefield and most of the Greek senior officers murdered by treachery, newly appointed generals (including the thirty-year-old Xenophon) had to lead the remnants of the army through what is today Iraq, the mountains of Kurdistan, and eastern Turkey to the Black Sea. About twenty years later, Xenophon wrote his account in the third person – a model for later autobiography, and praiseworthy for the attempt at objectivity.

During the fourth century important public autobiographies appeared in different forms. The orator Isocrates, charged with tax evasion, did what modern defense attorneys do so well – he represented himself as a victim of a terrible conspiracy. In his speech *Antidosis* (354 BCE), the orator makes himself into another Socrates persecuted for teaching young Athenians in an unconventional way. In the process he looks back on his long life as an educator and speechwriter and thus provides an autobiography of his public life. A few decades later, the great Athenian orator and statesman Demosthenes, in his speech *On the Crown* (330 BCE), gives an autobiographical account of his entire career of opposing Philip of Macedon. Athens had fought the Macedonians, and lost, and Demosthenes tries to justify his life and the policies he supported. The other important autobiographical text of the fourth century is the remarkable *Seventh Letter* of Plato. (This letter is regarded sometimes as genuine, sometimes as a fabrication by Plato's school soon after his death. I follow Misch and Momigliano in regarding it as genuine.) It is the greatest autobiographical letter of antiquity: in it Plato reviews his political involvement in Sicily, where he hoped with the help of his protégé Dion to put into practice his idea of a perfect state ruled by a "philosopher-king." He reviews his actions in great detail – the letter is in fact longer than his early dialogues – and admits that he failed, and in the process relates his own goals to the historical developments in fourth-century Sicily.

Throughout the Hellenistic world, kings and generals continued to write memoirs, though none has survived. The most famous was by Aratos of Sicyon, who was elected sixteen times general of the Achaean League in the Peloponnesus. His autobiography, which was used by Polybius and Plutarch, also had an apologetic tone, since Aratos had made the disastrous mistake of inviting the Macedonians into the Peloponnesus to help the Achaeans against the Spartans. When the Macedonian army came, and then stayed, some Achaeans surely recalled that the original reason their League was formed was to repel Macedon. Hence Aratos' self-justifying memoir. There were many other works, including the day-by-day military diaries of Pyrrhus, the diaries of Alexander, and a bizarre hodgepodge of a personal diary by Ptolemy VIII, which was being read with pleasure centuries later. None of these books survives, but their existence demonstrates the Greek tradition that lay behind Roman auto-biography.

Hypomnema and *Commentarius*

During the late Republic the Roman political class turned enthu-siastically to autobiographical writing. They used several overlapping Greek and Latin terms for these autobiographies: the Greek *hypomnema* (any sort of memoir) and *ephemeris* (diary); and the Latin *commentarius* (private aide-memoire, or notes for later use). I will here use *hypomnema* for the political memoir and *commentarius* for the (supposedly) private journal. The political class at Rome was enormously competitive in their quest for office and honors. Hence it is only natural that reports sent back to Rome by its generals, which might lead to the bestowal of a triumph, would be carefully crafted. Some of these reports and reminiscences were preserved in family archives. When Julius Caesar commented that his *dignitas* was dearer to him than his life, he spoke for many aristocrats who wished to equal their ancestors and to be so remembered by their descendants. They would leave behind them what they could – inscriptions, honorific poems, letters, and diaries – to improve their posthumous reputation.

Though these documents were at first preserved in the family, by the second century BCE leading Romans published autobiographical documents. As early as 190 BCE Scipio Africanus published a pamphlet in letter form, probably in Greek, detailing his victories as a young man against the Carthaginians in Spain before he finally defeated Hannibal in north Africa. A generation later Cato, despite his expressed opposition to a cult of personality, incorporated auto-biographical material including speeches in the last books of his *Origines*. By the beginning of the first century BCE, it had become common for retired political figures to write and publish their memoirs (*hypomnemata*) to justify their political or military careers. The first was M. Aemilius Scaurus, consul of 115 and leader of the Senate for a quarter-century. Cicero praised the dignity and sincerity of his speech, though he clearly regarded it as more honorable than charming. He recognizes that the literary charm of Xenophon's timeless and idealized *Cyropaedia* was more generally appealing in 46 BCE than Scaurus' austere account of his political career:

> We have orations of his and the three books about his own life addressed to L. Fufidius; very well worth reading, though no one reads them. They prefer nowadays to read

the life and training of Cyrus, a splendid book no doubt, but not so suited to our conditions and not deserving to be preferred to Scaurus' encomium of himself.

(*Brutus* 112, tr. Hendrickson (Loeb))

About the same time as Scaurus, the former consul Q. Lutatius Catulus also tried to redress what he saw as unfair credit given to Marius for their joint campaigns in 101 BCE against German invaders into Italy. It wounded Catulus that Marius was generally regarded as the savior of Italy, so he wrote his own version in what Cicero called "a smooth Xenophontean style" (*Brutus* 132) and perhaps even intended it to be turned into an epic poem in his honor. P. Rutilius Rufus had a more justifiable grievance, since he was exiled in 92 BCE for his obstinate integrity in opposing equestrian corruption while serving as governor of Asia. He ostentatiously returned to serve his exile in Asia where the admiring citizens of Smyrna protected him during the Mithridatic Wars, when tens of thousands of Romans were murdered. Rufus, who was a Stoic and a member of the Scipionic circle, expressed his philosophy in his autobiography, where he bitterly attacked his enemies. Two centuries later his work was recalled when Tacitus bemoaned that in his day men were neither permitted to accomplish great deeds nor to memorialize them:

Many too thought that to write their own lives showed the confidence of integrity rather than presumption. Of Rutilius and Scaurus no one doubted their honesty or questioned their motives.

(*Agricola* 1)

Since Romans gave little weight to the virtue of modesty, the habit of writing autobiographical memoirs spread quickly among the Roman political elite.

The other form of autobiography (*commentarius*) grew from the private diary and pretended to be a personal memorandum of the bare facts. The hope was that an historian or biographer might later turn these notes into literary form. These were not apologetic, or literary in any way, but what Sulla later called "the raw material of history." These derive their form from the military diaries of Greek kings like Pyrrhus and their content from inscriptions left to memorialize the lives of famous Romans. While Greek funerary inscriptions recorded little more than name and family members,

Romans wished to list their offices, honors, and perhaps accomplishments. Cato apparently even enjoyed reading inscriptions as a way of learning about Roman heroism of the past. After T. Sempronius Gracchus, father of the famous Gracchi, put down a revolt in Sardinia in 177 BCE, he deposited a painting of his victory in the temple of Mater Matuta in commemoration:

> Under the command and auspices of T. Sempronius Gracchus the army of the Roman people conquered Sardinia. In this province more than 80,000 of the enemy were slain or captured. Having administered the state most happily, set free the allies, and restored the revenues, he brought the army home, safe and secure and enriched with booty: for the second time he entered the city of Rome in triumph. In commemoration of this event he set up this picture to Jupiter.
>
> (Livy 41, 28, 8)

It was traditional to describe one's achievement in the third person, and the occasional text in the first person seems especially arrogant, like a milestone found south of Naples. This large, four-foot high tablet does not give the dedicator's name, but we know it was P. Popillius Laenas, consul of 132:

> I built the road from Rhegium to Capua, and on this road I placed all the bridges, milestones, and direction-posts. [It then provides distances.] As governor of Sicily I captured fugitive slaves from Italy, and returned 917 of them. And I was also the first to ensure that shepherds gave place to farmers on stateland. I erected the Forum here and the public buildings.
>
> (Dessau, *Inscriptiones Latinae Selectae* 23)

Two centuries later Petronius satirized this custom when his *nouveau-riche* hero Trimalchio proposes an inscription for his tomb:

HERE LIES C. POMPEIUS TRIMALCHIO, FREEDMAN OF MAECENAS. THE DEGREE OF PRIEST OF AUGUSTUS WAS CONFERRED UPON HIM IN HIS ABSENCE. HE MIGHT HAVE BEEN AN ATTENDANT ON ANY MAGISTRATE IN ROME, BUT REFUSED IT. GOD-FEARING, GALLANT, CONSTANT, HE STARTED WITH VERY LITTLE AND LEFT THIRTY MILLIONS. HE NEVER LISTENED TO A PHILOSOPHER.

FARE YOU WELL, TRIMALCHIO, AND YOU TOO,
PASSER-BY.

(Satyricon 71)

Sulla was the first political leader to use his *commentarii* to establish
a charismatic image of himself. Though he claimed they were raw
material for another to elaborate, his twenty-three books of diaries
even included dreams, and divine portents of his rise to power. It
was primarily a record of his military campaigns with little on
politics and almost nothing on his private life. The surviving fragments show that it was written in unadorned Latin, yet this
composition effectively presented Sulla's case and was much used by
later historians and biographers. Plutarch drew upon it not only for
his life of Sulla but for his (correspondingly unfavorable) life of
Marius as well. Though Sulla deprecated this book, it was clearly
intended for public readership and must have inspired Cicero and
Caesar to follow his example. Cicero likewise assembled such an
elaborate *commentarius* on the year of his consulship that when he
asked his friend Poseidonius to turn it into proper history, the
Greek deftly evaded the responsibility by telling Cicero that he
could not possibly improve upon it.

While Cicero hoped to entice a poet or historian to celebrate his
consulship and suppression of Catiline's revolt, he actually left
substantial autobiographical writings even if they are not properly
in the genre of autobiography. The *Brutus* is an account of his
education as an orator, but perhaps the most self-revealing work by
any pagan Roman is Cicero's books of letters to his close friend
Atticus. These letters range from Cicero's involvement in the
highest affairs of state to the most intimate family matters. In them
his conflicts and confusions become clear, and his weaknesses are
revealed. We come closer to knowing his inner self than that of any
other Roman before Augustine of Hippo. His display of weakness
and vacillation, of pride and shame, of deception and self-deception,
finally makes Cicero a more interesting and even more noble political figure than his self-serving public orations would ever have
allowed us to appreciate.

C. Julius Caesar's *Commentarii*

Life and works

Gaius Julius Caesar (100–44 BCE) is one of the best-known political and military figures of all antiquity – both from ancient sources and from later depictions in drama, art, and film. Though he had few prominent ancestors in historical times, the Julian family traced its line through Romulus to Julus, the son of Aeneas, and hence to Aeneas' mother, the goddess Venus. The goddess played an important role in Caesar's propaganda, and he built a temple of Venus Genetrix ("Venus the Begetter of the Family") in the new Forum he built at Rome. He made much of his mythological ancestors and his divine roots to deflect attention from the paucity of distinguished consuls and censors.

Despite his aristocratic background, Caesar aligned himself with the popular forces against senatorial conservatives. His early career progressed slowly; he reached the praetorship in 62 BCE and served as proconsul of Spain the following year. It was there, according to one story, that he saw a statue of Alexander the Great and lamented that the Greek had already conquered the world and died long before he reached Caesar's age of thirty-nine. Since the cost of his early political career had plunged him deep into debt, he returned to Rome determined to gain the consulship and a proconsular governorship that would allow him to recoup his finances. He formed an alliance – later called the First Triumvirate – with the general Pompey and the financier Crassus, which gave Caesar the consulship for 59 BCE. From 58 to 50 he was absent from Rome serving as governor of the Roman provinces of Gaul, which then included only northern Italy and modern Provence in southeastern France. He soon used a variety of pretexts to move into other parts of Gaul and by the end of the decade he had subjugated an enormous province to Roman rule. In this period he honed his military skills and developed a taste for power; he also became a great general who could arouse intense loyalty among his soldiers.

While Caesar fought in Gaul, the political situation in Rome was one of bitter political rivalry between Crassus and Pompey, and even gang warfare in the streets. As his command in Gaul expired, Caesar expected another consulship, but his enemies denied it in the expectation that he could then be prosecuted for abuse of office. In January of 49 BCE he marched his troops across the Rubicon river into Italy and thus began four years of civil war against the forces of the Senate. He defeated Pompey in Greece in 48, Cato in Africa in 46, and the remaining Republican forces in Spain in 45. When he pursued the fleeing Pompey to Egypt, Caesar became enmeshed in a dynastic struggle where he sided with the young queen Cleopatra. When he returned to Rome, she came as his mistress. On March 15 of 44 BCE, soon after he had been proclaimed dictator for life, Caesar was murdered at a meeting of the Senate.

What is less well known is Caesar's remarkable literary reputation. He was a poet, an essayist, and an orator who even impressed his great political rival, Cicero. In Cicero's history of Roman oratory, the *Brutus*, he has his friend Atticus praise Caesar as the most elegant speaker of Latin of all orators and suggests that Cicero agrees with his judgment. Caesar's essay on the use of Latin, *On Analogy*, argued for a purer Latin with fewer imported words; it was dedicated to Cicero, who certainly did not agree with its arguments. While Cicero preferred the rhetorical and poetic elaboration of Latin through colorful vocabulary, Caesar was known as an Atticist who preferred the spare style associated with Athenian writers like Thucydides. Caesar also wrote a tragedy on Oedipus and a political pamphlet against his Republican enemies, the *Anti-Cato*. None of these works has come down to us.

Caesar's surviving works are his *commentarii* on the Gallic War and on the Civil War. The seven books of the *Gallic War* were probably written year by year and circulated in Rome while Caesar remained in Gaul. (An eighth book was added by Caesar's aide Hirtius.) The three books of the *Civil War* seem unfinished; they may have been published in 46 BCE. Histories of Caesar's Alexandrian War, African War, and Spanish War have survived; Hirtius wrote the Alexandrian War but the authors of the others are unknown.

Gallic War

Book 1 Description of Gaul. Campaign against Helvetians and Ariovistus. (58 BCE).

Book 2 Campaigns in northern Gaul. (57 BCE).

Book 3 Naval campaign in Brittany. (56 BCE).

Book 4 Campaign against Germans. First invasion of Britain. (55 BCE).

Book 5 Second expedition in Britain War against Belgae. (54 BCE).

Book 6 Campaign against the Germans. Cultural digression. (53 BCE).

Book 7   General revolt under Vercingetorix; siege of Alesia. (52 BCE).

Book 8   Final operations; written by Hirtius. (51 BCE).

Civil War

Book 1   Causes of the war. Caesar crosses Rubicon and conquers Italy.

Book 2   Caesar's victories in Spain and southern Gaul.

Book 3   Defeat of Pompey at Pharsalus. His death in Alexandria.

Caesar wrote in an unadorned prose style; even Cicero, hardly sympathetic to this so-called Attic spareness, in his *Brutus* had his friend Atticus compliment Caesar as "the purest user of the Latin tongue" (252) while his future assassin Brutus says: "His orations certainly seem to me very admirable; I have read a number of them, as well as the *Commentaries* which he wrote about his own deeds" (262). The use of the third person endows the books with a plain-spoken objectivity typical of a general's dispatch from the field. The economy of style is not the jarring brevity of Sallust; Caesar's narrative flows smoothly and rapidly, only occasionally raising the emotional temperature with a flash of drama. All long speeches, with a single exception in Book 7, are delivered in indirect discourse and thus prove less of an interruption in the narrative flow. Most ancient historians are primarily interested in character, morality, or political context; Caesar's interest is focused on action. Hence his narrative is among the most effective, and the deceptive simplicity lends great conviction to this remarkably skillful text. It provides one of the greatest literary examples of the Latin epigram, *ars est celare artem* ("Art lies in concealing artifice"). Yet, after his death, Caesar's *Commentaries* went largely unread in favor of more literary histories of Sallust and Livy.

The nature of Caesar's Commentarii

Even in his own lifetime it was recognized that Caesar achieved a literary *tour de force* with his *commentarii*, for he used a non-literary form of aide-memoire and turned it into a remarkably effective political document. In many ways he avoided the obvious character-istics of history: rhetorical artifice and moralizing. The books begin without a prologue; the *Gallic War* opens with Caesar's famous description of the land and peoples of Gaul – "All Gaul is divided into three parts...." History in both Greek and Latin opens with the author's prologue – from Herodotus and Thucydides to Sallust, Livy, and Tacitus. Caesar's impassive and detached beginning conveys a new impression of objectivity.

On the other hand, there are some literary elements that would be out of place in a mere *commentarius*. The literary model that lies behind Caesar is Xenophon's *Anabasis*. Like that model, Caesar refers to himself in the third person and includes many speeches, though most are in the less intrusive form of indirect discourse. Caesar also includes several digressions on the geography and customs of Gauls and Germans. These elements – speeches and digressions – had been associated with the genre of history from its very beginning with Herodotus. (It should be said that the digressions are so inferior to the rest of the book that some scholars believe they are not from Caesar's pen but were added later.) It seems that Caesar was stretching the limits of the genre of *commentarius*; he wished his books to be taken as objective reports, but he certainly did not expect another historian to adapt them. It was a very skillful literary and political invention of a new form. Cicero, who was no innocent when it came to pulling the wool over the reader's eyes, said of Caesar in 46 BCE:

> His aim was to furnish others with material for writing history, and perhaps he has succeeded in gratifying the inept, who may wish to apply their curling irons to his material; but men of sound judgment he has deterred from writing, since in history there is nothing more pleasing than brevity clear and correct.
>
> (*Brutus* 262, tr. Hendrickson (Loeb))

Caesar's aide and continuator, Aulus Hirtius, consul of 43, wrote in a similar vein about his master's *commentarii* when he added the eighth book:

> For it is universally agreed that nothing was ever so elaborately finished by others that is not surpassed by the refinement of these Commentaries. They have been published that historians may not lack knowledge of those great achievements; and so strong is the unanimous verdict

of approval as to make it appear that historians have been robbed of an opportunity rather than enriched with one.

(*Gallic War* 8, *praef.*, tr. Edwards (Loeb))

The purpose of the *Gallic War* was, of course, political – Caesar did very little in his mature life that was not politically motivated. Each of the first seven books describes an annual campaign; they were most probably written the following winter and forwarded to Rome to keep Caesar's achievements fresh in the minds of the Senate and people during his long absence. Some scholars have argued that Caesar could not misrepresent the facts, since eventually his soldiers would return to Rome and the truth would be disclosed. This is an interesting perspective, of which the logical conclusion would be that politicians never lie since eventually they will be discovered. Perhaps it might be better to suggest that Caesar did not engage in bald-faced falsifications, but his account certainly shaped the narrative to his advantage: Caesar merely acted defensively; the forces of his enemies were especially fearsome; Caesar bestows praise generously on his troops; Caesar is never responsible for military reverses which are attributed either to his subordinates or to ill fortune; Caesar was admired and beloved by all his soldiers. There are certainly omissions and misrepresentations of Caesar's own mistakes, but the presentation is deft and convincing.

What were the virtues of Caesar conveyed in these books? Certainly his intelligence, his military genius, his ability to move quickly, and, in political terms, his common sense. The gods play no role; Caesar himself is the only superhuman figure in these pages. That image of decisive swiftness together with clemency toward former opponents would play an important role in Caesarian propaganda during the civil war. Of course, the genocide in which over 250,000 Helvetian men, women and children were killed (*Gallic War* 1, 29), the Roman cavalry cutting down fleeing German women and children (*Gallic War* 4, 14), or the amputation of the hands of Gallic opponents at the siege of Uxellodunum (*Gallic War* 8, 44) would not in Roman eyes have affected Caesar's reputation for clemency; after all, his opponents were only barbarians.

The *Civil War* is more overtly partisan, but even here Caesar shrewdly includes speeches by his opponents. This work is far more restrained than the slanderous anti-Caesarian pamphlets (like Brutus' *Cato*), and is thus more persuasive. It was important to Caesar that he be perceived by the non-political classes of Rome and Italy as a moderate, neither a revolutionary like Catiline nor a greedy cut-throat like Sulla. Caesar tells of his suppression of Caelius, who had called for suspension of debts, to show the propertied classes had nothing to fear from him. He is less concerned to set out his own political program than to deride the corruption and indulgence of the senatorial ruling class: freshly cut turf and artificial bowers were brought to decorate senatorial tents on the field at Pharsalus. He shows his own respect for all Roman soldiers, even those opposing him, but he depicts his political opponents as overconfident fools. The night before the battle of Pharsalus Pompey's generals argued about who would get Caesar's priesthood, and they planned trials for those who had not fought with them:

> In short, all of them were concerned with either office, or monetary reward, or pursuit of their private enemies, and thought not about how they could achieve victory, but how they ought to use it.
>
> (*Civil War* 3, 83, tr. Carter)

Conclusion

Caesar's *Gallic War* is the only detailed account of ancient battles by the field commander and, not surprisingly, his descriptions are infinitely superior to any other ancient accounts. Despite the attempts of some modern scholars to see them as gross distortions, military historians attest to Caesar's general accuracy even when he naturally emphasizes his successes and distances himself from any reverses. Caesar's *commentarii* are not bare memoranda to be embellished by a literary historian. That is the pretense, but in fact Caesar creates through these masterpieces a new literary genre that is a far more effective tool of propaganda than overblown rhetorical bluster.

Caesar wrote his *Gallic War* not only for Romans but for the new Gallic elite. He never speaks of subjugation, but rather of the benefits of Roman rule to the Gauls. He was probably correct; without Roman intervention Gaul might well have been overrun by German tribes. In these texts, as in his bestowal of Roman citizenship in Cisalpine Gaul, and in the many cities he founded in the provinces, Caesar displayed his understanding that the senatorial system of provincial administration by a small Roman elite would have to be transformed. After his assassination, it would fall to his great-nephew and heir, Octavian-Augustus, to effect that transformation.

The autobiographies of Augustus

C. Octavius (63 BCE–14 CE), the future emperor Augustus, was raised by his mother Atia, since his father died a few years after his birth. Atia's maternal uncle, Julius Caesar, became fond of the boy and introduced him to public life, and he attended his great-uncle in the triumph of 46. When the eighteen-year-old youth learned of Caesar's assassination in 44 and his own designation in Caesar's will as Caesar's adopted son and heir, he took the adoptive name C. Julius Caesar Octavianus (thus called "Octavian") and recruited Caesar's veterans to fight for vengeance. At first he sought the support of the senatorial forces, but he finally allied himself with Caesar's deputy Marc Antony. It was under Antony's military leadership that the "triumvirs" crushed the forces of Caesar's murderers at Philippi. After a decade of uneasy alliance, Octavian defeated Antony and his ally, the Egyptian queen Cleopatra, in 30.

In 27 Octavian took the name of "Augustus" and such a collection of powers that this might be said to be the beginning of the Roman Empire. Augustus brought Egypt into the Empire and himself ruled over the entire Mediterranean for two generations. His principal concerns were to settle the vast armies, his own and his rivals', that were left after the civil wars, to create a new administrative and financial structure, and to secure the succession within the Julian family. This ruthlessly ambitious young man later was portrayed as patron of the arts, upholder of morality, and the benevolent father of his country. Though he had always been sickly and often was desperately ill, Augustus outlived at least four designated successors until his death in 14 CE brought his stepson Tiberius to power.

De vita sua (Autobiography of Augustus)

Under the Empire, just as triumphs could only be celebrated by the emperor or his family, so there were few private military memoirs. Nearly all autobiographies were written by emperors or members of the imperial family. Augustus wrote an autobiography of his early life of which Suetonius says:

> [Augustus] wrote some of an Autobiography, giving an account of his life in thirteen books up to the time of the Cantabrian War, but no further.
>
> (Suetonius, *Augustus* 85)

This autobiography (*de vita sua*) must be distinguished from the *Res Gestae*, which will be discussed below. Though the autobiography, which was dedicated to Maecenas and Agrippa, has been lost, two dozen surviving fragments permit some reconstruction.

Why did Augustus write this autobiography and why did he stop in 25 BCE with the triumph after the Spanish wars? The fragments, which are primarily found in Suetonius, Plutarch, and Appian, make clear that the autobiography was a polemical work, aimed at rebutting accusations of his political enemies during the civil wars between 44 and 31 BCE. Some of these accusations can be found in Suetonius' *Life of Augustus*, where he also reports Augustus' denial of them. Some of Augustus' assertions may not seem important to a modern reader, but they were crucial to a Roman leader: nobility of ancestry and early recognition of his talents. Since Antony taunted him with his low-born ancestors, Augustus wrote of his distinguished equestrian lineage before his father entered the Senate (Suetonius, *Augustus* 2). The favorable portents at Augustus' birth and in his boyhood that appear in various ancient writers probably also originate in his autobiography.

The most important accusations dealt with in the autobiography were the charges of cruelty and treachery, and a feeble performance on the battlefield. There is little doubt that in the years after Caesar's death the young Octavian developed a terrible reputation: he hired assassins to kill Marc Antony in 44; he cooperated in the proscriptions of 43, which killed Cicero; he took the head of Brutus to Rome after Philippi in 42; and after the insurrection at Perugia he selected three hundred senators and equestrians to be sacrificed like so many animals on an altar of Julius Caesar on the Ides of March of 40 BCE. These rumors of his unparalleled barbarism circulated so widely that even Republicans found Antony a more sympathetic figure.

Whether any individual story was true or was rather a fiction of Antony's propaganda is now unknowable; but it is certainly believable that Octavian, being a young man whose political situation was insecure, deliberately acted to give the impression of ruthlessness. But in the 30s Octavian launched a publicity blitz to counter that impression and his autobiography formed an important part of that campaign. His emphasis was on his own loyalty, and on the clemency he showed even in the face of violence:

> When Quintus Gallius, a praetor, held some folded tablets
> under his robe as he was paying his respects, Augustus,

suspecting that he had a sword concealed there, did not dare to make a search on the spot for fear it should turn out to be something else; but a little later he had Gallius hustled from the tribunal by some centurions and soldiers, tortured him as if he was a slave, and though he made no confession, ordered his execution, first tearing out the man's eyes with his own hand. He himself writes, however, that Gallius made a treacherous attack on him after asking for an audience, and was haled to prison; and that after he was dismissed under sentence of banishment, he either lost his life by shipwreck or was waylaid by brigands.

(Suetonius, *Augustus* 27, 4)

Augustus also justified his lack of active involvement in the victory at Philippi, and even wrote that he divorced his pregnant wife Scribonia because of her shrewishness. Given the amount of criticism Augustus had to counter about his public and private behavior, it is no wonder that he also encouraged others, including Virgil and Horace, to write on his behalf.

After Actium and the "constitutional settlements" of 27 and 23 BCE eliminated all serious opposition, Augustus saw no further need to justify his early actions. The autobiography may not even have been published but only circulated privately, since some of the writers who cite it seem to have found the material in an intermediate source. Now the ruler turned from the present to the future and began to craft the political testament that would only be published after his death, the *Res Gestae*.

Res Gestae Divi Augusti
(Achievements of the Deified Augustus)

The *Res Gestae* of Augustus is the most important official document to survive from his long and pivotal reign. It is not a narrative autobiography but a first-person reckoning of his long stewardship of the Empire – a kind of balance sheet prepared in his final months to be disclosed to the Roman people on his death. We know from Suetonius that it was set up on bronze tablets in front of the emperor's mausoleum in Rome, but it only survives in a vast inscription in both Greek and Latin discovered on the walls of the temple of Roma and Augustus in Ankara – the *Monumentum Ancyranum*, known as "The Queen of Inscriptions." (Smaller fragments, which survive from two other sites in central Turkey, have enabled scholars to fill in most of the gaps.) It is likely that bronze copies, which have since been melted down, were set up throughout the provinces. These enormous eastern copies were probably modeled on the autobiographical inscriptions of Hellenistic kings (Ptolemy Euergetes and Antiochus I of Commagene), as well as much earlier texts carved on mountainsides by the Achaemenid Persian monarch Darius I.

The model for the content of the *Res Gestae* was the indigenous Roman tradition of texts inscribed on Roman triumphal arches, and the honorific texts (*elogia*) written for famous Romans. Such *elogia* go back to the third century BCE; Augustus himself set up 108 statues and *elogia* to honor great Romans of the past in the new Forum of Augustus, with an emphasis on his own ancestors back to Romulus and Aeneas. These *elogia* listed achievements and precedents that Augustus himself would equal or excel; all negative material was of course omitted. Such *elogia* were indeed the most specific model for the *Res Gestae*, which was drafted during the same years (20–2 BCE) that the Forum of Augustus was planned and constructed. The *Res Gestae*, however, is so much longer than any other *elogium* that it must be said to be in a class by itself.

The language of the *Res Gestae* is brief, almost telegraphic, with a seeming absence of emotional, ideological, or political argument. There is little of the overt boastfulness found in some funerary monuments. Augustus seems to be providing the straightforward accounting that a Roman magistrate presented to the Senate at the conclusion of his term in office, though the emperor is reporting on his entire fifty-six years in public life. For this reason Augustus only includes his official acts; there is no mention of his family except as they affected his public duties. The document was entirely drafted in final form by 2 BCE when Augustus was awarded the title of "Father of His Country" (*pater patriae*). It was slightly amended in his last year and an epilogue was added after his death in 14 CE. This public testament of Augustus is his challenge to future generations of Romans to judge him on his fiscal, political, and military achievements.

The structural organization of the text is clear. A brief preface and the two initial paragraphs provide an introduction, with an emphasis on Augustus' contributions to the Roman people – *populus* is mentioned three times and *res publica* five times:

Below is a copy of *The Achievements of the Deified Augustus*, by which he subjected the entire world to the imperial power of the Roman people, and of the expenses which he incurred for the republic and people of Rome; the original text has been inscribed on two bronze pillars set up at Rome.

1. When I was nineteen years old, on my own initiative and at my own expense I raised an army, with which I restored freedom for the republic which was oppressed by the power of a clique. For that reason the Senate passed honorary decrees enrolling me in its order, in the consulship of C. Pansa and A. Hirtius [43 BCE], granting me the privilege of speaking among the ex-consuls and giving me *imperium* – the right of military command. It ordered me, as a propraetor, to act together with the consuls to ensure that the state should suffer no harm. In the same year, when both consuls had fallen in battle, the people named me consul and appointed me one of a commission of three (*triumvir*) for the re-establishment of the republic.

2. I drove the murderers of my father into exile, and avenged their crime through legal tribunals; and afterwards, when they made war on the republic, I twice defeated them in battle.

After that introduction, the text is divided into three sections of two to three modern pages each. The first (3–14) concerns the honors gained by Augustus and the offices bestowed on him by the Senate and the Roman people, as well as the honors he gave to his grandsons. The second (15–25) is a numerical accounting of every sort: money spent, games sponsored, slaves captured, temples repaired, down to the 170 senators who held priesthoods and the 3,500 African beasts slaughtered in the arena. The third section (26–33) concerns the military and diplomatic triumphs that led to the expansion of Roman power.

The final two paragraphs return to the themes of the opening lines – Augustus' devotion to the interests of the Republic and the Roman people, and their gratitude to him:

34. In my sixth and seventh consulships (28–27 BCE), after I had extinguished civil war, and with the consent of all I was in complete control of affairs, I transferred the republic from my power to the authority of the senate and Roman people...

Thereafter I excelled all in authority, although I possessed no more official power than others who were my colleagues in each office.

35. In my thirteenth consulship (2 BCE), the senate, the equestrian order, and the entire Roman people called me "Father of His Country," and decreed that this title should be inscribed on the porch of my house, in the Senate House, and in the Forum of Augustus below the four-horse chariot which was placed there in my honor by decree of the senate. At the time of writing I was in my seventy-sixth year.

If the structure of the *Res Gestae* is relatively simple, its content is considerably more complex. Certain rhetorical tactics are obvious. There are over a hundred verbs in the first person, which together with adjectives and pronouns serve to focus attention on Augustus alone. The immense amount of quantitative material has its own rhetorical force. Other aspects are less overt. There is a remarkable absence of discussion on the vital decade between Philippi (42) and Actium (31 BCE), when Octavian grew from junior partner in a murderous coalition to the undisputed ruler of the Mediterranean world. While that was the turning point in his ascent to power, it was also the time of proscriptions and civil war as Romans killed other Romans. The omissions are an important part of the story.

Many scholars have criticized the hypocrisy in the *Res Gestae*'s omissions, not to mention Augustus' claim to have returned power to the Senate and Roman people. Others prefer to value the *Res Gestae* as a report of what Augustus thought important enough to place in this public record of his reign, rather than examine his hidden intentions. It should be seen as his final constitutional statement directed at both the Roman people and his successor: the Empire survives as a compact between *princeps* on the one hand and Senate and people on the other. He can justly claim to have saved the state after almost a century of civil conflict, and he restored the traditional forms of Roman government. Five centuries after Augustus, consuls and senators still existed. It is true enough that the *Res Gestae* has a magisterial disregard for the embarrassing details of the civil wars, so that the Republican leader Sextus Pompey is referred to simply as a pirate, Antony's name is never mentioned, and constitutional issues are blurred or distorted. Yet the *Res Gestae* does trace the important transition from naked power (*potestas*) to a widely accepted institutional framework that reduced the need for brute force.

There is no monarchy in the *Res Gestae*. Though Augustus certainly laid the foundation for a monarchy which endured, in

Constantinople, for fifteen hundred years, he himself sought power to preserve Republican institutions rather than to replace them. In an edict he expressed his hope that he "may be called the author of the best possible government, and bear with me the hope when I die that the foundations which I have laid for the State will remain unshaken." Suetonius then adds, "And he realized his hope by making every effort to prevent any dissatisfaction with the new regime" (*Augustus* 28, 2).

Augustus wrote this political testament to point out his mission in restoring peace and Republican government. This unique document — there is no real parallel to it — also contains his philosophy of government. He wrote almost half a century after the events, and his disregard for the constitutional niceties of the dying Republic was surely in his mind vindicated by the establishment of peace and prosperity. It is a glorification of his fifty-six years in public life, but the actual achievements of this greatest of all Roman rulers were so remarkable that he can be forgiven his final boast.

Later imperial autobiography

Though only members of the imperial family were permitted to write autobiography, some senators tried to evade such restrictions. The eminent general Cn. Domitius Corbulo wrote his memoirs during the reign of Nero, but this was numbered among the faults that drove him to suicide. The letters of the younger Pliny were autobiographical in content, if not in form, but his close friendship with Trajan doubtless emboldened him to publish them. Yet it was principally the emperors who followed Augustus' example with a series of autobiographies.

Tiberius had wide literary interests in both Latin and Greek and wrote poetry in both languages. We hear from Suetonius (*Domitian* 20) that the emperor's memoirs (*commentarii*) and papers (*acta*) were the only books Domitian bothered to read. It has been suggested that these books inspired Domitian's cruelties. Claudius began as an historian under Livy's guidance and initially planned a book on the civil war, until his mother Antonia (daughter of Marc Antony) and his grandmother Livia persuaded him that he would not be allowed to publish a true account of that sensitive period. He simply left a long lacuna. He then began again from the battle of Actium and produced forty-one books. Those are lost, as are his autobiography in eight books, though Robert Graves recreated them as *I, Claudius* and *Claudius the God*. The younger Agrippina also left an autobiography which was used by Tacitus. Since Agrippina was the incestuous sister of Caligula, final and perhaps fatal wife of Claudius, and mother of Nero, she certainly had stories to tell. How much she actually told we cannot judge. Likewise the lost Greek autobiography of the restless emperor Hadrian only survives in the brilliant fictional recreation of the French novelist Marguerite Yourcenar. No imperial autobiographies survive, except the philosophical memoir of the Stoic emperor Marcus Aurelius, and that was written in Greek.

8

HISTORICAL WRITING AT ROME

The forms of Roman history

The Romans, like the Greeks, sang and wrote about the past for as long as they produced poetry or written literature. How much of this can we regard as "historical writing?" In our own time, we would include not only conventional history but also much biography and autobiography. In recent years some ethnography, as well as many political, sociological and economic analyses, also command attention as works of history. But we firmly exclude "fiction" – novels, poetry, dramas, and mythic stories – from our conception of history.

Other cultures define "history" differently, so that poetic gene-alogies in traditional Africa might be as genuinely historical as the Homeric poems were for the ancient Greeks. The Romans regarded *historia* more narrowly still, as a genre separate from the genres of biography and autobiography. But if the ancient critics were more rigorous in defining genres than modern readers, Roman readers were less strict in differentiating between fiction and historical fact. Naevius' epic poem on the Punic War was regarded as the earliest historical writing, and the development of prose history never completely supplanted the historical epics of Ennius and Virgil as primary sources of Rome's history. The historical epic continued into the Empire: Lucan, writing in the reign of Nero, described the civil wars between Caesar and Pompey in his poem *Pharsalia*. Even the professional educator Quintilian regarded historical research as mere pedantry, and saw no serious difference between what he learned of the Trojan War from Virgil and what he read of the Punic Wars in Livy. The millennium that passed between those two conflicts was of less consequence to Quintilian than the style of the poet or historian.

In the wake of Alexander's conquest of Egypt and much of Asia, fantastic histories appeared, in which miraculous events occurred in exotic locales with the traditional embellishments of Greek myth. Suetonius tells us that the emperor Tiberius was much taken with such stories, and the learned Aulus Gellius complained that in his own day, the second century CE, fantastic histories so filled the book-shops of Brundisium that serious books of history could not be found (*Noctes Atticae* 9, 14). This popularity ensured that fabulous elements would appear in conventional history, as when the Sicilian Diodorus, writing in Greek in the age of Augustus, describes utopias on the islands of Corsica and Sardinia as if they really existed. This fasci-nating stream in ancient historiography directly contributed to the miraculous and exotic stories found in the ancient novel. Lucian paro-died such fantasies in his account of a trip to the moon in *A True History* – perhaps the first instance of "science fiction." The popu-larity of fantasy was so great that the ascetic emperor Julian wished to ban all history that contained fantasy or eroticism, and he was also concerned with the proliferation of Christian saints' lives, in which fantastic and miraculous elements abounded.

It was not only in works of pseudo-history that exotic elements were to be found. From the time of Herodotus and his forebears, geography and ethnography had been a popular way to introduce strange and awe-inspiring material into history. Genuine knowledge of faraway places was so limited that geographical digressions inevitably contained a mixture of fact and fancy. The first Latin historian, Cato, included the geography, customs, and marvels of Italy in the early books of his *Origines*. Sallust's *Jugurtha* even uses Carthaginian sources in its descriptions of North Africa. Similar exotic fantasies appear in the elder Pliny's treatment of Taprobane (modern Sri Lanka), as well as Tacitus' *Germania* or his digression on the Egyptian phoenix (*Annals* 6, 28). This strain of ethnographic interest continues throughout Roman historians, to the extended, and sometimes puzzling, digressions included by Ammianus in his history. The Roman historian knew as well as the epic poet that his audience was much entertained by geographical digressions, and both made effective use of them.

After the Hellenistic idea of scholarly compilations reached Rome with Atticus' and Nepos' chronological compendia, Romans began to collect historical anecdotes. Suetonius recounts that Augustus liked to copy precepts and examples from his reading and send them when appropriate to members of his household or to his generals (*Augustus* 89). In the reign of Tiberius, Valerius Maximus published *Memorable Deeds and Words*, which contained almost a thousand anecdotes classified under such headings as dreams, miracles, public games, and omens, as well as virtues and vices like chastity, bravery, and cruelty. Valerius, who particularly relied on Cicero, Livy and Nepos, makes it clear that his work is intended as a shortcut to spare his reader the onerous task of reading entire historical works. Used by orators much as Bartlett's *Quotations* has been used by politicians and banquet speakers in modern times, Valerius' compendium attained great popularity in the Middle Ages and survives in more Renaissance manuscripts than any other ancient work.

We tend to be scornful of compendia, since the subtle analysis of the historian is inevitably lost in such excerpts. For the Romans, however, history was either a literary work or a collection of useful stories, not an overall work of analysis. Other Romans also provided abridged versions of history: Florus compared his *Epitome* to a pocket map prepared for travelers, while Justin boasted in the fourth century CE that his excerpts of Pompeius Trogus' universal history had omitted all that was unpleasant to know or unnecessary to imitate. This pragmatic, and sanitized, view of historical writing became popular in the later Empire and had great influence on centuries of Byzantine scholars who excerpted books. Yet we must be grateful, since only through Justin has Trogus been preserved, and the same is true for many other important historians.

The art of writing history

In the ancient world, history was a branch of literature, and the historian was above all a literary artist. First he would gather basic information from contemporary witnesses or from books, and then reshape this material into his own story and recast it in his own words. This form of historical writing remained enormously popular through the nineteenth century. Even in our own century, some writers have published similar works of history, but they are usually not professional (or academic) historians. Winston Churchill's *A History of the English-Speaking Peoples* did not rely on primary research into archives; those volumes are a elegant synthesis of other books, much in the style of Livy. That Churchill won the Nobel Prize for Literature in 1949 was not inappropriate, for his great, multi-volume synthesis relies more on his political vision, literary craft, and personal style than it does on historical research. Likewise, Will and Ariel Durant's traversal of Western civilization in more than a dozen volumes is wonderfully entertaining, but now appears like something from another age. Only in textbooks do most professional historians attempt to reach a truly wide audience; otherwise they usually write original, carefully researched history directed primarily at other professional historians.

From the time of Herodotus' public readings of his compositions, Greek historians appealed to their readers by entertaining them. By the Hellenistic age, some historians resorted to shock and horror to induce that pleasurable pity and revulsion that modern readers derive from tabloid journalism and the Gothic novels of Stephen King. Lucian condemned such extravagant poetic history for its artificial beauty. Roman annalists present a decided contrast. Stylists like Cicero were disappointed in them because he expected the historian to be an "embellisher of events," whose elaboration of the story would bring pleasure to the reader. Similarly, Quintilian described history as "a poem in prose" and suggested that the historian's task was "to tell and not to prove" – narration took precedence over analysis. Even the most careful of Roman historians, Tacitus and Ammianus, did not forgo literary techniques, but deployed their considerable stylistic and rhetorical skills to present historical truth more convincingly.

By the first century BCE, Roman education consisted almost exclusively of instruction in literature and rhetoric, and all the great Roman historical writers from Caesar to Ammianus display their rhetorical training. Since Roman historians followed their Greek predecessors in introducing speeches into their narrations, rhetorical training was especially useful. For the monarchy and the early Republic, there were probably no surviving actual speeches. But even though such speeches were composed by the historian, certain themes must have been transmitted through Rome's very tenacious oral tradition. In Livy's account of Rome's conquest of the East, his speeches can be checked against the Greek versions in Polybius, who was a contemporary of those events. At times Livy reliably retained the substance of the speech, but at other times he created both the occasion and the speech. It is Tacitus who provides the only opportunity to check his version of Claudius' speech on Gallic senators against the text as recorded on a bronze tablet. Here we can see that Tacitus' version (*Annals* 11, 24) preserved the substance of the emperor's speech, while immeasurably improving its rhetorical force.

For ancient historians, speeches were not only part of the narration, but also served as a method of analysis by which the motives of a character, a political faction, or an entire people could be made explicit. A modern historian delivers analytical judgments in his own voice, but ancient historians preferred the dramatic and rhetorical mask of a speech. Hence occasions for speeches and debates were sometimes invented to allow the historian to synthesize and analyze the reasons for a course of action. One recurring occasion is the speech given to the troops on the eve of a great battle. When the speech is given by a barbarian general like Hannibal or the Briton Calgacus, we know that it is wholly invented as a formulaic diatribe against the enemy. And yet the best of such speeches – such as Achilles' speech to Hector in Homer's *Iliad* or King Henry V's speech before Agincourt in Shakespeare – convey a psychological truth of the motivation that leads men to risk their lives in battle. Even in our own century, speeches and memorable maxims have been attributed to charismatic commanders like Patton and MacArthur, Montgomery and Lawrence of Arabia. Such encouragement, passed orally from soldier to soldier to bolster morale, must have existed from time immemorial.

In Athens or Republican Rome, a speech was above all a public political act, and it is as such that Sallust records the debate between Caesar and Cato over the fate of the Catilinarian conspirators. Later the autocratic power of the emperors reduced speeches to occasions for display rather than for genuine persuasion. In an autocracy, speeches, indeed words in general, are used to disguise and conceal rather than to reveal the truth; hence the imperial historians Tacitus and Ammianus used speeches far less frequently and usually where a speech was actually delivered.

The use of rhetoric in Roman historical writing goes far beyond the construction of speeches to the organization of episodes, the structure of argument, and the use of language. Tacitus characterizes by juxtaposition when he makes Nero and his mother Agrippina resemble Tiberius and Livia, and Sallust's Catiline is echoed by Tacitus' portrait of Sejanus. These portraits, together with certain formulaic scenes (death scenes, battles, trials), appealed to the reader's own rhetorical training and thus enriched the texture of the historical narrative. As a literary artist, the Roman historian exercised great care over his prose style, since the Latin itself revealed the author's attitudes. Livy's literary richness is well suited to a master storyteller of heroic achievements, while Sallust and Tacitus use a leaner, harsher, and more intense Latin to uncover political realities. If Livy's congenial narrative suited the exploits of Rome's past, the grim contemporary history of the late Republic and early Empire required more biting and wittily epigrammatic prose.

Another important literary device in Roman historiography is the use of drama. Though this technique goes back to Herodotus, it was the Hellenistic historians who vastly expanded the use of drama and passed these traditions on to Rome. Since history, like tragedy, intended to recount the deeds of great men (real or mythical), there is a similar preference for personalities and the human element. Livy's account of the sack of Alba Longa paints an almost cinematic picture of personal and communal destruction. But it is Tacitus who employs the full array of dramatic devices: the dramatic prologue to an episode; foreboding built up by omens as well as mood; reversals of fate and dramatic irony. His story of Germanicus' death in *Annals* is a more effective tragedy than any written for theatrical performance in the early Empire. It is no surprise that the French classical dramatists Corneille and Racine found much tragic material in the Roman historians.

The literary recreation of the past found in a Roman historian like Livy might seem to a modern reader to be akin to an historical novel. Livy himself would be greatly offended by the suggestion that he was writing fiction. He was indeed constrained by what he could know: characters, events, institutions, traditions, and ethical values. His imagination in depicting a siege and his *inventio* in finding themes for speeches were his ways of recreating the past, of putting meat on the skeleton of early Roman history. In our own time, literary skill is regarded as almost as irrelevant to the writing of sound history as it is to other disciplines in the sciences and the social sciences. Yet in the last century Charles Darwin and Thomas Huxley had their enormous impact on biology in part through their literary skills, just as Sigmund Freud's imaginative skills were no less important than his medical observations in transforming psychology and creating the discipline of psychoanalysis. Our contemporary tendency is to devalue the artistic and imaginative side of historical writing, but we must be aware that in doing so we are defining the genre of history in a different way from Herodotus, Polybius, and Tacitus.

The craft of history

Greek historians often discussed their research in methodological prefaces; it was a way to assert the value of their history. Since their Roman counterparts rested their authority on their public career, they rarely spelled out their research techniques; they and their readers expected them to make use of the data already easily available. There was little documentary evidence for the earliest Republic, though for the later period oral traditions could in theory be checked against preserved treaties, census records, laws, and decrees. During the first century BCE, Sulla built an enormous public record office, and Julius Caesar had the minutes of the Senate's proceedings recorded. Yet most Roman historians still had limited interest in primary documentary material and preferred to gather material from the works of other historians. On several occasions Livy even alludes to documents still available in Rome that he has not bothered to consult personally. Though the greatest historians so impressed their conception and style on the material as to change it radically, the fact remains that there was little genuine research on primary material. History was, in most cases, written from eye-witnesses or from other books.

How accurate were the Roman historians? We have already seen the contrast between Cicero's high-minded goals for history – "an author must not dare to tell anything but the truth" (*De orat.* 2, 62) – and his appeal to his friend Lucceius: "Indulge your affection for me a trifle more than even strict truth would allow" (*Epist. ad fam.* 5, 12, 3). The gap between ideal theory and actual practice might seem to be considerable in the highly politicized world of the Roman elite. But Cicero was not a practicing historian. In urging Lucceius to bend the truth, he sacrificed none of his own integrity. The genuine historians, whose reputations rested on their writings, were far more scrupulous in combining investigation with story-telling. They understood the need for credibility and, unlike the epic or tragic poets, they were self-conscious about untrustworthy aspects of their narrative. Tacitus found the incestuous relationship between Nero and his mother Agrippina so horrifying that he carefully reported contradictory sources on whether Nero or Agrippina instigated it, before following Cluvius' account that it was most likely Agrippina (*Annals* 14, 2). He cannot simply report this morally outrageous episode as an epic poet would do.

Thucydides' impartiality and his passion for accuracy have been regarded in modern times as ideal qualities for an historian. But we forget that in this respect Thucydides was exceptional; other Greek and Roman historians placed readability at least on a par with exactitude. Even when Roman historians sincerely desired to avoid untruths, in some cases they did not have the critical skills to evaluate inconsistent evidence, and they made no serious distinction between primary and secondary sources. Quite simply, if a source reported a probable story, it was accepted without much question. Moreover, what was essential was not only truth itself but also verisimilitude – the appearance of truth. Teachers of rhetoric had long instilled in their pupils the importance of probability in constructing a persuasive narrative. Sometimes this was helpful to the historian, as when he rejected stories of divine intervention on the battlefield. But how was the historian to deal with well-attested, but seemingly unbelievable, stories? When Tacitus reports that the empress Messalina contracted a marriage to Silius while her husband Claudius was away for a day in Ostia, he addresses the preposterousness of the account:

> I am well aware that it will seem a fable that any persons in the world could have been so obtuse in a city which knows everything and hides nothing, much more, that these persons should have been a consul-elect and the emperor's wife...But this is no story to excite wonder; I do but relate what I have heard and what our fathers have recorded.
>
> (*Annales* 11, 27)

This episode reveals the historian's quandary when the improbability of his account will strain the reader's credulity.

Livy often accepts stories, believable and dubious, at face value since they had occurred as much as seven centuries earlier. Like Herodotus in reporting stories he heard in Egypt, Livy explicitly says that he cannot vouch for the accuracy of all these traditions, but he believed it was important to preserve them. Today we are grateful that legends and myths have been preserved, but we still suspect Livy of insufficient rigor. In our time, for example, the cosmological myths and early legends of native American peoples are regarded as vitally important for understanding their values, social structure, and even early migrations, but we do not expect the myths to be preserved in books of history. They are collected elsewhere. For Livy, there was no "elsewhere." What he did not include in his massive book might well be lost, and we must appreciate his difficulty when he preserved what he did not necessarily believe was true.

For Roman historians the important issues were always political and moral, not the accuracy of names and dates. Thus some historians concealed the fact that the Etruscan Porsenna may have reconquered Rome after 509 BCE, and that the Gauls had actually captured the Roman Capitol in 390 BCE. Cicero arbitrarily chose one of several versions of the death of Coriolanus to prove his point – that is the way of lawyers and politicians; at least Livy makes clear that he knew there were several versions. And Tacitus, through his language, dramatic construction, and use of innuendo, created a powerful picture quite at variance with the facts that he accurately reported. Tacitus was writing a moral history to address the larger truths of tyranny and political freedom. Concern with minor details was for a pedantic antiquarian, not an historian.

Senators as historians

Cato the Elder's apparently immodest comment that history, unlike poetry, was written by great men simply means that his contemporaries who wrote history were members of the senatorial elite who had held high public office. Only senators would have had access to state and family archives, and only they, who alone had held high magistracies and military commands, had sufficient leadership authority to write convincingly on political matters. Thus nearly all early Roman historians were senators or members of senatorial families. Since they wrote for other members of the same class, their histories display a constant focus on the political battles of the Forum and the senate house.

In the highly partisan atmosphere of the late Republic, it is not surprising that some historians were allied with various political factions: Antias with the Valerii; Sisenna with Sulla; and several (writing in both Greek and Latin) with Pompey. Though literary patronage was widespread in Hellenistic Greece, it is uncharacteristic of Roman historiography, since the writers are themselves members of a political elite. Roman poets sought out and flattered patrons, but among historians only Livy relied on a patron, Augustus, and he was, perhaps for this reason, the least political of major historians. Otherwise the greatest Roman historians – Cato, Caesar, Sallust, Asinius Pollio, Tacitus, and Ammianus – were all men who, whatever their birth, had carved out their public niches through their own political or military achievements. Since the senatorial order were the losers in the civil wars of the first century BCE, senators under the Empire naturally looked back to the Republic as a golden age of power and influence for their class. Decision-making was no longer done in public meetings, but by the emperor alone and his advisors. Historians, like other senators, were now outside the circle of power.

Although the histories were still primarily intended for the political elite, the growth of interest from a wider audience led to public readings by historians. Originally intended for small private parties, these recitations later moved to the theaters and the baths, sometimes with large audiences in attendance. Oral recitations afforded publicity to the historian and entertainment to his audience and were particularly appropriate in a society in which even private reading was done aloud. Such diffusion led to Livy's fame in Spain, and Tacitus was known to readers (or hearers) in Gaul.

Censorship and the suppression of history

Though the English word "censorship" derives from the Roman censor, who exercised moral as well as fiscal scrutiny over the membership roll of the Senate, the modern conception of state censorship did not exist in the Roman Republic. The earliest Roman law code, the Twelve Tables, compiled about 450 BCE, contained a prohibition against defamatory songs that carried the death penalty, but that (as in all early Roman law) was a matter for civil litigation by the aggrieved party. Likewise, the poet Naevius was not imprisoned by the state, but by the aristocrats whom he had lampooned. The wide authority of magistrates under the Republic may have been sufficient to deter critical writings about contemporaries; Cicero hints that this is the reason he avoided writing history. Tacitus regarded truth as a privilege of the Republic. He looked back to that earlier time when historians wrote "with equal eloquence and freedom," and saw Actium as the dividing point after which historians wrote either with excessive flattery for living emperors, or excessive pent-up hostility to dead emperors (*Histories* 1, 1).

While Julius Caesar responded to vicious Republican pamphlets with words of his own, like his *Anti-Cato*, there are reports that his successors banned and burned critical or offensive writings. It is important not to exaggerate these stories. Augustus was friendly with the Republican-sympathizer Livy, and even attended a reading of Cremutius Cordus despite the historian's praise for Brutus and Cassius. Suetonius reports the advice of Augustus to his successor: "My dear Tiberius, you must not...take it to heart if anyone speaks ill of me; let us be satisfied if we can achieve it that nobody is able to do us any harm" (*Augustus* 51, 3). When the historian Timagenes of Alexandria was banished from the imperial palace for jibes against Augustus and his family, he continued to live in Rome in the house of Pollio. Though Pollio offered to expel the sarcastic Greek, he was told it was unnecessary. (Timagenes seems to have burned his account of Augustus' accession as an act of spite.) Titus Labienus was another difficult fellow; the elder Seneca reports that he savaged all classes so viciously that he was called "Rabienus" —

from the Latin *rabies* ("anger"). When his books were burned, that fierce historian preferred to die with them – but the books were burned by the decree of his many enemies in the Senate rather than by persecution of the emperor. Suetonius and the elder Seneca both repeatedly praise the license for criticism allowed in the reign of Augustus. But if there is little evidence for censorship under Augustus, there may well have been a great deal of wariness since he and Antony had once treated their enemies with frightening cruelty. A witticism survives: "It is not easy to write (*scribere*) against one who can kill (*proscribere*) you." Later Seneca remarked on Cicero's good fortune that the triumvirs were content to kill him, and let all his books survive. Though Augustus occasionally responded to personal attacks, as in the case of Ovid, that was nothing new. Scurrilous poetry had long been prosecuted, even under the Republic.

Under Tiberius writers were prosecuted under the newly revived *lex maiestatis*, which functioned like a treason law. Cremutius Cordus was the first historian to be tried for treason on the basis of his published work. In 25 CE, sixty-eight years after the Ides of March, Cremutius was charged before the Senate for praising Brutus and Cassius in his history. In his defense, Cremutius pointed out that Livy had praised Pompey and remained a friend of Augustus, while Asinius Pollio praised the tyrannicides and lived peaceably afterward. He goes on to say, in Tacitus' long report on the trial, that among the Romans:

> there has always been complete, uncensored freedom to speak about those whom death has placed beyond hate or favor...They have their place in the historian's pages. Posterity gives everyone his due honor. If I am condemned, people will remember me as well as Cassius and Brutus.
>
> (*Annales* 4, 35)

Cremutius was correct; it is for this that he has been remembered. But the accusation was probably a smokescreen. Cremutius seems to have offended a crony of the praetorian prefect Sejanus, and this case was contrived against him. He was, like so many of those prosecuted under Tiberius, the victim of private enmity rather than any actual offense. Cremutius, Labienus, and other banned authors were republished under Caligula, who claimed that he wished future generations to have access to all the historical facts. This view is strange coming from the same emperor who contemplated suppressing Livy's history for its inordinate length.

Claudius was the only emperor who actually wrote history (as opposed to autobiography), so it is not surprising that there is no evidence of censorship in his reign. Perhaps the memory of his aborted history of the civil war and Augustus' tolerance for his old teacher Livy made Claudius more indulgent. The truth is that little history was actually suppressed under the Julio-Claudians; even the final Republican diatribe of the younger Cato remained a popular oration for schoolroom study. We cannot know, however, to what degree the writers of the age were muzzled by their own fear.

The Flavian era witnessed expulsions of philosophers and astrologers from Rome, and laudatory biographies of the Stoic dissidents Thrasea Paetus and Helvidius Priscus were burned. The Greek Josephus took the precaution of submitting his *Jewish War* to the court to gain permission for publication. But an even more gruesome story is told of Hermogenes of Tarsus, who died under Domitian for some incautious allusions in his history. The emperor ordered that even the slaves who had copied the book be crucified.

The Antonine emperors ushered in a new era of toleration. Historical accounts of the horrors of the preceding century could only glorify the new Golden Age, so Tacitus and the Greek historians writing at the time claimed to have had few restraints or fears. But Tacitus never did write the history of his own time that he once promised; perhaps even in an age of "good emperors" he thought it best to be prudently silent.

The function of history

Throughout this book I have tried to take Roman historical writing on its own terms; to do otherwise is to apply inappropriately anachronistic standards. Yet in conclusion it might be useful to review the functions of history in our own time in order to highlight similarities and differences of Roman historical practice. Most contemporary historians would recognize three principal functions of history today, though they might disagree vigorously about the relative importance of each.

The civic or political function of history   Every society uses history to introduce the young to the past events that have shaped their communal political and social institutions. In some cases this promotes prejudice and hatred, which can range from the narrow sectarianism of religious education, to warmongering, and the brainwashing of totalitarian regimes. On the positive side, education in history can play an important role in nation-building (nineteenth-century republican France); and there is even what might be called "therapeutic history," through which post-war German children have confronted Nazism and the Holocaust. Recent debates over multiculturalism in the United States focus on providing heroic models and objects of pride for women, African-Americans, and other groups. The current dispute over the treatment of the destruction of Nanking in Japanese textbooks demonstrates the perceived importance of history as a political statement. One purpose of George Soros' multinational Central European University in Budapest is to overcome the contradictory, and defiantly nationalistic, histories which continue to cause friction in central and eastern Europe.

The moral function of history   While many societies use religion to inculcate moral values, theological principles are usually regarded as overly abstract. Hence moral examples drawn from history are a more effective method of providing the young (and old) with heroes and villains. Here too, history may be created, as when the Rev'd Joseph Weems, twenty years after George Washington's death, invented the story of George ("I cannot tell a lie") and the cherry tree. Heroes in war and peace may exemplify patriotism, courage, loyalty, generosity, love of family, faith, and honesty – whatever personal virtues the society wishes to instill. A more sophisticated view of history may also teach the terrible costs of war, inflation, famine, civil disturbances, etc. This practical morality drawn from history can shape the behavior of future generations.

The intellectual function of history   While politics and morality may be drawn from anecdotal or textbook history, there is a deeper function that requires thought and careful analysis. History can expose its reader to a wealth of experience otherwise unattainable. For example, though civil war is of great importance in many countries today, American and British students can only experience their own civil wars through the study of history. Students can learn to evaluate primary sources, to analyze contradictory testimony, and to see how history itself has been abused for political expediency by both sides in a civil war. A proper understanding of history of many peoples may allow fruitful comparisons of the success or failure of political, economic, and social systems. Thucydides' idea of learning from history is the most notable instance of this intellectual function in the ancient world.

*   *   *

Roman historiography grew out of the political life of the city. Save for their ethnographic digressions, Roman historians centered their interest resolutely on the public life of the Roman people, whether in the Forum, in the senate house, on the Palatine, or on military campaigns. Duty was defined through historical examples, and stories of courageous Romans like Lucretia and Horatius spelled out family piety as well as public duty. Since their concern was Rome, the historians rarely found it necessary to leave the city in quest of evidence. Chauvinism and a resulting xenophobia were endemic, and there was little interest in the universal history that had inspired some Greek writers.

These political concerns were closely intertwined with moral issues in the Roman mind, and the linkage between the two led Roman historians to themes of great public importance. They looked nostalgically to a lost Golden Age and repeatedly explored the decline of Republican Rome. Rome had not been conquered and her Empire was larger than ever, but, in the common view first promoted by Sallust, her moral values and political institutions had been eroded from within. Scipio Africanus had defeated the great Hannibal, but he also behaved in untraditional ways and helped introduce Greek culture to Rome. The Romans, and their historians, wrestled with the moral price of political success. Conquest, wealth, and perhaps civilization itself had corrupted the free Roman people and left them subject first to civil war and then subjects of a new monarchy. And, centuries later, even that monarchy eventually fell for moral reasons – a point adumbrated by Tacitus and much later developed by Edward Gibbon.

Moral historiography became the conscience of the Roman people, and it is in Sallust, Livy, Tacitus, and Ammianus that we find the most cogent Roman discussions of freedom versus tyranny, the corrupting effect of individual or civic power, and the decline of political and social institutions. There are of course considerable differences in approach, but the continuities over five centuries are far more extraordinary: though rhetorical in expression and parochial in its scope, Roman historiography never lost its lasting concern with the moral dimensions of political issues. And these remain central issues for the historian of any age.

If the Roman historians were deeply devoted to the moral and political functions of history, they are seemingly less interested in the intellectual uses to which history can be put. Greek historians wished to challenge their readers and force them to think; most Romans would have found history a strange place for such speculation.

Romans would have agreed with Plutarch, who denounced Herodotus for impiety when he ascribed political motivation to the oracle at Delphi. Thucydides' impartiality toward his own homeland would have seemed treason to the Romans, and his pragmatic analysis of political tactics would have seemed amoral. The provocative relativism of Herodotus and Thucydides appeals to the modern reader far more than to the Romans. And yet, at their greatest moments, Roman historians pose questions in political and moral terms that challenge fundamental assumptions: the cost of imperialism; the construction of political mythology; and the political role of language. At those points they too challenge the minds of their readers and require intellectual engagement in the quest for historical truth.

Conclusion

The genre of history occupies an important place in Latin literature, but Roman historiography is more than a literary record of the past; it is an extension of political life. Speeches were political acts in Republican Rome and Tacitus did not turn to history to escape into the past but to take a political stance in his own time. The language of history functioned as a principal mechanism of political discourse and social analysis. It thus served as the anthropology, the sociology, the psychology, and the political science of the time. It was indeed the social science of ancient Rome, that is, their attempt to understand and improve society.

Roman historians learned much from their Greek predecessors. Like the Greeks, they preferred to study the remote past or contemporary history, but they had more difficulty with intermediate periods. Their defensiveness in the face of the more advanced Greek culture led to the competitive chauvinism that permeates Roman historical writing. Thus it was the Romans who transmitted to the Renaissance their carefully crafted idea of national history, which would then be taken up throughout the nations of Europe. The tradition of competing national history survives to the present day as the result of this heritage.

The Roman historians continue to be read both for what they say and for who they are. They have preserved in their pages the great adventure that changed the face of half the globe. When the Romans conquered Italy, the Mediterranean, and western Europe, they spread Latin to areas where it has been adapted and exported so that more than a billion people speak languages based upon it. Rome's creation of a Greco-Roman *oikoumene* allowed Greek-speaking Christians to spread the new religion throughout the Mediterranean basin and into Europe. In addition to language and religion, Rome has bequeathed its art, law, architecture, military tactics, engineering, and urban planning to the Western world. Roman historians thus are read for what they preserve of the beginnings of the European civilization.

The historians are also read for who they are and what they have achieved, for when a great mind encounters an important subject it leaves an ineradicable result. Livy's story of the honor of Lucretia, or Hannibal's crossing of the Alps, or Tacitus' account of the effects of political paranoia under Tiberius survive not only as recreations of the past but in their own terms. Lucretia, Hannibal, and Tiberius take on their own historical force as surely as do Achilles, Oedipus, or Dido. The creative aspect of Roman historical writing allows these books to transcend the mere recording of the past.

During the centuries literary genres have changed, and other kinds of writers and scholars have taken over some functions of history. The social sciences now analyze in far more technical ways aspects of contemporary civilization. Novelists, especially the great novelists of the nineteenth century, chose to educate and entertain their readers as Livy had once done. As Cato had once expunged the names of magistrates to emphasize the collective achievement of the Roman people, Leo Tolstoy's *War and Peace* is a great argument for the inexorable force of people against Thomas Carlyle's emphasis on the importance of the charismatic "great man." The destiny of the Roman people is woven through Livy's immense history like the divine plan that many modern peoples have claimed for their own history.

From antiquity to the present day Roman history has been read for its examples of heroic conduct. In it virtues and vices seem to be writ larger than life, as Cato originally intended his history to be. Succeeding peoples have commemorated the Romans in poetry, drama, and painting. This goes beyond nostalgia; these texts kept the dream of liberty alive to be reborn in Cola di Rienzo's medieval Roman republic (1347–54), the Italian communes of the Renaissance, and revolutionary America and France. Machiavelli and Montesquieu used Livy and Tacitus to understand how men could free themselves of tyrants, and Jacques-Louis David's *Oath of the Horatii* brings Livy into the attempt to create modern democracy. Tacitus believed that the function of history is to affect the future and, by that standard, Roman historiography succeeded and continues to succeed. It remains, as Cicero hoped it would be, "the witness of the past, the light of truth, the survival of memory, the teacher of life, the message of antiquity" (*De orat.* 2, 36).

NOTES

1 Origins of Roman historiography

1 For a more extensive treatment, cf. T.J. Luce, *The Greek Historians* (London, 1997), 123–41.

2 Sallust

1 Translations of Sallust from J.C. Rolfe, Loeb Classical Library (London, 1921).

3 Livy

1 Translations of Livy adapted from William Roberts (London, 1912–24).

4 Tacitus

1 Translations adapted from A.J. Church and W.J. Brodribb (London, 1886).

5 Ammianus Marcellinus

1 Translated by Walter Hamilton (Harmondsworth, 1986).

6 Roman biography

1 Translated by J.C. Rolfe, Loeb Classical Library, 1929.
2 Translated by J.C. Rolfe, Loeb Classical Library, 1914.
3 Translated by David Magie, Loeb Classical Library, 1922, 1924, 1932.

FURTHER READING

Translations

Modern translations of the most important texts are available in paperback from Penguin books: Livy (4 vols); Sallust; Caesar (2 vols); Tacitus (3 vols); Ammianus (selections); Suetonius; and selected lives from the *Historia Augusta*.

The Loeb Classical Library (Harvard University Press) keeps in print almost five hundred volumes of Greek and Latin authors in bilingual editions, with Latin (or Greek) and English on facing pages. The following are available: Livy (14 vols); Sallust; Caesar (2 vols); Tacitus (5 vols); Ammianus (3 vols); Suetonius (2 vols); *Historia Augusta* (3 vols); Cornelius Nepos; and the *Res Gestae*.

General books

Conte, G-B. *Latin Literature: A History*, tr. J. Solodow (Baltimore and London, 1994).

Dorey, T.A. (ed.) *Latin Historians* (London, 1966) (essays on Caesar, Sallust, Livy, and Ammianus).

Fornara, C.W. *The Nature of History in Ancient Greece and Rome* (Berkeley, 1983).

Kraus, C.S. and Woodman, A.J. *Latin Historians*, Greece and Rome: New Surveys in the Classics (Oxford, 1997).

Laistner, M.L.W. *The Greater Roman Historians* (Berkeley, 1947).

Marincola, J. *Authority and Tradition in Ancient Historiography* (Cambridge, 1997).

Wiseman, T.P. *Clio's Cosmetics* (Leicester, 1979).

Woodman, A.J. *Rhetoric in Classical Historiography* (London, 1988).

Origins of Roman historiography

Badian, E. "The Roman Annalists," in *Latin Historians* (ed. T.A. Dorey) (London, 1966), 1–38.
Leeman, A.D. *Orationis Ratio* (Amsterdam, 1963), 2 volumes.
Oakley, S.P. *A Commentary on Livy Books VI-X*, I (Oxford, 1997).

Sallust

Earl, D.C. *The Political Thought of Sallust* (Cambridge, 1961).
McGushin, P. *Sallust: The Histories* (Oxford, 1992, 1994), 2 volumes.
Syme, R. *Sallust* (Berkeley, 1964).

Livy

Luce, T.J. *Livy: The Composition of His History* (Princeton, 1977).
Miles, G. *Livy: Reconstructing Early Rome* (Ithaca and London, 1995).
Syme, R. "Livy and Augustus," *Harvard Studies in Classical Philology*, 1959.
Walsh, P.J. *Livy: His Historical Aims and Methods* (Cambridge, 1961).

Tacitus

Dorey, T.A. (ed.) *Tacitus* (London, 1969).
Martin, R. *Tacitus* (Berkeley, 1981).
Mellor, R. *Tacitus* (New York, 1993).
Syme, R. *Tacitus* (Oxford, 1958), 2 volumes.

Ammianus Marcellinus

Matthews, J. *The Roman Empire of Ammianus Marcellinus* (London, 1989).
Syme, R. *Ammianus and the Historia Augusta* (Oxford, 1968).
Thompson, E.A. *The Historical Work of Ammianus Marcellinus* (Cambridge, 1947).

Biography

Dorey, T.A. *Latin Biography* (New York, 1967) (essays on Nepos, Suetonius, and the *Historia Augusta*).
Momigliano, A.D. *The Development of Greek Biography* (Cambridge, MA., 1971).
Stuart, D.R. *Epochs of Greek and Roman Biography* (Berkeley, 1928).

Cornelius Nepos

Dionisotti, C. "Nepos and the Generals," *Journal of Roman Studies* 78, 1988, 35–49.

Geiger, J. *Cornelius Nepos and Ancient Political Biography* (Wiesbaden, 1985), *Historia* Einselschriften 47.

Millar, F. "Cornelius Nepos 'Atticus' and the Roman Revolution," *Greece and Rome* 35, 1988.

Suetonius

Baldwin, B. *Suetonius* (Amsterdam, 1983).

Wallace-Hadrill, A. *Suetonius: The Scholar and His Caesars* (London, 1983).

Augustan history

Barnes, T.D. *The Sources of the Historia Augusta* (Brussels, 1978), *Latomus* Supp. 165.

Momigliano, A.D. "An Unsolved Problem of Historical Forgery: The *Scriptores Historiae Augustae*," *Journal of the Warburg and Courtauld Institutes* 17, 1954, 22–46.

Syme, R. *Emperors and Biography* (Oxford, 1971).

Autobiography

Brunt, P.A. and Moore, J.M. *Res Gestae Divi Augusti* (Oxford, 1967).

Misch, G. *A History of Autobiography in Antiquity*, tr. E. Dickes (London, 1950).

Ramage, E. *The Nature and Purpose of Augustus' "Res Gestae"* (Wiesbaden, 1987), *Historia* Einselschriften 54.

Yavetz, Z. "The *Res Gestae* and Augustus' Public Image," in F. Millar and E. Segal (eds) *Caesar Augustus: Seven Aspects* (Oxford, 1984).

INDEX